Hartmut Mayer and Henri Vogt (*editors*)
A RESPONSIBLE EUROPE?
Ethical Foundations of EU External Affairs

Lauren M. McLaren
IDENTITY, INTERESTS AND ATTITUDES TO EUROPEAN INTEGRATION

Justus Schönlau
DRAFTING THE EU CHARTER
Rights, Legitimacy and Process

Forthcoming titles in the series include:

Ian Bache and Andrew Jordan (*editors*)
THE EUROPEANIZATION OF BRITISH POLITICS

Palgrave Studies in European Union Politics
Series Standing Order ISBN 1-4039-9511-7 (hardback) and ISBN 1-4039-9512-5
(paperback)

You can receive future titles in this series as they are published by placing a standing order.
Please contact your bookseller or, in case of difficulty, write to us at the address below with
your name and address, the title of the series and one of the ISBNs quoted above.

Customer Services Department, Macmillan Distribution Ltd, Houndmills, Basingstoke,
Hampshire RG21 6XS, England

A Responsible Europe?

Ethical Foundations of EU External Affairs

Edited by

Hartmut Mayer

Fellow and Lecturer in Politics, St. Peter's College, University of Oxford, UK

and

Henri Vogt

Research Fellow, University of Helsinki, Finland

First published 2006 by
PALGRAVE MACMILLAN
Houndmills, Basingstoke, Hampshire RG21 6XS and
175 Fifth Avenue, New York, N.Y. 10010
Companies and representatives throughout the world

PALGRAVE MACMILLAN is the global academic imprint of the Palgrave Macmillan division of St. Martin's Press, LLC and of Palgrave Macmillan Ltd. Macmillan® is a registered trademark in the United States, United Kingdom and other countries. Palgrave is a registered trademark in the European Union and other countries.

ISBN-13: 978-1-4039-8816-4   hardback
ISBN-10: 1-4039-8816-1   hardback

This book is printed on paper suitable for recycling and made from fully managed and sustained forest sources.

A catalogue record for this book is available from the British Library.

Library of Congress Cataloging-in-Publication Data

A responsible Europe? ethical foundations of EU external affairs / edited by
    Hartmut Mayer and Henri Vogt.
        p. cm.
    ISBN 1-4039-8816-1 (cloth)
    1. European Union. 2. Globalization—Moral and ethical aspects—European Union countries. 3. Security, International—Moral and ethical aspects. 4. International relations—Moral and ethical aspects. 5. European Union countries—Foreign relations. I. Mayer, Hartmut. II. Vogt, Henri, 1967–

JN30.R47 2006
172'.4094—dc22   2006046254

10   9   8   7   6   5   4   3   2   1
15   14   13   12   11   10   09   08   07   06

Printed and bound in Great Britain by
Antony Rowe Ltd, Chippenham and Eastbourne

Contents

List of Tables and Figures

Tables

Figures

Acknowledgements

We got the idea for this book in the autumn of 2003 as we together pondered upon the scope and publication goals of Henri Vogt's current research project 'The Dialogue between the EU and Africa'. The project was generously funded by the Finnish Ministry for Foreign Affairs and placed at the Finnish Institute of International Affairs (FIIA; 2002–2004).

That project also sponsored the two brainstorming sessions that we organised for the book, the first at St Peter's College, University of Oxford, and the second at FIIA. In the final editing stage we also received financial support from our respective current academic homes, St Peter's College (Mayer) and the Department of Political Science, University of Helsinki (Vogt). We wish to thank all the above-mentioned institutions and their staff for support, encouragement and assistance over many years, and – as we both have come to experience on several occasions – hospitality.

Earlier versions of some of the chapters of this book were presented in the Annual Convention of the International Studies Association in Honolulu in March 2005. We are grateful for all the comments that we received from our panel in that Convention. As editors of the book, we also wish to thank collectively all those 'outsiders', who have contributed to the finalisation of the individual chapters.

We are also thankful to Palgrave Macmillan, and particularly Alison Howson and Ann Marangos, for smooth cooperation in bringing the text into print.

Finally, we wish to express our deepest gratitude to all the contributors of the book, for their enthusiasm and intellectual curiosity and, above all, for their patience towards our perhaps not so clear comments and ideas that we bombarded them with in order to help the project reach the end station.

Hartmut Mayer and Henri Vogt

Notes on Contributors

Pami Aalto is Research Fellow in the Aleksanteri Institute, University of Helsinki, Finland. He was a Visiting Fellow in the School of International Relations, St Petersburg State University during autumn 2004 and the 2005/2006 term. He has a PhD in International Relations from the University of Helsinki, and his publications include *Constructing Post-Soviet Geopolitics in Estonia* (2003), *European Union and the Making of a Wider Northern Europe* (2006), and articles in *Cooperation and Conflict, Geopolitics, Journal of Peace Research* and *Space & Polity*.

Joakim Ekman holds a PhD in political science from the University of Örebro, Sweden, where he also currently teaches. His research interests comprise European politics, democratisation and political socialisation, and his works include *National Identity in Divided and Unified Germany* (PhD thesis, 2001) and *The Handbook of Political Change in Eastern Europe*, 2nd edn (co-edited and co-authored with Sten Berglund and Frank H. Aarebrot, 2004). His works have also appeared in the *European Journal of Political Research* and the *Journal of Communist Studies and Transition Politics*.

Elena Jurado is an administrator at the Council of Europe's Secretariat of the Framework Convention for the Protection of National Minorities in Strasbourg, France. Between 2000 and 2004 she was a Junior Research Fellow and Politics Tutor at Oriel College and Christ Church, the University of Oxford. She holds a DPhil. in International Relations from the University of Oxford. She has published articles on European institutions, minority rights and political developments in the Baltic States in the *Journal of Baltic Studies, Democratization, The Bulletin of the Association for the Study of Ethnicity and Nationalism*, and *Claves de Razón Práctica*, a Spanish journal of philosophy and political science.

Rieko Karatani has been an Associate Professor in Politics and International Relations at Kyushu University, Japan, since 2000. She received a DPhil. from the University of Oxford (St Antony's College), an MA from Sophia University, a BL from Kobe University and a BA from Kobe College. She has been writing on immigration and refugee policy in Britain and the EU, and her latest publication is *Defining British Citizenship: Empire, Commonwealth and Modern Britain* (2003).

Hartmut Mayer has been a Fellow and Lecturer in Politics (International Relations) at St Peter's College, University of Oxford, since 1998. He holds a DPhil. from St Antony's College, University of Oxford, an MPhil. from Gonville and Caius College, University of Cambridge, an MALD from the Fletcher School of Law and Diplomacy, Tufts University and the equivalent of a BA from the Free University of Berlin. He has been a visiting researcher at the European University Institute in Florence and the German Institute for International and Security Affairs (SWP) in Berlin. His recent publications include a book on German–British relations and various book chapters and articles on European security policy, German foreign policy, and the external relations of the EU.

Hanna Ojanen is a Senior Researcher at the Finnish Institute of International Affairs. She holds a PhD in Political and Social Sciences from the European University Institute in Florence. Her publications include 'If in "Europe", then in its "core"? Finland', in Kaiser, Wolfram & Jürgen Elvert (eds), *European Union Enlargement: A Comparative History* (2004); *The ESDP and the Nordic Countries: Four Variations on a Theme* (co-authored with Nina Græger and Henrik Larsen; Programme on the Northern Dimension of the CFSP, Finnish Institute of International Affairs and Institut für Europäische Politik, Helsinki 2002); and *The Plurality of Truth: A Critique of Research on the State and European Integration* (1998).

Terry O'Shaugnessy is a Fellow in Economics at St Anne's College, University of Oxford. Previously he was a Research Fellow at King's College, Cambridge. He holds an MPhil. and PhD from Cambridge. He has published research in a number of areas, including macroeconomic theory, econometric modelling, trade policy and the economics of education. He also has an interest in the history of economic thought and recently contributed an essay on Richard Kahn to *The Biographical Dictionary of British Economists*.

Kristi Raik is Researcher at the Finnish Institute of International Affairs. She holds a PhD from the University of Turku, Finland. Her publications include *Democratic Politics or the Implementation of Inevitabilities? Estonia's Democracy and Integration into the European Union* (2003); 'EU Accession of Central and Eastern European Countries: Democracy and Integration as Conflicting Logics', *East European Politics and Societies* 18:4 (2004); and 'Bureaucratisation or strengthening of the political? Estonian institutions and integration into the European Union', *Cooperation and Conflict* 37:2 (2002).

András Szigeti has been Rector's Research Fellow at Central European University since 2004 where he is also completing his PhD thesis on the philosophy of moral responsibility. He received his Lizentiat (the equivalent of an MA) from the University of Basel in 2000. In 2003/2004, he was a FCO/Chevening Visiting Scholar at Oriel College, Oxford University. His latest publication is 'Freedom: A Global Theory?' in the *Croatian Journal of Philosophy*, vol. V: no. 13, 2005.

Henri Vogt is Research Fellow at the Centre for European Studies, Department of Political Science, University of Helsinki, Finland. He holds a DPhil. in politics from the University of Oxford. In 2002–2004 he was Senior Researcher at the Finnish Institute of International Affairs. His books include *Between Utopia and Disillusionment: A Narrative of the Political Transformation in Eastern Europe* (2005), *Challenges to Democracy: Eastern Europe Ten Years after the Collapse of Communism* (co-authored with S. Berglund, F. Aarebrot and G. Karasimeonov, 2001), and *The Making of the European Union: Foundations, Institutions and Future Trends* (co-authored with S. Berglund, J. Ekman and F. Aarebrot, 2006). His current research is funded by the Academy of Finland (project number 108239).

List of Abbreviations

AAMS	Associated African and Malagasy States
ACP	African, Caribbean and Pacific countries
AEFP	People's Forum of Asian and European NGOs
ASEAN	Association of Southeast Asian Nations
ASEM	Asia-Europe Meeting
CAEC	Council for Asia-Europe Cooperation
CAP	Common Agricultural Policy
CAT	Convention Against Torture and Other Cruel, Inhuman or Degrading Treatment or Punishment
CBC	Cross Border Cooperation
CEDAW	Convention on the Elimination on All Forms of Discrimination Against Women
CEES	Common European Economic Space
CERD	International Convention on the Elimination of All Forms of Racial Discrimination
CFSP	Common Foreign and Security Policy
CIS	Commonwealth of Independent States
CRC	Convention on the Rights of the Child
CSDP	Common Security and Defence Policy
CSR	Common Strategy on Russia
EABC	European-American Business Council
EADI	European Association of Development Research and Training Institutes
EC	European Community
ECHR	European Convention on Human Rights
ECtHR	European Court of Human Rights
ECJ	European Court of Justice
EDA	European Defence Agency
EDF	European Development Fund
EEC	European Economic Community
ENP	European Neighbourhood Policy
EPA	Economic Partnership Agreement
EPC	European Political Cooperation
ESDP	European Security and Defence Policy
ESS	European Security Strategy
EU	European Union
EUMC	European Monitoring Centre on Racism and Xenophobia
FTAA	Free Trade Areas of the Americas
GATT	General Agreement on Tariffs and Trade

GNI	Gross National Income
GUAM	Georgia, Ukraine, Azerbaijan and Moldova
ICC	International Criminal Court
ICCPR	International Covenant on Civil and Political Rights
ICESC	International Covenant on Economic, Social and Cultural Rights
INGO	International non-governmental organisation
IR	International Relations
JHA	Justice and Home Affairs
LDC	Less Developed Countries
NATO	North Atlantic Treaty Organisation
ND	Northern Dimension
NDEP	Northern Dimension Environmental Partnership
NEPAD	New Partnership for Africa's Development
NGO	Non-governmental organisations
NIS	Newly Independent States
NTA	New Transatlantic Agenda
ODA	Official development assistance
OSCE	Organisation for Security and Cooperation in Europe
PACE	Parliamentary Assembly of The Council of Europe
PCA	Partnership and Cooperation Agreement
SEA	Single European Act
UN	United Nations
UNHCR	United Nations High Commissioner for Refugees
WEU	Western European Union
WTO	World Trade Organisation

Introduction

Henri Vogt

This book reviews the external affairs of the European Union (EU) from a very distinct perspective. Different from existing literature on the EU's international role, we seek to find moral and ethical arguments and justifications on which the Union ought to base its global policies. We ask, in other words, what ethical foundations might there be for developing a larger role for the EU in regional politics and global governance or, conversely, what moral factors could potentially limit the scope of the EU's external ambitions? What should or should not the EU do in international arenas and, above all, why? By posing these questions we hope to open new avenues of research within the already rich and inspiring literature on the EU's global role. In addition, the book seeks to put forward a set of moral principles which we hope could function as practical guidelines for the formulation of EU activities in international affairs.

To do all this, we depart from the notion of responsibility. This may appear problematic and not particularly original, given the current fashionableness of the notion. Politicians, bureaucrats, journalists, businessmen and civic activists use it in numerous contexts and with a great number of meanings in mind, albeit often without a precise understanding of all these meanings. The term of course varies – obligation, duty, pledge, moral commitment, necessity, promise, or even 'common values' – but they all seem to represent the same phenomenon, an attempt to find a moral ground, moral guidelines, moral legitimacy for politics in an era in which no such ground or guidelines are believed to exist.

Let us illuminate this with a few examples. Globalisation debates are now full of references to 'responsibility'. In the United Nations Millennium Declaration, the heads of state assert, among other things, that 'we have a collective responsibility to uphold the principles of human dignity, equality and equity at the global level. As leaders we have a duty therefore to all the world's people, especially the most vulnerable and, in particular, the children of the world, to whom the future belongs.' In 2000, the International Law Commission, a United Nations (UN) body, started a long-term work on the

'Responsibility of international organisations'. By the end of 2004, it had published a number of draft legal articles on the issue. The forces of global capitalism have also been subjugated to the discourse of moral duties. Those who are seeking to give globalisation a more human face, now organise conferences on 'Corporate Social Responsibility'.[1]

Security policy no longer survives without 'responsibility' either. The doctrines of humanitarian intervention and pre-emptive strikes are often defended in the name of it. The 2001 Report of the International Commission on Intervention and State Sovereignty, working in close cooperation with the UN, even turned the 'right of humanitarian intervention' into 'Responsibility to Protect', or R2P; a legal right was transformed into a moral, subjective, political duty. The current US administration has used, and often misused, moral-based argumentation very openly and prominently. Its prime doctrine seems to read: 'It is the United States' responsibility to protect democracy and freedom in the world'.[2]

In the context of EU policy formation the discourse of responsibility has also infiltrated countless agendas, declarations and speeches – even more systematically than we realised when we started planning this book in late 2003. The European Security Strategy of 2003 explicitly mentions responsibility as one of its guiding principles, and many leading EU politicians have repeatedly emphasised that the EU needs to be globally strong but nevertheless responsible.[3] In the spring of 2004, Eurostep, the network of European development organisations, launched a programme called 'Vision of a Responsible Europe'. In Germany, the European Association of Development Research and Training Institutes (EADI) organised a series of top-level discussions under the title 'Europe's Responsibility in the One World' in 2004.[4]

What these examples obviously show is that there is no single mode of understanding 'responsibility' in today's world affairs, but it has become a catchword for many different things. It is invariably used as a political notion or a moral one or both, and often it is impossible to know where the line between these categories should be drawn. What is more important, however, is that the promoters of 'responsibility' generally do not seem to ponder upon the ultimate sources of these responsibilities. Why, in the final analysis, should A be responsible towards B? And to what degree? And if we can indeed decide upon the reason why A bears a responsibility towards B, how can A best fulfil it? In more concrete terms, if rich countries have promised to halve poverty in the world by 2015, what actual measures are they morally required to take in order to succeed in this?

Dealing with this elasticity of different meanings of 'responsibility' obviously poses a major challenge to this volume, namely, how to bring at least a degree of conceptual clarity into the analysis. We will explain how we have sought to achieve this shortly. But this volume also enriches some of the larger and more traditional debates in international affairs. There are at least three such debates; they deserve to be reviewed briefly.

Three debates

The debate on *the European Union as a global actor* is implicit in all the ensuing chapters. This debate has intensified dramatically after the end of the Cold War as the Union has been enlarging and assuming new tasks. This has fed people's expectations about the worldwide influence of the Union, often formulated in the language of responsibilities and duties. The genocide in Rwanda and the crises in former Yugoslavia painfully brought forth the question whether the EU should be more willing and capable to act outside its own borders; many believed that it had a duty to do more, much more. With the US-led 'wars' in Afghanistan and Iraq, the argument that it is Europe's responsibility to share the burden of such crises, and if needed, counterbalance the dominance of the United States has become, for some, almost axiomatic.[5] The 2004 big-bang enlargement of the Union may have become possible because to some extent it was seen as the old member states' moral duty to finally end the artificial division of the continent. As a result, the Union is now faced with a new set of responsibilities towards its new neighbours, such countries as Ukraine, Belarus and Turkey.

The frequent demands for a strengthened global role, spiced up with references to responsibility, have often been intertwined with a positive, norm-based self-image of the EU. Many Europeans truly believe the Union to be the world's leading moral authority. They are convinced that it can, and most often does, lead by example when it comes to a number of issues of global governance, for example the Kyoto Protocol, trade negotiations in the World Trade Organisation (WTO) or the realisation of the Millennium Development Goals. They also consider this brave new Europe capable of bearing its historical responsibility towards its former colonies and, as one of the most prosperous regions in the world, its moral responsibility to fight against poverty in other continents. This positive self-understanding has also been codified. In the consolidated version of the Draft Treaty establishing a Constitution for Europe, the European Union's role in the world is defined as follows:

> In its relations with the wider world, the Union shall uphold and promote its values and interests. It shall contribute to peace, security, the sustainable development of the Earth, solidarity and mutual respect among peoples, free and fair trade, eradication of poverty and protection of human rights and in particular the rights of the child, as well as to strict observance and to development of international law, including respect for the principles of the United Nations Charter. (Article I-3-4)

It is not realistic to expect that these ambitions and expectations regarding the global presence of the EU would lose their appeal in the foreseeable future. Assuming new member states and the current constitutional process, if and when successfully completed, are likely to further strengthen the Union's international standing. However, this development is by no means inevitable, nor does it follow a predestined path: there are various alternative types of global actor that the EU could be or develop into. The above passage from the Constitutional Treaty, for example, remains silent about the means with which the EU seeks to 'contribute to peace'; and at what cost; and why; or with whom. What is important, then, is that whatever the future global role of the Union, its construction should be a very deliberate process, a process based on well thought-out premises and arguments. One task of this book is to explore what these premises and arguments should or could be. Our aim is thus not simply to describe institutional developments or particular EU policies, but also to define such norms and values that could guide the EU towards more consistent and coherent policies, and help it in the setting of policy priorities.

*   *   *

The second major intellectual debate that we would like to contribute to concerns *the moral agency of international institutions* in general, *and the constraints of this agency* in particular. While we in this book focus on the EU, it is obvious that similar reasoning could be applied to, say, the *G8*, WTO or perhaps even Amnesty International as they all assume special responsibilities by pursuing their global activities. This is in fact a fairly new debate in the field of International Relations (IR) and political science more generally. The field has been for far too long been dominated by the realist paradigm with its explicit limits with regard to the moral dimensions of world affairs.[6]

What has been widely and for a long time discussed, however, is the individual's responsibility as a member of a system, organisation or social structure. Hannah Arendt's by now classic analysis of Adolf Eichmann's responsibility as a servant of the Nazi regime is no doubt the best known contribution to this debate. We believe that the logic of assigning responsibilities to institutions is not necessarily that different from the way in which we assess a single person's responsibilities, responsibilities that are defined by her individual freedom on the one hand, and by systemic constraints, on the other. Institutions, too, are constrained by their own practices, norms and traditions as well as by other institutions, but also they normally possess a certain degree of freedom of action. Indeed, as the contributors to this book argue, it is justified to regard institutions, including the European Union, as moral agents, and therefore bearers of a great number of responsibilities towards both individuals and other institutions.[7] The current age of globalisation may have made this moral *institutional* agency particularly significant: the problems of the global, interdependent world are so complex that no individual can understand or be aware of all their implications. Often only institutions can be expected to bear such a comprehensive knowledge.[8]

It is worth noting that the principles of institutional responsibility have evoked increasing attention in International Law in recent years.[9] As was mentioned at the outset, the International Law Commission has also undertaken the codification of these principles, but it is still premature to draw any conclusions as to the direction that this codification will take. We will return to the issue of agency below as we introduce some of the central concepts of this book.

*   *   *

The third debate we would see our book as being part of is less explicit in the ensuing chapters but still very important; it could be called 'Normative Globalisation'.[10] We ask, in other words, which norms and values inform or could inform various globalisation processes, and how we could possibly harness these processes to ensure that they benefit the majority of humankind, instead of only filling the pockets of the rich and the beautiful.

Globalisation is a worldwide, continuous, and possibly still accelerating, structuration process. More and more relations, linkages and interdependencies between actors from different parts of the world are created, and these are determined by a great number of different rules, norms, beliefs, habits, traditions and desires. Europe – the EU, its member states, as well as other European states and regional organisations – constitutes a very powerful actor in this process. The legitimacy and therefore the influence of this actor in the eyes of others, as well as European citizens themselves, is dependent on the nature of its international activities and the values that inform them. The crucial questions are: Who defines these norms and rules and forms of action? How are they defined? Who do they benefit and why? We believe that by shaping its activities, in a conscious and deliberate manner, around the concept of responsibility, the EU can better contribute towards making globalisation a more regulated process, and perhaps a more just one as well.[11]

This leads to an important point. The majority of studies on the EU's international agency have implicitly adopted an inside-out perspective: developments within the Union are the primary context of their analyses and if they seek to employ a normative perspective, the starting point tends to be 'what is good for Europe, is good for the world'. We believe, instead, that only an outside-in perspective makes sense today – and can be morally justified: 'what is good for the world is good for Europe.' Indeed, a global rather than strictly European perspective should inform most decisions made by the Union – it should be the ideal even though it may never become the reality – and this will be beneficial for the Union itself in the long run.

Finally, any attempt to analyse the EU's global role must include a discussion of the nature of the world order. How should the EU contribute to the post-bipolar and post-9/11 world order? We obviously cannot say anything conclusive on the issue, but the reader should bear in mind that we have a normative point of departure in this respect: we want to make a plea for what we call *cooperative regionalism* as opposed to US dominance, unilateralism, competitive bloc politics, or 'the West against the rest' attitude.

Conceptual starting points and existing literature

In order to avoid, or at least downplay, the elasticity of 'responsibility' and to transform it into a truly analytical notion, we apply a specific conceptual and theoretical framework in this book. The framework asks: *if an agent* (for example, the EU) *potentially incurs responsibility towards another agent* (or a policy sector or geographical area), *what are the sources of this responsibility?* We identify six such sources, or as we call them 'moral principles that incur responsibilities': *contribution, community, beneficiary, capacity, legitimate expectations* and *consent principles.* András Szigeti develops these in detail in Chapter 1. The eight policy-specific chapters all use these principles as their point of departure and analytical angle. The overriding idea is that in its policies the Union ought to be aware of the multiplicity of these different sources of responsibility. Duties can emerge through a number of different mechanisms. When applied in the specific context of EU responsibilities, these principles also yield largely convergent results. Not just one normative principle but several support and often accentuate the claim that the EU has a certain duty in certain situations. Moreover, the EU's nature as a voluntarily established association with clearly declared objectives creates specific responsibilities for the EU and gives these responsibilities particular weight.

In addition to 'responsibility', three other concepts are particularly relevant for the analyses of this volume, although their role may not always be explicit: *agency* and the nature of the Union as a multilayered organisation; *power* and its different forms in international relations; and the way global agency determines *European identity.* Through the brief discussions of these concepts below we also introduce in passing some of the existing literature with which this book wishes to converse.

EU agency

The European Union is both vertically and horizontally unique, *sui generis.* On the one hand, more powerfully than any other regional organisation in the world, it challenges and transforms the nation-state system and creates a new level of politics and policy-making. The division of labour between the EU as an independent, unified body and its member states is not always clear, however, but intermingled in numerous ways, both official and unofficial. Using Niilo Kauppi's terminology, a two-way structuration process between the national and European polities shapes the nature and development of both of these entities.[12] On the other hand, although the Union is 'only' an international organisation and not (yet) a state, it is involved in a great variety of different policy fields. The number of these fields is significantly higher than that of other regional organisations in the world, and it is still growing.

This uniqueness is, of course, significant as we think about the international role of the Union in light of the notion of responsibility. Vertically, the EU is a combination of the activities of the Union and its member-states – hence shared agency, and shared responsibility. In the field of external relations, member states have remained the dominant partner of this combination; they have not been willing to give away their power to the community level. In the definition of foreign policy objectives (as opposed to their implementation) in particular, the member states have played a more important role than the European Commission. Because of this inclination of the member states to safeguard their own particularistic interests, the EU's foreign policy has often been reactionary, not a matter of consciously and independently outlined objectives.

This does not mean, however, and as Karen E. Smith remarks in her *European Union Foreign Policy in a Changing World*, that there would be no 'Brussels element' in EU foreign policy.[13] As the practices of EU foreign policy have developed, the independence of the Union-level in these matters has increased; the instruments which the EU has at its disposal to pursue its objectives have come to cover so wide a range – agreements, conventions, conditionality, persuasion – that they no doubt guarantee an increasing amount of independence to the Union. If the new Constitution (including, e.g. an EU foreign minister) were to enter into force some day, this independence would most likely become even more meaningful. Be that is it may, what is important in the context of this book is that assigning responsibility to somebody or something, thus making him/her/it a moral agent, requires that we define as accurately as possible who or what this agent actually is.[14]

The division of labour between the EU and other possible institutional agents is another important question here. France's possible responsibilities in the genocide of Rwanda in1994 may help making sense of this point. In her excellent article on the crisis, Daniela Kroslak concludes that 'The combined fulfilment of the three criteria – extensive knowledge, heavy involvement, and ample capability – shows that the French government bears a great responsibility for not averting the genocide in Rwanda.'[15] This may indeed be an adequate conclusion, but we can also ask: Were there no other outside actors equally responsible, for they might have fulfilled the same criteria? Or were not the other member states of the EU also responsible? And if the French can be blamed for their inaction in Rwanda, is not the whole Western world responsible for letting people being killed in Darfur in 2004–2005? In other words, we not only need to know who can act (or could have acted) but also who *the most suitable actor* is. This is often a very tall order; in the EU context, for example, we cannot necessarily know whether individual member states would act more effectively than the Union itself. Yet the difficulty of knowing who the most appropriate actor is should not lead to a situation where the issue of responsibility is not tackled at all. It is conceivable that an agent should act even though it does not seem to be the 'appropriate' actor.[16]

The other aspect of uniqueness – involvement in a great number of policy fields and activities worldwide – is also highly relevant here. It does not seem to be difficult for the EU to act responsibly in some policy sectors and irresponsibly in some others. This lack of coherence, and also temporal consistency, may distort the Union's agency in the long run.[17] Charlotte Bretherton and John Vogler pay attention to this as they conclude in *The European Union as a Global Actor* that 'it has become apparent in reviewing the Union's external policies that breadth of policy coverage may not always be matched by clarity, consistency and coherence'.[18] One of the important points of this book is, then, that in some fields, rather than assuming new tasks, the Union should seek cooperation with other relevant actors, especially such European actors as the Council of Europe or the Organisation for Security and Cooperation in Europe (OSCE). In the foreseeable future, this may be the only way for the Union to minimise its policy incoherence – and thereby act in as responsible a manner as possible. This kind of cooperation might also protect the idea of European plurality; there would be no all-powerful concentration of power.

Finally, although we concentrate explicitly on the EU's external policies, this does not mean that domestic policies would not be relevant as one tries to understand the nature of the Union's global role. Without diving too deep into a familiar debate, the EU's domestic agricultural subsidies are possibly the most important – and in many people's view the most fatal – feature of the Union's global agency. In the age of globalisation external and internal policies are indeed intertwined.

Different forms of EU power

The nature of the EU and the form of power it exerts towards others has been a subject of intense debate over the past few decades. The traditionally dominant view has been that the EU is a 'civilian power'.[19] Economic carrots rather than political sticks, persuasion rather than coercion, have been its way of influencing other actors. This changed, at least to a certain degree, in the 1990s. The Union started to build up its common foreign and security policy and even the use of military force began to look acceptable. In this respect, the EU has increasingly become a traditional, state-like, power-political actor. Many argue, however, that this new military/power-political dimension only complements and does not replace the former civilian nature of the EU. The primary idea so far has been to increase the EU's capacity in the field of crisis management, primarily civilian crisis management that may also require military strength.[20]

There are also other, more complicated forms of power that are relevant in the context of the EU. Ian Manners, among others, has emphasised the normative power of the EU, that is, the Union's capacity to influence through its values and norms and this way control the dominant discourses of the world – and thereby action.[21] It is obvious, however, that this discursive form of power only becomes possible when economic and coercive forms of power are available and potentially in use, too. A further possible form of power applicable to the EU is what is sometimes referred to as 'model' or structural power. The EU possesses a certain amount of power simply because it represents 'Europe', the historically dominant continent, or because it seems to be an alternative to the US. In the EU's own discourse, this has often been expressed as 'Leading by example'. All in all, at least four (or maybe eight) forms of power can easily be connected to the EU: civilian/ economic; military/ political; normative/ discursive; and model/ structural.

The relationship between these forms is obviously a complicated matter. They can, and often do, enforce one another, but it is equally possible that they do just the opposite. For the analyses of this volume, however, the crucial question is: What form or forms of power are needed to fulfil certain responsibilities? What kind of power is required to achieve those goals and visions that have been set? In general, increases in power and capacity also tend to mean increasing responsibilities. For example, if the EU's military dimension becomes stronger, this may bring about new obligations for the Union, duties that it cannot possibly fulfil in practice. From this perspective, there is a good case to be made for the EU to preserve its nature as a civilian power, and through civilian means develop its foreign policy. The temporal perspective is also important here: from a short-term perspective, the required form of power may be totally different from that which is needed when the time span is longer.

European identity

The empirical chapters of the book do not primarily focus on the issue of an emerging European identity; we try to define principles of responsibility that go further than if derived from a pure identity discourse. Two identity-related questions, however, appear highly relevant for our analyses. Firstly, how does the EU's global role shape the identity of Europeans? More precisely, to the extent that the EU truly is or becomes a responsible actor (or an irresponsible one), what kind of impact would this have on European identity? Secondly, to what extent will the identity of Europeans (provided that we can speak of it in the singular) determine the nature of the Union's role as a global actor in the future?

Many *debateurs* in today's Europe seem to believe that the connection between the possibly emerging European identity and the EU's international position is intimate, and that the development of this identity would follow the path of nation-state identity. They fear, for instance, that if Europe's military might does not match that of the United States or if Europe's economic competitiveness lies behind the Asian Tigers, this might create a sense of inferiority among Europeans, which would then have an impact on their identity – or indeed hamper the development of this identity altogether and thereby stop the whole European project.

In reality the logic is hardly this simple. Even though identities in many respects develop in relation to others – in social science terminology, the Other – 'European identity' is still so unstable and vague that it makes little sense to talk about it purely and primarily in relation to others; it is still first and foremost an identity for Europeans themselves. The EU's foreign policy decisions should therefore not be justified by appealing to the requirements of some sort of mystical Europeanness. It is worth noting, however, that in some EU member states a certain – let us call it 'responsible' – attitude towards the rest of the world has truly become an element of national identity or national ethos; Sweden is perhaps the most obvious case.[22] Whether for example the idea of 'a civilian power Europe' can assume the same position at the European level remains to be seen; if it will, it certainly is a matter of decades rather than years.

The problem of exclusion–inclusion may be more relevant in this context. In fact, the pattern with which the Union includes ones and excludes others will essentially define the nature of European identity in the coming decades – and the acts of excluding some and including others definitely actualises the question of responsibility. Lars-Erik Cederman puts the problem excellently:

> Those who try to forge a European identity and to put forward European ideals and values abroad need to consider not only the respective merits of 'deepening' and 'widening' but also the negative effects of 'exclusion' and 'dilution'. On the one hand, defining too narrow an identity for Europe risks excluding foreign goods, immigrants, and entire countries. On the other hand, a wide and unfocused definition of 'Europe' may dilute the very values that the European identity was intended to protect and project in the first place.[23]

From our perspective the crucial issue is how the idea of responsibility, of a responsible global agency, can relocate the limits of exclusion and dilution. On the one hand, if indeed the idea of responsibility were part of a European identity, one could imagine that the field of exclusion would be fairly small; a 'fortress Europe' would not exist. On the other hand, 'full inclusion', that is, letting all potential immigrants to enter the Union might so weaken the Union that it would prevent it from helping the rest of the world. And if the EU managed to help the poor of the world in their home countries in line with the demands of 'responsibility', exclusion (or inclusion) might not be as burning a problem as at the moment.

The structure of the book

While the six principles incurring responsibilities hold the book together, the individual empirical chapters assume either a regional or functional approach or in some cases both. Chapters 2 through 9 explore a number of key external policy fields of the European Union and they can be divided into four thematic pairs.

The first pair discusses, broadly speaking, the EU's emerging security and defence role. Hanna Ojanen starts with the fact that the European Union has recently expressed its intention to take on a number of responsibilities in the field of security policy. Whether the Union can credibly fulfil the expectations raised by this intention depends crucially on two questions: its *capacities* and its degree of independence as an agent. The development of capabilities may thus not be enough, but the agent also needs to be sufficiently independent from other agents to be held responsible. The chapter therefore tackles the question of the EU's independence from the member states, from NATO, and from the UN. It argues that the EU is pushed towards assuming functions of both states and defence alliances at a pace which might temporarily worsen rather than improve overall security, but may in the long run be the only effective way to handle security policy.

In Chapter 3, Hartmut Mayer analyses some larger aspects of the EU's transatlantic relations in the post-9/11 world. He argues that the EU has different layers of responsibility towards the transatlantic alliance. The EU has to continue to play its normative role as the most vocal advocate of multilateralism and the rule of law. It also has to promote the idea of 'co-operative regionalism' and 'co-operative multipolarity' as the basis of global order. At the same time the Union has the responsibility of shared leadership with the United States in creating and sustaining this order. Acknowledging the different layers of responsibility, the chapter will make the case that the EU must give priority to global norms and the rule of law over transatlantic solidarity whenever a 'conflict of responsibility' emerges.

The next two chapters are concerned with the EU's role in Eastern Europe and Russia, that is, with the new neighbours of the Union. Kristi Raik explores the ways in which the EU practices extended governance over its neighbours and extends its rules and norms beyond its borders. This may be problematic from the viewpoint of responsibility, however, because it obscures agency and power on the side of the EU, establishes an asymmetric power relation between the parties, restricts the development of democracy and self-determination in the neighbouring countries, favours countries that are the fittest to adopt the whole set of EU norms, and excludes those that do not share them. Hence, in order to act as a responsible regional power, the EU must not let 'objective' norms and criteria replace (political) responsibility, political dialogue.

Pami Aalto argues in Chapter 5 that the difficult question of the EU's responsibilities towards Russia is best approached as a problem of *community*. Applying a broad notion of the wider European community can make it easier for the Union to be sensitive *vis-à-vis* its gigantic eastern neighbour and, as a consequence, to define its policies towards it. The issues of identity and belonging are thus fundamental to delineating the Union's responsibilities towards Russia regardless of whether we speak of the EU–Russia strategic partnership or regional cooperation level, the two main levels of analysis in the chapter.

Elena Jurado's and Rieko Karatani's chapters deal with the EU's role in two international regimes, human rights and migration, respectively. Jurado's starting point is the 'capacity principle': whichever agent can bring about change most effectively should do so. This means that to the extent the EU has instruments needed to promote human rights, it is not only justified but morally required to use them. The EU's responsibility in the global system of human rights stems from its impressive economic resources, which give it enormous political leverage over third states dependent on cooperation with the EU. However, economic incentives are insufficient instruments for ensuring compliance with international human rights standards. Whilst the response of most observers is to call on the EU to develop the full range of instruments needed to promote human rights effectively, the chapter argues that it is neither feasible nor in fact advisable for the EU to do this. Instead, a responsible EU should seek to coordinate its activities with other agents, in particular the Council of Europe and the UN.

Rieko Karatani highlights an area of 'failed responsibility' of the EU. She notes that a clear reduction in migration rights has taken place in recent years, and the EU has significantly contributed to this development; in fact, the Union's focus on inter-regional cooperation shifts migration control to a new level, to a degree beyond democratic control. She takes the Asia–Europe Meeting (ASEM) as an example, and argues that it is a new institutional mechanism that justifies and intensifies a more restrictive drive in the EU's immigration policy. The ASEM framework does not allow for non-governmental organisations (NGO) representation and this lack of advocacy on behalf of migrants by civil rights groups clearly shifts the balance towards restrictive measures and governmental interests in ASEM, also in the international migration regime more generally.

The final pair of policy-sector chapters deals with what could be called 'globalisation and development'. Henri Vogt analyses the trends and images of the EU's development policy particularly in the context of the cooperation with African, Caribbean and Pacific states. His main argument is that both the recent changes of EU development policy and the images that it necessarily has of itself, and that others have, constrain and determine the Union's possibilities to be a responsible actor in the world. The EU needs to understand the contradictory aspects of its activities and the principles it follows in its development policies, and that its image in the world may vary a great deal despite its own positive self-understanding. Awareness of these contradictions might create a Union that can enter into dialogue with its partners in a modest, humble manner – and thus make responsible agency possible.

Terry O'Shaugnessy evaluates the EU's role in the international trading system with the help of three case studies – the disputes settlement procedure within the WTO, agricultural trade reform and the EU's trading relationships with developing countries. The case studies show that the EU has attempted to act responsibly, but has not always done so consistently. To some extent, this is inevitable. After all, different responsibilities are in conflict and some are invoked rhetorically so that interests are obscured rather than described clearly. The chapter concludes by arguing that clarity and consistency in trade policy (and a little less rhetoric) are keys to ensuring that the EU behaves responsibly in its trading relations with others.

In the final chapter, Chapter 10, Joakim Ekman seeks to put the empirical findings of the preceding chapters into the context of European public attitudes, by reviewing existing surveys on European integration. It is important to understand that whatever Europe does in the world, these activities should be supported by EU citizens. Only by anchoring its politics and policies in public opinion, the European Union itself can act in a democratic, legitimate way, decrease its democratic deficit, and thereby become a respected and responsible actor in world politics. Ekman concludes that EU citizens clearly favour an active role for the Union in the world, but this role should be significantly different from that of the current United States.

The conclusion of the book synthesises the main 'findings' of the preceding chapters and assesses to what extent the EU has fulfilled its responsibilities towards the rest of world, and whether it should possibly do something differently in the future. It defines a set of policy priorities which the two editors believe could guide the EU to use its available resources and considerable strengths in a more responsible manner.

The contributors of this volume represent a number of different fields of the social sciences, as well as different academic traditions and nationalities. While our shared principles of responsibility provide the indispensable glue of the study, each author was given room for a reasonable individual application and interpretation of these principles. We believe that this is a strength rather than weakness. Creative thinking on issues of great importance for the future of the world requires a substantial degree of liberty – without the constraints of academic compartmentalisation.

Notes

1. The references in this paragraph: United Nations Millennium Declaration 55/2, Chapter 1, Article 2; www.un.org/millennium/. See e.g. European Multi Stakeholder Forum on Corporate Social Responsibility. Results – June 2004; http://europe.eu. int/comm/enterprise/csr/documents/final_draft_forum_report_290604.pdf (9/7/2004). International Law Commission, fifty-fifth session (2003). www.un.org/ law/ilc/. See also European Commission's Non-Paper for Discussion: Responsibility of international organisations: the case of the European Community. Brussels, 19 May 2003; www.eu.int.
2. It is easy to find examples of this pattern of argumentation in the speeches of George W. Bush. For example in a speech in Washington on 26 February 2003 on the Future of Iraq, he argued as follows:

   Much is asked of America in this year 2003. The work ahead is demanding. It will be difficult to help freedom take hold in a country that has known three decades of dictatorship, secret police, internal divisions, and war. It will be difficult to cultivate liberty and peace in the Middle East, after so many generations of strife. Yet, the security of our nation and the hope of millions depend on us, and Americans do not turn way from duties because they are hard. http://www.themoderntribune.com/george_bush_speech_february_26,_2003_ plans_for_iraq_and_iraq_war.htm; visited on 15 August 2005

3. See, for example, the speeches of Erkki Tuomioja, Foreign Minister of Finland, on www.formin.fi.
4. See www.eadi.org.

5. In recent years a number of good articles and volumes on EU's external affairs have been published, see e.g. Cameron 1998; Bretherton & Vogler 1999; Ginsberg 2001; Jupille and Caporaso 1998; Larsen 2002; Rhodes 1998; Manners 2002; Smith K. 2003; Smith M. 2004; Hill & Smith (eds) 2005.

6. In this respect the recent volume, *Can Institutions Have Responsibilities?*, edited by Toni Erskine (2003), is truly significant; it has been an important source of inspiration for the present book. It is also worth noting that in IR, a number of books have been published recently that more or less explicitly deal with ethics and normative values in relation to international agents. Perhaps we could even talk about a normative turn in IR. See e.g. Frost 1996; Cochran 2000.

7. We are therefore also inclined to think that methodological individualism – the idea that all political objectives and acts can be addressed to a certain individual – is often a problematic interpretative perspective: most individuals, those who are not 'heroes', are constrained by the practices of the institution or social structure that they belong to or represent. See e.g. Haskell 1998, Chapter10.

8. Cf. Erskine 2003.

9. See e.g. Petman 2003; Klabbers 2004.

10. See e.g. Nicolaïdis & Lacroix 2002.

11. One way of conceptualising the different paths which normative globalisation can take is to make a distinction between cosmopolitanism and communitarianism; both seek an alternative to present globalisation but the former takes the individual and his/her potential to be a global citizen as the starting point, whereas the latter emphasises the role of the political community to resist the facelessness of globalisation. See e.g. Cochran 2000.

12. Kauppi 2005.

13. K. Smith 2003, 196.

14. Toni Erskine also pays attention to this in the Introduction of *Can Institutions Have Responsibilities?* by arguing that 'the language of responsibility in international politics [. . .] is impoverished when it comes to the expression of one very important concept: moral agency. This is the concept that would allow us to consider who *can* act in response to ethical reasoning, before we engage in questions of who should act.' (Or in the past tense: 'who acted → who could have acted → who should have acted'.)

15. Kroslak 2003, 170.

16. Cf. Barry 2003, 222.

17. In an interesting article from 1998, Joseph Jupille and James A. Caporaso analysed the EU's role in the Rio Earth Summit of 1992 in the light of four concepts that in their view determine actor capacity: *recognition* – other actors allow the presence of a particular actor; *authority* – the actor has a legal competence to act; *autonomy* – distinctiveness from other actors; and *cohesion* of pursued policies.

18. Bretherton and Vogler 1999, 250.

19. Duchêne 1973; Maull 2005.

20. See e.g. Larsen 2002.

21. Manners 2002.

22. Trägårdh 2002.

23. Cederman 2001, 3.

Bibliography

Barry Christian, 'Global Justice: Aims, Arrangements, and Responsibilities', in Toni Erskine (ed.), *Can Institutions Have Responsibilities?: Collective Moral Agency and International Relations* (Basingstoke and New York: Palgrave, 2003).

Bretherton, Charlotte and John Vogler, *The European Union as a Global Actor* (London and New York: Routledge, 1999).

Cameron, Fraser, 'The European Union as a Global Actor: Far from Pushing Its Political Weight Around', in Carolyn Rhodes (ed.), *The European Union in the World Community* (Boulder & London: Lynne Rienner Publishers, 1998).

Cederman, Lars-Erik, 'Political Boundaries and Identity Trade-Offs', in Lars-Erik Cederman (ed.), *Constructing Europe's Identity. The External Dimension* (Boulder and London: Lynne Rienner Publishers, 2001).

Cochran, Molly, *Normative Theory in International Relations. A Pragmatic Approach* (Cambridge: Cambridge University Press, 2000).

Duchêne, François, 'Die Rolle Europas im Weltsystem: Von der regionalen zur planetarischen Interdependenz', in Max Kohnstamm and Wolfgang Hager (eds), *Zivilmacht Europa: Supermacht oder Partner?* (Frankfurt am Main: Suhrkamp, 1973).

Erskine, Toni, 'Making Sense of "Responsibility" in International Relations: Key Questions and Concepts', in Toni Erskine (ed.), *Can Institutions Have Responsibilities?: Collective Moral Agency and International Relations* (Basingstoke and New York: Palgrave, 2003).

Frost, *Mervyn, Ethics in International Relations: a Constitutive Theory* (Cambridge: Cambridge University Press, 1996).

Ginsberg, Roy H., *The European Union in International Politics: Baptism by Fire* (Lanham *et al.*: Rowman & Littlefield Publishers, 2001).

Haskell, Thomas L., *Objectivity Is Not Neutrality. Explanatory Schemes in History* (Baltimore and Chicago: The Johns Hopkins University Press, 1998).

Hill, Christopher and Michael Smith, *International Relations and the European Union* (Oxford and New York: Oxford University Press, 2005).

Kauppi, Niilo, *Democracy, Social Resources and Political Power in the European Union.* (Manchester and New York: Manchester University Press, 2005).

Klabbers, Jan, *An Introduction to International Institutional Law* (Cambridge: Cambridge University Press, 2003).

Kroslak, Daniela, 'The Responsibility of Collective External Bystanders in Cases of Genocide: The French in Rwanda', in Toni Erskine (ed.), *Can Institutions Have Responsibilities?: Collective Moral Agency and International Relations.* (Basingstoke and New York: Palgrave, 2003).

Jupille, Joseph & James A. Caporaso 'States, Agency, and Rules: The European Union in Global Environmental Politics', in Carolyn Rhodes (ed.), *The European Union in the World Community* (Boulder and London: Lynne Rienner Publishers, 1998).

Larsen, Henrik, 'The EU: A Global Military Actor?' *Cooperation and Conflict*, vol. 37, no. 3 (2002).

Manners, Ian, 'Normative Power Europe: A Contradiction in Terms?', *Journal of Common Market Studies*, vol. 40, no. 2 (2002).

Maull, Hans W., 'Europe and the New Balance of Global Order', *International Affairs*, vol. 81, no. 4 (2005).

Nicolaïdis, Kalypso and Justine Lacroix, 'Order and Justice Beyond the Nation-State: Europe's Competing Paradigms', in Rosemary Foot, John Gaddis, and Andrew Hurrell (eds), *Order and Justice in International Relations* (Oxford: Oxford University Press, 2002).

Petman, Jarna, 'The Problem of Evil and International Law', in Jarna Petman & Jan Klabbers (eds), *Nordic Cosmopolitanism: Essays in International Law for Martti Koskenniemi* (Leiden Martinus Nijhoff Publishers/Brill Academic Publishers, 2003).

Rhodes, Carolyn (ed.), *The European Union in the World Community* (Boulder & London: Lynne Rienner Publishers, 1998).

Smith, Karen E., *The European Union Foreign Policy in a Changing World* (Cambridge: Polity 2003).

Smith, Michael E., 'Institutionalization, Policy Adaptation and European Foreign Policy Cooperation'. *European Journal of International Relations*, vol. 10, no. 1 (2004).

Trägårdh, Lars, 'Sweden and the EU: welfare state nationalism and the spectre of "Europe"', in Lene Hansen and Ole Wæver (eds), *European Integration and National Identity: The Challenge of the Nordic States* (London and New York: Routledge, 2002).

1

The Problem of Institutional Responsibility and the European Union

András Szigeti

In order to provide an analytical foundation for this volume on the EU's global role, my aim in this chapter is to outline a conceptual framework that enables us to assess institutional action in moral terms. It is hoped that this can help to understand what is normatively entailed by the more specific claims made in subsequent chapters about the EU as a *responsible* actor in international affairs. I will try to show that once we get a grip on the notion of institutional agency and the concomitant notion of institutional responsibility, it will be much easier to make headway on what specific responsibilities the EU may have and what failings and achievements it can be held responsible for in retrospect. It seems to me that we should say not only that institutions are in many cases better equipped than individuals to discharge certain duties, but also that some institutions are clearly better equipped to do so than others. Should we find that this also holds true for the EU in certain areas, then we may be able to draw conclusions directly relevant to policy-making.

As a point of departure, I will argue that there is no conceptual difficulty involved in holding institutions morally responsible. If it is justified to hold individuals morally responsible for their actions, then it is also justified to hold institutions morally responsible in much the same ways. Furthermore, if it is right to say that individuals incur special duties in certain situations, then it must also be right to say that institutions incur special duties in certain situations. For instance, we clearly have the duty of rescuing a drowning child when no one else is around and we are in no way endangered by our doing so. Given this, why would an institution not shoulder a similar duty to intervene on behalf of those in need, if no one else is there to do the job and the other vital functions of the institution are in no way endangered by it doing so? In fact, it seems that in a significant number of cases institutions are better equipped to perform certain duties and to respond to certain needs than individuals. What reason is there *against* holding them responsible for failing to do so?

Once it is established that institutions indeed hold certain responsibilities, a further question arises. Which institution or agent is to be held responsible

17

for a particular course of action? Of course, there are often many actors around, individuals as well as institutions, who could do the job in question. Equally often, it is unclear who or what is really capable of doing that job at the first place. So it has been argued, for instance, that the EU does not incur certain responsibilities because there are others better positioned to look after the given problem. And it is said even more frequently that the EU is simply not capable of performing certain duties and hence incurs no responsibility to do so.

This is of course not to say that once all the conceptual work is done we can draw up an unambiguous list of special duties to be discharged specifically by the EU, let alone hold court over EU policies of the past and the future. At the very least, however, conceptual distinctions can help to make it clear that talk of moral responsibility in connection with an institution such as the EU is by no means misguided.

The chapter can be broadly divided into two main parts. The first part discusses different forms of responsibility and establishes the core argument that institutions or international organisations can be deemed to be moral agents. The latter part in its turn presents the primary conceptual framework of this book, a framework of six distributive principles for the allocation of responsibilities to potential actors including, and in particular, the EU.

Terminological distinctions: varieties of responsibility and varieties of institutions

Scepticism about institutional responsibility has been principally fuelled by worries about two questions: (i) can institutions be said to act, and if yes, (ii) can institutional action be assessed in moral terms? I would like to argue that both questions should be answered in the positive. Those positive answers raise a further question: (iii) what is the source of the special responsibilities institutions have? Put differently, on what grounds can we single out institutions as falling under specific moral requirements?

Before turning to these questions, however, a note on an important terminological distinction is necessary. The term 'responsibility' is used in a confusing variety of ways in the literature, even if we restrict ourselves to *moral* responsibility only. Three distinctive senses of the term appear to me to be of central importance in this particular area: responsibility as capacity, prospective (role) responsibility and retrospective responsibility.[1]

The notion of responsibility as capacity refers to the criteria in terms of which one is judged to be a responsible agent. What we mean when we say that an agent is responsible in this sense is that she is capable of 'standing up for her action', to give reasons why she did what she did, etc. More precisely, every agent has to meet certain conditions to be fit to be held responsible. Serious mental illness, being a child, or the inability to grasp fundamental moral concepts are usually regarded as undermining the basic capacity

requisite to being a responsible agent. In sum, if an agent is said to be responsible in the capacity sense of responsibility, then no such responsibility-
undermining conditions obtain.[2]

Prospective responsibility, by contrast, is a collective term to refer to all the
special responsibilities an agent may have in the short or long run in virtue
of her given situation and in virtue of what or where she is. When talking
about this notion, it is very common to use the plural form 'responsibilities' –
responsibilities that one has in the present and in the future. These responsibilities often arise from the fact that the agent voluntarily shoulders or
is involuntarily saddled with certain functions, roles and offices (hence the
term 'role responsibility'). These functions, roles and offices can impose
various moral requirements on the agent's behaviour. Thus it is said to be
a parental responsibility to look after one's children and it is said to be among
the captain's responsibilities to ensure the safety of the passengers on board.
It is also in this sense that the newer international relations literature has
raised important questions. Toni Erskine, for example, asks, in the title of her
recent book, 'Can Institutions Have Responsibilities?' and thereby rightly
distinguishes it from the question whether institutions can be blamed or
punished for failures and wrongdoings of various sorts – a question that
belongs to the area of retrospective responsibility as pointed out below.[3]

It is equally possible however, and perhaps less confusing, to talk about
'special duties' rather than 'responsibilities' in the context of prospective
responsibility. This would be more convenient as it would also allow us to
distinguish this area from that of retrospective responsibility which I am
going to come to in the next paragraph. But since this distinction is seldom
respected, I will not adhere to it religiously in the following either. I will use
the term 'duties' and the plural 'responsibilities' interchangeably, while sometimes using both together in the formulation 'responsibilities/duties' when
this seems necessary to avoid further confusion. But the difference between
prospective responsibilities – duties as opposed to retrospective responsibility (as below) should always be borne in mind.

Strictly speaking, what an agent is *held* responsible for is the *violation* or
fulfilment of duties and obligations. This area is covered by the third notion,
that of retrospective responsibility. It is in this sense that Jones is said to be
morally responsible for breaking his promise to dine with Susan, or Thomas
for failing to rescue a drowning child. In short, ascriptions of retrospective
responsibility concern what the agent has done or has failed to do.[4] If an
agent is held morally responsible for her action in this backward-looking
sense, then she may incur blame or praise and may even be said to *deserve*
punishment or reward for her action.[5]

These distinctions are important for the following reason. When we
raise questions such as (i)–(iii) above, then we are largely concerned with the
prospective responsibilities of institutions. In other words, when we ask whether
institutions can act, and if yes, whether they can act morally, and if yes, what

specific moral requirements they should conform to, we want to know about the special responsibilities/duties incurred by institutions and the normative source(s) of these special responsibilities/duties. Very bluntly, we want to single out institutions, if we can, for performing tasks that we think they are morally required to perform. It is another question whether and in what shape or form institutions can be blamed, praised, punished or rewarded *ex post* for failing or not failing to look after these special tasks.[6]

Let me also note that the term 'institution' is used only in a restricted sense in this paper. It is to denote organisations with a complex and relatively stable internal structure, a structure which is expressly designed to integrate the constitutive members of the institution. Such organisations are expected to rely at least in part on formalised and rational procedures to reach decisions and determine policies. Ritualised and rule-governed forms of social interaction, for example, marriage, sport events or the etiquette of diplomatic exchange, are also often described as institutions, but clearly this cannot be the sense of the term we are concerned with when looking into the possibility of institutional action.[7]

Institutional agency

Can institutions be said to *act?* Is institutional agency not a mere figure of speech, one that is often convenient but also dangerous on account of disguising the fact that in truth only individuals can act. A number of authors appear to think so.[8] In the eyes of these people, also referred to as eliminativists, when we say that an institution did this or that, we simply help ourselves to a metaphor which serves to express that some or all members of that institution performed a certain action. Thus, for instance, journalists may describe the EU as taking action against immigration or intervening in Macedonia, but in reality it is the decision-makers of the EU, the specific member states, individual members of the Council of Ministers or the High Representative for the Common Foreign and Security Policy (CFSP) who act. If none of these people, then those officials who carry out the decisions of these bodies on the ground, or all of these people in combination or whoever, but certainly not the institution of the EU as such.

This scepticism about institutional agency does not lack intuitive appeal. After all, has anyone ever seen the EU as such in action? Or for that matter, has anyone ever seen an institution *qua* institution to act? What we inevitably see is certain individuals acting. They may act in a group or on behalf of others. But again, what we perceive is individuals making statements, raising their hands or signing pieces of paper even if they happen to act in concert.

A further worry is that admitting that institutions can act seems to entail the ascription of capabilities to institutions which we are accustomed to ascribing only to persons: perception, decision-making, deliberation, and so on. Can we really say that institutions have beliefs and feel emotions? Neither groups in general, nor institutions in the narrow sense appear to have consciousness or display features that presuppose consciousness. Nor can groups have the kind of unified, internal and subjective perspective on the world that is often said to be the truly distinctive feature of individual agency. Fortunately, however, consciousness is not a necessary condition of agency as I would like to show in the following.

Note first of all that institutions, or at least some of the institutions which are formal organisations in the sense defined above, display a series of important characteristics that they share with individual agents. Many institutions are able to (i) absorb and process information; (ii) adjust their policies for inconsistencies should new information require them to do so; (iii) implement their policies in a reliable fashion; and (iv) to do so independently from other agents (individual or institutional).[9]

One may insist, however, that even though (i)–(iv) can indeed be ascribed to at least some institutions, this is not enough because we can still only ascribe these properties to institutions in a metaphorical sense. This is because, strictly speaking, (a) only individual human beings can act, and (b) only individual human beings possess the kind of reflective unity that enables one to form intentions.[10]

In response to the second complaint, the 'objection from unity', I want to defend the claim that belief in the reflective or rational unity of individual agency turns out to be a mere fiction, not only in practice but also in principle. That individual actors are never perfectly rational in practice seems easily confirmable, but there is also the further point that it seems *theoretically* impossible to imagine an agent who would not have to act under imperfect information and on at least partially opaque motives which are to some extent beyond the reach of her control. Consequently, if reflective or rational unity were indeed required for the ability to act, then not only no institution but also no individual agent could ever be said to act. Moreover, individual action appears to presuppose the existence of institutions just as much as the functioning of institutions presupposes the existence of individuals. As noted by Onora O'Neill, '[decisions and policies] are never produced by individuals in the abstract: an institutionally embodied context of cognitive capacities and powers of actions is needed for functioning individuals'.[11]

Given their mutual dependence on one another, it seems therefore artificial to draw a sharp boundary between individual and institutional agency. The upshot of this is that the methodological or conceptual priority of individual action to institutional action is a mere chimera because the ability of individual human beings to deliberate and to act is importantly shaped by the existence of institutions.[12]

But what of the first objection mentioned above? Perhaps no such methodological or conceptual priority obtains but it may still be true that O'Neill's reference above to already existing and formative institutional contexts for individual action is once again an indirect way of referring to what is in reality just the pre-established context of other individuals' actions. What creates the semblance of the continued and independent identity of institutions is in fact merely a long sequence of individual actions. I believe, however, that individuals and (at least some) institutions share crucial characteristics in the light of which talk of independent institutional action is entirely legitimate. Given those characteristics – roughly, the ability to act upon reasons consonant with the available information and the ability to act freely – institutions can be said to be capable of purposive action.

Clearly, not all institutions, let alone all groups, are in possession of this capability. Thus many institutions are not in a position to absorb and process information in the required sense because their structural design simply disables them from doing so. Nor are many institutions able to settle upon determinate policies of action. Arguably, however, what renders at least some institutions capable of doing these things comparably well is their having a complexly structured internal organisation with well-defined decision procedures.[13]

The ability to act in a consistent and purposeful fashion presupposes that the given institution has an independent, non-elusive and fairly permanent identity that is not merely the sum of the identities of its constituents. Thus such institutions will strive for consistency not only synchronically (trying to accommodate as many individual preferences as possible) but also strive for consistency over time: present and future policies are to be consistent at least to some extent with policies adopted in the past.

Without trying to provide a complete list of the characteristics owned by institutions capable of purposive action, we can now ask whether the EU qualifies as such an institution. I think there can be no doubt that it has indeed been *intended* and *designed* to be such. A great deal of effort has been spent on trying to make its bureaucracy capable of absorbing and processing information, a great deal of effort too on trying to enhance the connection between information-gathering and policy-making units, and finally a great deal of effort on streamlining internal deliberative and decision-making structures.[14] Also, it might not be entirely idealistic to attribute something resembling a permanent identity to the EU. The question of identity is often reduced to how people living in member countries feel about being a 'European citizen'. But a more important question is, I believe, whether the EU has an institutional identity in the sense discussed here, that is, an identity that is not reducible to the identity of its constituents.

Admittedly, all of these efforts may have only been partly successful. The EU's institutional agency has often been found to be weak and fraught with inconsistencies leaving much to be desired in terms of unity and resolution. But now it at least seems clear what is required to turn the EU into an institution capable of purposive action in the full sense of the word.

Can institutional agents be held to moral requirements?

Let us accept that at least some institutions are capable of acting in a robust, non-metaphorical sense. But can institutional action be held to moral requirements? Are institutional agents *moral* agents?

Perhaps it should be noted once again that this question can be taken in at least two different senses, the second depending on the first in some ways: First, do institutions, genuine agents as they may be, ever incur moral duties and obligations? More broadly, ought moral considerations ever to influence the actions of institutions? Second, is it reasonable to subject the actions of institutions as such (that is, *not* decision-makers or other individual members of institutions but the institution as a collective actor) to moral criticism, to blame, praise and possibly even to punish or reward institutions for their actions?[15]

I will focus here mainly on the first (prospective) understanding of the question concerning moral institutional agency. Those who return a negative answer to this question hold that there can be institutional action but institutions cannot be expected to respond to moral requirements but only, at best, '[. . .] to restricted types of practical discourse established by their constitution and charter'.[16]

This objection is articulated in a way that has special relevance to our present concerns by adherents of the position that has come to be known as 'statism' in international relations. The argument goes roughly as follows: (i) there is only one type of institution capable of acting effectively in world affairs: the (nation-)state, (ii) states are not moral agents, (iii) therefore: no institution can be qualified as having moral agency in the context of international relations.

More specifically, what statism denies is that intergovernmental organisations possess the kind of robust (non-subsidiary, non-parasitic) institutional agency which they would need to have if they were to pursue independent political aims on the global stage (premise i). And, second, statism claims that the institutions – nation-states – that do possess this kind of robust institutional agency are not to be regarded as moral agents (premise ii).

I believe that both premise (i) and premise (ii) are false.

Consider the arguments usually given in support of the first premise. Once it has been granted that institutional agency does make sense (which point must of necessity be granted if we suppose states to be full-blown institutional agents), why should we not admit that institutions other than the state can take effective action to influence international affairs? The first, 'optimistic' statist answer to this question might be that since all moral issues arise within state boundaries, they are to be solved within state boundaries too.[17] There is simply no need to attend to moral issues in international contexts because all requirements of morality – including matters of citizenship and distributive justice – can and should be solved domestically. But this is clearly wrong. The processes of globalisation have put in sharp relief the fact that individual states are unable and often also unwilling to deal with a series of grave injustices, human rights violations, and so on. Moreover, as it has become painfully clear by now, many of these injustices and violations are caused by states themselves.[18]

A second, more 'realist' way of supporting premise one is to say that intergovernmental political institutions cannot be regarded as possessing robust institutional agency, because they are ultimately formed and run by their member states who will use all the power at their disposal to render such institutions subservient to their particular national interests.[19] Note, once again, that even if this claim were true, it would only show that intergovernmental political organisations did not have robust institutional agency. It would still say nothing about the kind of agency attributable to other kinds of institutions, political or economic, some of which may even be active on the international stage (e.g. multinational companies, international NGOs and other networking organisations).

In any case, the EU is indeed the kind of intergovernmental organisation that statism thinks is incapable of possessing robust institutional agency. To what extent should we therefore be worried about this realist version of the statist argument? Answering this question in full would require a detailed analysis of the politics of the European Union which I cannot provide here. It is certainly true that the history of the European Union has been characteristically marked by a 'tension between the drive to act collectively on the world stage and the desire to retain national autonomy',[20] a tension which is reflected in EU policies as well as in a wide range of institutional arrangements within the EU. At the same time, and this is the crucial point, an interpretation that reduces EU policies and practices wholesale to the particular national interests of member countries would be just implausibly pessimistic.

One significant reason for this is that – whatever one's position in the intergovernmentalism/functionalism/europeanisation debate may be – the European integration process cannot be understood as exclusively driven forward by governments acting in the pursuit of national interests. Even intergovernmentalists are prepared to recognise that governments tend to bargain across policies, i.e. one government may be willing to make concessions on one issue in exchange for winning votes in its favour on other issues. More importantly, there is a good case to be made that governments in many cases respond to the *fait accompli* of historical, social and cultural integration rather than act as the driving force behind integration. If political integration ran counter to such historical, social and cultural processes, then it would be (or will be) highly unlikely to succeed, no matter how much governments insisted upon integration. In other words, the relative success of political integration at its current stage can be taken as an indication that integration is not merely the outcome of intergovernmental bargaining.

The general upshot of these considerations is that the first premise of the statist 'objection' has to be rejected as unacceptably restrictive: at least some international political organisations, one of which is I believe the EU, may indeed lay a legitimate claim to having a robust and independent institutional agency.

What about the second premise? Is it true that states are deaf to the calls of morality? The strongest, and in my opinion most interesting, argument put forward in favour of a positive answer to this question is that states *ought to be* non-responsive to moral requirements of any kind, because their only acceptable reason for action can be the furthering of national interests. The point is not that states are *unable* – given the kind of institution they are – to respond to moral considerations.[21] It is rather that they *should* not be responsive because by doing so they would undercut their very *raison d'être*.[22]

Why should realists think that to be the case? One explanation that has been given in the past is that the international arena can be described as being in a Hobbesian state of nature where every state is left to its own resources. But certainly more complex explanations are available too. For instance, if the actions of a democratic state are in question, the second premise of the statist argument may appear initially more plausible since governments of such states are by definition accountable to their electorates and can therefore be expected to give priority to the interests of those electorates.

In any case, now that we have seen that the first premise is false, that is, states are not the only institutional agents to be reckoned with in international relations, we can widen the discussion concerning the second premise to include international organisations as well. So, to rephrase the question, is it true that institutional agents capable of effective action in international contexts – whether nation-states or other international organisations – ought to turn a deaf ear to moral considerations because they are first and foremost required to represent the interests of their constitutive members (who may be individuals or other institutions)?

The answer seems to be clearly 'no'. First, the separation between particularistic, selfish interests, on the one hand, and other-regarding moral requirements, on the other, is a highly artificial one. This holds true of both states and institutions. Moral duty and interest often go hand in hand. For instance, humanitarian intervention in a region where severe human rights violations occur may be in the interest of outside parties but at the same time intervening can be a moral duty too. Intervention can restore stability and economic prosperity in the region, but it can also put an end to human rights violations which is why intervention is morally required in the first place.

Second, it is unclear why actual accountability to constitutive members (for example, to electorates of democratic countries) or even the broader obligation to pursue prudential interests should *always* outweigh moral duties incurred by institutional agents in international relations. When talking about humanitarian intervention – an important but certainly also a rather extreme course of action in international politics – Bernard Williams is surely right in emphasising that the decision to intervene is always a political one;[23] it must be authorised by the relevant bodies within the state or international organisation at issue. Moreover, the decision can hardly be completely at odds with the interest of those represented because otherwise those represented would be likely to resist the effort to put the decision into practice.

In fact, the point about intervention can be generalised. We can certainly agree with 'pragmatic realists' in that strictly political, or if you like 'selfish', considerations must be taken into account when institutional agents, states or intergovernmental organisations, seek to determine whether and how to respond to what appear to be moral calls for action. What will the effects be on other priorities of a more prudential kind (balance of power, economic interests, etc.)? Will the decision be supported by the constitutive members? Is it realistic to expect them to do so?

Having said that, it is difficult to see why institutions should not take moral reasons for action into account if they are perfectly capable of acting upon those reasons. Consider, once again, the case of the drowning child. It is incumbent upon an individual agent to try to rescue the child if she is the only one in the vicinity and doing so does not put her at risk. Now if it is institutional action that can rescue the drowning child, why would the mere fact that an institution rather than an individual is to act render the duty of rescue invalid?

These ideas are especially relevant to the assessment of institutions that have expressly pledged to give serious weight to moral considerations in shaping their policies. The EU has unambiguously identified itself as such an institution. The European Community's development policy lists fighting poverty, the promotion of democracy and human rights among its principal objectives. Similarly, the Common Foreign and Security Policy is expressly aimed at developing and consolidating democracy, the rule of law and respect for human rights, and more specifically at 'contributing to the prevention and settlement of conflicts, and to more effective, international coordination of emergency situations', and even at 'promoting good government' – as for instance stated in the June 1992 declaration by foreign ministers of EU member countries.[24] These commitments make it absolutely clear that the 'statist' objection cannot be invoked in order to justify morally questionable EU policies. It is another question (to be tackled in the next section) whether the EU has been successful or not in pursuing policies which prioritise such moral considerations. In any case, the definition of its central objectives leaves no room for saying that it should not even try.

I conclude, therefore, that the statist objection fails on both counts: it is false that states are the only significant actors in international relations, and it is false that institutional actors must ignore moral considerations.

Distributive principles for the allocation of responsibilities/duties

Our interim conclusion that states as well as intergovernmental institutions can be considered to be moral agents leaves us, however, with what appears to be an even more difficult problem. What is the normative source of the special (prospective) responsibilities incurred by institutions?[25] Or more simply, what are the specific moral duties of institutions and what grounds are there for assigning these duties to them?

The problem is essentially a distributive one. In contrast, however, to the question the theories of distributive justice are more commonly preoccupied with – who is entitled to certain goods and on what grounds – what we ask here is: who or what incurs certain moral duties.[26] In the words of David Miller, 'the issue is how to identify one particular agent, or group of agents, as having a particular responsibility'.[27]

It is very seldom the case that there is only one person standing on the shore of the lake in which a child is drowning. It is equally rare that an institution clearly stands out as alone being capable of discharging a certain moral duty. There are usually many people on the beach, and there are (even more frequently) many institutions that could take care of a certain problem. One person, however, has to be found to wade into the water and it better be quick. By the same token, it is hoped that some means of identifying those (institutional) agents that are *saliently* related to the problem can be found and found quickly.

Several distributive principles for the allocation of duties have been suggested. David Miller and Christian Barry have put forward four: (i) the contribution principle, (ii) the beneficiary principle, (iii) the community principle, and (iv) the capacity principle. I will add another two: (v) the legitimate expectations principle, and (vi) the consent principle.

All of these principles serve to identify those agents who or which stand out as most likely candidates incurring certain duties. I will not be able to go here into the details of each of these principles, nor indeed to explore various connections and possible overlaps among them. The relevance of these principles to the problem of institutional agency and the specific case of the EU will be discussed through a series of examples following the abstract definitions of the principles below:[28]

(i) The *contribution principle* holds that a duty is incurred by those who are causally, or at least indirectly by omission, responsible for bringing about the situation in which the duty arises. Most commonly, what is specifically meant is causal contribution to harm or loss suffered by someone. It is argued that in such situations the causal contributor has the duty to mitigate the harmful consequences of the action.

(ii) The *beneficiary principle* applies to situations in which someone has benefited from a situation which at the same time involves a loss or is harmful to others. In such cases, the principle stipulates that the beneficiary incurs a duty to alleviate the harm or reduce the loss, or if that is not possible, to compensate those disadvantaged in some other ways. Thus, according to this principle, if the rich have become rich at the expense of the poor, then they are duty bound to lessen the plight of the latter (and this is so even if the ways in which they gained their riches at the expense of the poor was not itself morally objectionable).[29]

(iii) The *community principle* states that membership in a community or group singles out agents as incurring certain duties. Community membership can mean here everything from membership in the same family to membership in any group with a distinct identity. In fact, on some accounts the mere fact of one's membership of the human race in itself may generate certain duties. This debatable generalisation aside, the basic idea is that agents owe various things to those who belong to the same group as they do, for example parents to their children, members of a sports team to each other, everyone to his or her compatriots, etc.

(iv) According to the *capacity principle*, if there is a valid duty to do X, then all those who are capable of doing X incur a duty to do X. Stated in such a general form, it is not shared by too many people, although some forms of consequentialism may actually accept it. But when limited to situations in which somebody suffers a serious deprivation or loss, it gains considerably more support. Everyone who is capable of rescuing the drowning child, has a duty to do so.[30]

These four principles, suggested by Miller and Barry, do not cover all kinds of normative reasons that we might have for allocating duties in certain ways – not even if we take them in combination. One problem is that they have been put forward to cover situations in which someone has suffered or could potentially suffer serious and immediate harm (as Miller or Barry were only interested in remedial responsibilities arising in cases of extreme need). But duties can arise in different situations as well. Here is, for instance, a further principle that may apply to cases in which no one is seriously deprived and no one suffers from an acute need:

(v) The *legitimate expectations principle* states that one has a duty to do X, if others legitimately expect one to do X. Various reasons can make the expectation legitimate in this sense – even without express consent. For instance, my behaviour can be clearly indicative of my intention to do X in which case you can hold me responsible for failing to do X (without me ever expressly stating that I will do X). More controversially, the mere fact that I have repeatedly and consistently done X may not only give you reasons to expect me to do X on the next possible occasion, but also justify your holding me responsible should I fail to do X. If I meet you for lunch every single day even if we do not agree in advance to do so, then you may hold me responsible for not turning up one day without prior warning of any kind.

Furthermore, the above principles (including the one just discussed) suffer from the added limitation that they cover non-voluntarily acquired duties only. But we may voluntarily shoulder duties as well. In line with the practice to be found in at least some parts of the pertaining literature, let us distinguish, therefore, such voluntarily shouldered duties from the rest by calling them *obligations*. For instance, making a promise is a paradigmatic way of acquiring an obligation. Hence we obtain the following principle:

(vi) The *consent principle*: one is obliged (that is, shoulders a voluntarily-acquired duty) to do X, if one has consented to doing X or has expressly stated her intention to do X.

Needless to say, each of these principles can be shown to have various shortcomings. One general problem affecting *all* of them is that they do not necessarily solve the problem of salience, that is, the problem of unambiguously identifying the bearers of responsibilities/duties (not even when discharging the duty is extremely pressing) – which is the problem these principles have been intended to solve at the first place. Contrary to appearances, not even principle (vi) is completely immune to this objection as more than one agent may have consented to doing X.

Consider, in particular, the frequently discussed capacity principle. As remarked above the mere fact that an agent is capable of performing a duty cannot automatically mean that the agent ought to perform that duty. First, several agents may have that capability and thus be equally well-positioned to perform the given duty. Moreover, second, the agent may have more pressing duties.

Thus the ability to do X is a necessary but not a sufficient condition for having the duty to do X. This is a trivial point. A more debatable point is this: It could be argued that even if the duty in question is more pressing than any of the agent's other duties, the agent will not necessarily incur that duty. I may have a duty to feed my starving neighbour, but I may not have the *duty* to rescue a starving child in Africa, even if my doing so would involve exactly the same costs as feeding my starving neighbour! In other words, it could be morally commendable for me to do so but it is not morally obligatory in the way feeding my neighbour is obligatory. Or so at least some people argue.

Another considerable difficulty arising in connection with principles (i)–(vi) is that, despite frequent overlaps, these distributive principles may apply only to specific *types* of situations but not to others. But the most serious issue of all concerns the relationship or ranking of these principles when several or all of them appear to be pertinent to a given situation. What if several agents have contributed to the situation at hand? What if one agent has causally contributed to it, but someone else benefited from it? What if one agent both causally contributed to and benefited from a given situation, and on top of that, is closely related to the person(s) most afflicted by the situation, and yet is incapable of performing what she is required to do, whereas another agent to whom none of these conditions apply would be easily able to do so?

Such questions could be multiplied *ad nauseam*. Some, David Miller in particular, have drawn the conclusion from this that none of these principles is clearly prior to the others. In other words, we may have to adopt a pluralistic approach and choose whichever principle (or principles) identifies the most salient agent in a given situation without aiming to provide a universally applicable formula for ranking them.

I cannot even begin to address these difficulties here. What I would like to look at in closing, however, is how these principles, all of which are at least *prima facie* admissible principles for allocating responsibilities/duties, could bear on the responsibilities/duties of an institution such as the European Union. This is, I believe, an issue well worth looking into to answer the question what institutional roles the EU should be legitimately expected to take on. All of the principles discussed have been cited at one point or another to establish that the EU has a responsibility/duty to pursue a given policy.

Let us consider the principles listed above one by one:

(i)   *Contribution principle:* Though looking back on a much shorter history than its member countries, the EU already has a not insignificant record of failures and mismanagement on the global scene. For instance, it is often said that its infelicitous policies seriously contributed to the exacerbation of the crisis in Yugoslavia.[31] Although it clearly shares this responsibility with the UN,[32] NATO as well as several other organisations, states and individuals (not the least the nationalist forces in the ex-republics of Yugoslavia themselves), the contribution principle singles out the EU as incurring at least some responsibility for seeking to alleviate the harmful consequences of those failed policies. A hostile attitude towards refugees or a refusal to contribute to the reconstruction of that area would, however, amount to an unacceptable denial of such a responsibility.

(ii) *Beneficiary principle:* This principle is very often cited in connection with prosperous Western countries. It is often said for instance that, alongside with the US and Japan, the EU benefits from manipulating free trade agreements, patent laws and agricultural regulations to its own advantage when dealing with the developing countries of the Third World. If this is true and to the extent it is true, the beneficiary principle points to the EU as having the responsibility to try and curb the negative effects of such domineering policies.

(iii) *Community principle:* Since the EU enshrines a communitarian understanding of itself in its very name, it is hard to escape the thought that this principle ought to play an important role in defining EU responsibilities as well. We need not be all too idealistic about a shared European identity, history or culture to agree that some of the EU's specific tasks and duties are owed, among others, to other non-member European countries merely by virtue of their being part of a broader European community.[33]

(iv) *Capacity principle:* It is a hotly debated issue what the EU is capable of doing and what it ought to leave to others. What I wanted to show through the discussion of institutional agency in the preceding sections was this: institutions are better suited to discharge certain kinds of duties than individuals, and some institutions are better suited to discharge certain kinds of duties than other institutions. If it is found that a given institution is *uniquely* capable of taking care of a serious problem or responding to a grave need, then it is incumbent upon that institution to do so. If it is found, therefore, that the EU possesses such a unique capability in a given area, then it incurs the duty of putting that cap-ability to use in that area.

Let me also note that there is a pessimistic and an optimistic understanding of the capacity principle. Upon finding that the EU is unable to pursue important tasks or even to contribute to their solution, the pessimistic interpretation argues that it should leave those tasks to other, more capable organisations or possibly states. The ambitious, optimistic interpretation suggests instead that the EU should reform itself so that it can contribute more effectively to the solution of those problems.

(v) *Legitimate expectations principle:* I believe that this principle may well be argued to throw an unfavourable light on quite a few of the EU's strategic decisions and policies. There is a good case to be made that over-confident 'expansion' rhetoric and a host of unfounded promises have induced legitimate expectations in many non-member European states, expectations which the EU has not met, and more gravely, has never even genuinely intended to meet.[34]

(vi) *Consent principle:* Arguably, this principle is of particular significance for an institution such as the EU which owes its existence to the unanimous will of the member countries. It is true that there is a great deal of obscurity and unwelcome flexibility when it comes to the precise determination of priorities.[35] It is also true that the history of the EU as well as that of its institutional predecessors is marked by deep-running disagreements and serious setbacks. At the same time, the principal objectives of the organisation were laid down in constitutive documents and were confirmed repeatedly by all (or almost all) member countries.

As already noted, these objectives give pride of place, among others, to the promotion of human rights, democracy and the reduction of poverty within the EU and throughout the world. In the light of these commitments, there is a good case to be made that the consent principle singles out the EU as shouldering specific responsibilities in the respective areas of human-rights issues, democratisation and the reduction of poverty (and possibly in other related areas too).

If you will, the EU would incur these responsibilities even without its express commitment to take them on, but *given that emphatic commitment* it can hardly opt out of them without exposing itself to well-deserved moral criticism and possibly even an implosion of its core identity.

I believe that this query yields three major conclusions. Firstly, when applied in the specific context of EU responsibilities, the principles will yield largely convergent results. The claim that the EU incurs certain duties will be supported not just by one of these principles but several of them simultaneously. Secondly, the fact that the EU is a voluntarily-established association with clearly defined objectives and priorities creates specific responsibilities or roles for the EU and gives these responsibilities and roles particular weight. How actual policies should be shaped in order to reflect the recognition of the special significance of these roles and responsibilities by policy-makers in the EU will be a much discussed topic throughout this book.

Thirdly, and finally, on a more cautious note: the discussion of such distributive principles on its own is incapable of showing what specific projects and undertakings ought to enjoy priority. Most of the examples discussed in the preceding sections involved cases of extreme need and deprivation, that is, cases in which duties were by definition of the greatest urgency and could not plausibly be said to be overridden by other duties. That is hardly ever the case in the real world. Or what is worse, there are many duties 'out there' that appear to be of the greatest urgency and that would require immediate attention. Moreover, slightly less 'burning' duties are manifold and they require long-term commitment as well. The above principles for allocating responsibilities/duties can provide useful criteria for singling out institutional agents *once the weight and urgency of needs and claims have been established*, but they cannot help in ranking those needs and claims themselves.

Notes

1. Hart offers the definitive classification of various senses of the term 'responsibility' in the 'Postscript Responsibility and Retribution' to Hart 1968. I will not take up here, however, all the meanings of responsibility discussed by Hart.
2. The notion of responsibility as capacity is interestingly connected to the capacity principle which will be discussed in the latter half of the chapter. The core idea of that principle is that the mere possession of certain capacities by an agent can constitute a sufficient reason to hold that agent to be under a duty.
3. Erskine 2003. The same usage can be found, for example, in Smith 2003: 'With the end of the Cold War, the Community was increasingly expected to take on international *responsibilities*, such as spreading peace and security to Eastern Europe.' [my italics – A. Sz.]
4. The concept of retrospective responsibility is only tangentially relevant to the tortuous and highly specific problem of historical responsibility. Of course, historical responsibility (if it is at all meaningful to talk about such a thing) is usually assumed to be backward-looking. But you can also bear retrospective responsibility for something you did five minutes ago, while talk of historical responsibility typically refers to a series of collective actions of large groups in particular historical situations over a longer period of time.
5. Note that retrospective responsibility presupposes responsibility as capacity. In order for the agent to qualify as a suitable object of attributions of retrospective

responsibility, she is to have been in the possession of certain capacities typically associated with rational agency (e.g. the ability to form intentions and to act in accordance with those intentions, etc.) at the time of her action. The converse is not true, however. The agent may be said to be capacity-responsible and she may nevertheless not be retrospectively responsible for a certain action (see also the following footnote).

6. As I will try to argue later on (cf. note 15 below), prospective and retrospective responsibility are closely related concepts. But the route from prospective responsibility to retrospective responsibility is anything but straightforward. One of the several complexities in establishing the precise nature of the connection between the two concepts is this: One may have the prospective responsibility (duty) to do X and yet not be fit to be held retrospectively responsible for *failing* to do X. This is because one may be excused on various grounds – ignorance, duress, necessity, physical compulsion, etc. – from bearing retrospective responsibility for not doing X. For instance, an agent may have been forcibly prevented by someone else from doing X. In such a case, (other things being equal) X is not to be held retrospectively responsible for her failure to do X, even though it was that agent's prospective responsibility to do X.

7. Cf. Erskine 2003, 5–6.

8. Cf. Quinton 1975.

9. I have taken and adopted some of these features from O'Neill's discussion of the institutional agency attributable to nation-states in O'Neill 1986, 62. I will later argue that some organisations may possess a much more robust institutional agency than nation-states.

10. Erskine 2003, 6 & 15n19.

11. O'Neill 1986, 66.

12. In making this important point, I think O'Neill has predominantly *informal* institutions in mind. I concede that the dependence of individual agency on the existence of institutions as formal organisations (which is what we are concerned with here) is less obvious. But there is a good case to be made, I believe, that this latter kind of (inter-) dependence also obtains. We could perhaps just about *imagine* there being individual agency without there being any formal institutions, but the fact is that such institutions are abundant in any existing society and impact on individual action to an enormous extent. And that empirical fact is sufficent for the purposes of the argument made above.

13. Cf. French 1984.

14. For a discussion of cooperation among EU bodies on foreign policy and defence matters see Smith 2003, 234.

15. I differ here from Erskine 2003 in that I think it is rather strange to separate the two questions as she does. A complete separation of the two issues raises this worry: Is it meaningful to say that an agent has a duty but cannot be morally criticized retrospectively for failing to discharge it? In other words, can we have actors who incur duties but are immune to ascriptions of retrospective moral responsibility? The answer seems to be clearly no. But then the two issues – i.e. that of prospective and retrospective responsibility – appear to be related after all.

16. O'Neill 1986, 51.

17. Cf. O'Neill 1996, 369 and Barry 2003, 225–6.

18. Often requiring humanitarian intervention from outside (by other states and/or international organisations), cf. Walzer 1995, 53–66 & O'Neill, 1996.

19. Cf. especially Williams 1995, 67–75.

20. Smith 2003, 230.
21. Although one comes across this version of the argument as well, cf. O'Neill 1986, 59.
22. I am aware that this is an extremely sketchy reconstruction of what the realist theory has to say about the role of states in international relations. It ignores important differences to be found among those who embrace that general theoretical framework. In particular, it ignores the differences between classical realism and structural realism. The other reason why the above gloss is unsatisfying is because it says too little about *why* realists think that states ought not to respond to moral impulses. I give two possible reasons in the next paragraph but of course a more detailed analysis of the pertaining theories could bring to light more convincing reasons too.
23. And this is why considerations justifying the intervention in the affairs of another country cannot be analogous to those cited in support of the 'duty of easy rescue' as applying to individuals, cf. Williams 1995.
24. Smith 2003, 240–1.
25. It is worth remembering that in terms of the conceptual distinctions made in the beginning of the chapter, we are dealing here with prospective (or role) responsibilities. There is also the further issue of retrospective responsibility incurred by institutional agents for failing to discharge these duties that I cannot discuss here.
26. Saying that we are dealing with a distributive problem should not be taken to imply, however, that there is some kind of supreme institution in place which in fact assigns special duties to various institutional or individual agents. Nor does it automatically follow from the discussion in this section that such a supreme institution for the allocation of duties *should* be created. The conclusion that having distributive institution(s) of this kind would be a good thing does not necessarily follow, even if we could unambiguously identify the requisite distributive principles (which I think we cannot as will be seen below).
27. Miller 2001, 453.
28. Note also that other contributions to this book contain a number of direct or indirect references to these principles and their policy-relevant implications.
29. The reason why it is necessary to add this clause is this. If the rich *were* morally responsible and hence blameworthy for gaining their advantage over the poor, then the grounds for their having duties towards the poor would be their moral responsibility for bringing about their poverty through sheer exploitation and *not* the beneficiary principle as above.
30. Compare and contrast the notion of responsibility as capacity: the capacity principle says in effect that the mere capacity-responsibility of the agent can constitute a *sufficient* (and not just necessary) reason to hold that agent to be under a duty.
31. Smith 2003, 238.
32. On the specific issue of the UN's responsibility for one of the most tragic episodes of the Bosnian crisis, cf. Lang 2003, 183–203.
33. Representatives of the EU are keen to emphasise that the EU is to be seen as a genuine community based on much more than just temporarily shared economic interests. As Javier Solana, High Representative for CFSP, succinctly put it in a keynote speech: 'We are much more than a free trade area or an alliance of convenience. Ours is a union of values.' The speech was delivered to 58th Session of the UN Commission on Human Rights in Geneva on 19 March 2002.
34. References to the EU's 'historic responsibility' towards other countries or groups can now be understood as appeals to one or several of these principles, in particular principles (i), (ii), (iii) and (v).
35. Cf. Smith 2003, 241.

Bibliography

Barry, Christian, 'Global justice: aims, arrangements, and responsibilities', in Toni Erskine (ed.), *Can Institutions Have Responsibilities?* (Basingstoke and New York: Palgrave, 2003).

Erskine, Toni, 'Making sense of "responsibility" in international relations: key questions and concepts', in Toni Erskine (ed.), *Can Institutions Have Responsibilities?* (Basingstoke and New York: Palgrave, 2003).

French, Peter, *Collective and Corporate Responsibility* (New York: Columbia University Press, 1984).

Hart, Herbert L.A., 'Postscript Responsibility and Retribution', in Herbert L.A. Hart (ed.), *Punishment and Responsibility: Essays in the Philosophy of Law* (Oxford: Clarendon Press, 1968).

Lang, Anthony, Jr., 'The United Nations and the fall of Srebrenica: Meaningful responsibility and international society', in Toni Erskine (ed.), *Can Institutions Have Responsibilities?* (Basingstoke and New York: Palgrave, 2003).

Miller, David, 'Distributing responsibilities', *Journal of Political Philosophy* vol. 9, no. 4 (2001), 453–71.

O'Neill, Onora, 'Who can endeavour peace?', in Copp, David (ed.), *Nuclear Weapons, Deterrence, and Disarmament, Canadian Journal of Philosophy, Supplementary Volume 12*, University of Calgary Press, 1986, 41–73.

O'Neill, Onora, 'From statist to global conceptions of justice', in Hubig, Christoph (ed.), *Cognitio humana – Dynamik des Wissens und der Werte* (Leipzig: Akademie Verlag, 1996), 367–79.

Quinton, Anthony, *Social objects*. Proceedings of the Aristotelian Society 76, Oxford: Blackwell 1975, 1–27.

Runciman, David, 'Moral responsibility and the problem of representing the state', in Toni Erskine (ed.), *Can Institutions Have Responsibilities?* (Basingstoke and New York: Palgrave, 2003).

Smith, E. Karen, 'EU external relations', in Michelle Cini (ed.), *European Union Politics* (Oxford: Oxford University Press, 2003).

Walzer, Michael, 'The politics of rescue', *Social Research*, vol. LXII, no. 1 (1995), 53–66.

Williams, Bernard A.O., 'Is international rescue a moral issue?', *Social Research* vol. LXII no. 1 (1995), 67–75.

2
The EU's Responsibility for Global Security and Defence

Hanna Ojanen

With the development of the European Security and Defence Policy (ESDP), the EU is assuming both new tasks and new means – civilian and military – as an international security agent. Its ambitions are plainly expressed in the European Security Strategy of 2003, where the Union declares its 'readiness to share in the responsibility for global security'. In that document, the Union commits itself to acting in various ways: disciplining violators of international norms, supporting stability in the neighbourhood, preventing conflicts, and tackling a number of complex security threats. Moreover, it aims at assuming a role in the defence policies of its member states in that the Constitutional Treaty, in its existing form, includes a common defence clause and the establishment of the European Defence Agency. If taken literally, all these tasks together amount to an enormous burden of responsibility. Can the EU credibly take care of all this? What bearing does this shouldering of responsibility have on its actions in practice?

How the EU came to assume such a role in security policy can be fruitfully approached through the six general principles for the allocation of duties that guide all the chapters in this volume. The community principle holding that the members of a community shoulder certain duties to the other members, is particularly clear in a defence alliance such as NATO, but also clearly present in today's EU. This is well reflected by the fact that it encompasses in its draft constitutional treaty a solidarity clause and a common defence clause. The capacity principle, then, holds that an agent has the duty to act if such action can be considered a valid duty and if the agent possesses the capabilities for undertaking it. For a long time, the EU did not have concrete means and capacities at its disposal for taking care of security, at least not *military* capabilities. Over the past six or seven years, it has, however, more ambitiously worked to build up such capabilities; accordingly, it can be held responsible also on the basis of this principle. Two other sources of responsibility further help to conceptualise the EU's security and defence role: the legitimate expectations principle, and the consent principle. Growing expectations have been widely recognised as an important factor pushing the EU into more activism in external relations. To a large extent, the EU has itself fed these expectations by its own indications that it intends to be an efficient actor. Thus, the EU has consented to act by expressly stating its intentions. This is most explicit in the European Security Strategy that is analysed below.

The applicability of these principles proves how similar the security field is to the other external policy fields analysed in this book. Still, there are also clear differences. Security and defence are new to the EU's external role. In this area, the EU does not have the long history of integration that it has in, for instance, trade policy, and thus we are simply not used to thinking about the Union as a security and defence actor. The development over the past decade has been fast, almost so as to leave theorists and political commentators behind. Another difference is that in this field, there are *other and traditionally more important* international organisations to carry specific responsibilities, such as NATO and the UN. Thus, the EU has to find a place among these other agents that might contest the role the Union is claiming for itself. This makes the problem of *credibility* particularly acute.

Whether the Union at all can be said to be a credible agent to assume such responsibilities depends crucially on two questions: first, its capacities, and second, its degree of independence as an agent. In terms of capabilities, one could argue that the EU might not be the best organisation for carrying responsibility for security and defence when compared with such specialised organisations like NATO. Until very recently, the EU did not have any military means at its disposal. But even if an agent possesses all the required capabilities, this may not be enough for it to be held responsible; the agent also needs to be sufficiently independent from other agents. Thus, this chapter tackles the question of the EU's independence in relation to NATO and the UN.

The EU's new role in security and defence also touches upon the traditional perception of the position of the member states. Security and particularly defence have been seen to belong, more clearly than most other fields, to the exclusive competence of states, to the domain of their sovereign decision-making. Many see that the EU's independence as an agent is clearly limited by the states still retaining their position. Yet, the constellation is changing. The distinction between security and defence has become more blurred as defence loses its territorial connotation and increasingly denotes activities carried out somewhere else than on the territory to be defended. Together with the development of EU agency in security policy, also a security thinking specific to this new agent might be taking form, challenging the states' power ultimately to define what security and defence mean and how security is pursued.

While the independence of the EU as a security and defence political agent is incomplete, it is clear that a noteworthy expansion of the EU's role and tasks has taken place in this field. This chapter sheds light on the process through which the EU came to assume such responsibility with the help of factors both internal and external to the Union. Among them, relations to the other agents of the field are paid particular attention to. The chapter argues that the EU is pushed to assuming functions of both states and defence alliances at a pace which might temporarily worsen rather than improve overall security. In the long run, however, the EU's new role may be crucial for any effective handling of issues of contemporary security.

The construction of a security political agent

Assuming new tasks

Security and defence policy did not originally belong to the competences of the European Community. Thus, formally speaking, it was not possible to hold the EC responsible for security and defence. In the field of defence, the member states of the Community cooperated within the frameworks of the Western European Union (WEU) and NATO. Such repartition of roles was confirmed in 1954 when the French National Assembly turned down the initiative for a European Defence Community. Even though a common external trade policy was formulated, and put under the exclusive competence of the Communities, the harmonisation of external *political* relations was not an immediate aim. Foreign political cooperation started only in 1970 in the form of European Political Cooperation (EPC), outside the community institutions. It consisted mainly of consultation; the aim was to formulate common positions on issues of common interest. As late as in the Single European Act (SEA) of 1986 was foreign policy cooperation brought into a legal document, binding, but not enforceable. The scope of EPC was not affected, however, and discussion of security matters was limited to political and economic aspects of security.[1]

For a long time, it was thought unlikely that the EU would ever expand to the field of security and defence policy. Indeed, theorists concentrated their efforts at finding explanations for the fact that this field was *not* integrated. Plausible reasons, such as the specificity of the field as the core of state sovereignty, were found, and theories of European integration came to reinforce the view that there would be no security political integration in the future either.

The end of the Cold War put into question the static conception of defence alliances directed against one another. The Warsaw Pact broke up. Security organisations in Europe needed to look for new tasks and roles. 'Crisis management' was introduced as a new notion, appropriate for the new security and defence related activities that reflected a broadening spectrum of security threats and increasingly consisted of operations outside the area of the organisations. In 1992, the previously largely dormant WEU was revitalised and defined crisis management as its new field of activity in the form of 'Petersberg tasks'. It would thus undertake humanitarian and rescue tasks, peacekeeping tasks and tasks of combat forces in crisis management, including peacemaking. In these, it would lean on NATO capabilities. Both NATO and the EU started to assume a role in crisis management, too, including both civilian and military activities. The EU envisaged getting the required new capacities from WEU. In the Maastricht Treaty of 1991, WEU was made into an 'integral part of the development of the Union'. The EU was to use WEU to elaborate and implement decisions and actions of the Union which have defence implications (article J.4.2). WEU got a double identity in that it was also a 'European pillar' of NATO. Eventually, in 2000, the EU took over WEU's operational parts as part of its own capacity-building.

As the European Communities transformed into the European Union, a common foreign and security policy seemed to fall quite naturally as one of its main constituent parts. A CFSP was formally established in the Maastricht Treaty of 1991. According to article J.4.1, the policy was to include 'all questions related to the security of the Union, including the eventual framing of a common defence policy, which might in time lead to a common defence.' Such a wording seemed at that time over-ambitious, if not utopian. Factors working *against* a common policy in these areas – in particular quite diverging national standpoints – seemed clearly to outnumber eventual factors that would work *for it*.

Indeed, it came as a surprise to most observers that security and defence integration within the EU started gathering pace in the late 1990s. The Amsterdam Treaty of 1997 introduced an important novelty in incorporating crisis management in the Union's tasks. The 'Petersberg tasks' of WEU were now a new definition also for the EU's external role and opened the door for the use of military force by the Union.[2]

Already before the Amsterdam Treaty entered into force, however, the United Kingdom and France agreed in a bilateral summit in St Malo in 1998 on a declaration that underlined the need for EU's *autonomous* crisis management capabilities. The declaration stated, *inter alia*, that

> The European Union *needs to be in a position to play its full role on the international stage*. [. . .] To this end, the Union *must have the capacity for autonomous action*, backed up by credible military forces, the means to decide to use them, and a readiness to do so, in order to respond to international crises. [. . .] In order for the European Union to take decisions and approve military action where the Alliance as a whole is not engaged, the Union must be given appropriate structures and a capacity for analysis of situations, sources of intelligence, and a capability for relevant strategic planning, without unnecessary duplication, taking account of the existing assets of the WEU and the evolution of its relations with the EU. In this regard, the European Union will also need to have recourse to suitable military means (European capabilities pre-designated within NATO's European pillar or national or multinational European means outside the NATO framework). Europe needs strengthened armed forces that can react rapidly to the new risks, and which are supported by a strong and competitive European defence industry and technology.[3]

This put the crisis management role into a new perspective: the EU would now aim at acting independently, instead of leaning on other actors. A consensus was quite rapidly formed on a new conception of the EU's international agency, on the EU's need to have an independent action capability in the world, including also the possession and use of military means. The 'full role on the international stage' that the EU needed to play was from now on much more than responding to crises if no other organisation responded. It also went beyond crisis management to encompass strategic planning and joint efforts at strengthening the European defence industry.

The EU's development took, thus, quite a sudden turn, but it was triggered by several different factors concomitantly. Expectations of the EU playing a more important role were growing, in particular in crises within Europe to which the EU was expected to react.[4] Public opinion played a role here and signalled its acceptance to the EU's increasingly prominent role (cf. Ekman's chapter). Actors that might earlier on have taken care of certain tasks were seen as inadequate or were redefining their roles. WEU was for practical purposes integrated into the EU; NATO was looking for new tasks and geographical focuses.

Thus, other organisations may have left 'space' and tasks to the EU, or indeed invited it to perform a certain role. Of considerable importance has also been the very logic of integration: a gap emerges as integration proceeds in other realms while the intergovernmental foreign and security political side lags behind. This causes confusion when the EU's total performance as an international agent is evaluated. Finally, single countries' aim at improving their relative position within the Union often also results in further integration. A case in point is Tony Blair's United Kingdom in 1997–98 and its emphasis on military cooperation as a new focal point for the EU because it was a domain in which the UK could assume a leading position. In all, the reasons working for a strengthened EU role in security policy are not necessarily related to security and defence at all, but often to union-building and integration dynamics in general.

Collecting capabilities and putting them to use

Once the EU has been established as an agent with specific security-related tasks, its credibility in playing this role depends on its capabilities: autonomous action presupposes means that can be used independently of other actors. The declaration of St Malo that called for such capabilities was put into practice without delay. In the Helsinki European Council of December 1999, the member states set themselves the 'Helsinki Headline Goal' of being able by the year 2003 to deploy and sustain forces 'capable of the full range of Petersberg tasks' in operations up to the level of 50,000–60,000 troops. 60 days was set as the time within which they should be able to deploy these forces, but also more rapid elements were to be included. The member countries committed themselves to sustaining these troops for the duration of at least one year. In reality, primarily as a result of the two capabilities commitment conferences in 2000 and 2001, these numbers have easily been achieved and even surpassed.[5] The work is ongoing: a new Headline Goal 2010 was set for the member states in 2003 to guide the capabilities development further.

In the conception of what the EU's crisis management should be like, rapidity and efficiency have increasingly been valued and sought for. The rapid reaction elements were taken up in the preparation of the Constitutional Treaty by France and the United Kingdom in spring 2004 in the form of EU 'battle groups'. Once again, the popularity of the initiative was surprising. Even though the idea was first connected to the notion of permanent structured cooperation in security and defence, limited to the most able and willing member states, in the end, few wanted to be left behind.[6] In November 2004, the EU was able to agree on as many as 13 different battle group formations of 1,500 troops each. The member countries were willing to contribute more forces than what was thought, and also quicker than thought, and there was consensus on the battle groups becoming reality already in 2005, independently of the fate of the constitutional treaty that 'introduces' them.[7]

Similar action was taken on civilian crisis management capabilities. In June 2000, the Santa Maria da Feira European Council agreed on an Action Plan in the areas of police cooperation, rule of law, civilian administration and civil protection. A Helsinki Headline Catalogue was approved in the autumn of that year, stipulating that the EU would create by 2003 a pool of 5,000 police officers, 200 judges, prosecutors and other experts and intervention teams consisting of up to 2,000 people to be deployed at short notice and able to assist humanitarian actors.

Again, collecting the commitments was not difficult. Committing troops was a way of showing Europeanness – even applicant countries and outsiders contributed. Besides, the same troops were already committed elsewhere: being simply 'double-hatted', they did not imply any extra cost. While the EU has managed to reach the set targets in terms of numbers in both the civilian and the military side, there are still many shortfalls, too. For instance, the ambition to set up integrated civilian rapid reaction units consisting of all the elements listed above, and in cooperation with the military forces, is still far away.[8] Yet, the commitment process has been consequential. It has laid the basis for the EU's claim to be an independent agent, and also affected the capabilities of other agents. As the capabilities committed to the EU are the same that are committed to other organisations' similar activities, when effectively used by the EU, they cannot be used by any other agent simultaneously.

The next step for the EU has been to prove that it really can put the capabilities to use, and start undertaking crisis management operations as envisaged. The record so far is promising. The EU carried out its first crisis management operations in 2003 – the target year set in 1999: a police mission in Bosnia-Herzegovina, and military crisis management operation in Macedonia ('Concordia'), followed later on by a police mission ('Proxima'), and a military operation in the Democratic Republic of Congo ('Artemis').[9] In 2004, a rule of law operation in Georgia ('EUJUST Themis') and a joint military–civilian operation in Bosnia ('Althea') started. The size of the operations has been growing. The first operations were of a modest size, comprising some hundreds of troops, limited to months, and to some clearly defined tasks, but operation Althea mobilises already some 7,000 troops, will last for at least one year, and involves a range of different duties.[10] Increasing expectations are directed towards the Union from its inside as well as from the outside to be present in, for instance, Sudan, and alongside new police and security sector operations in Congo, the EU has also started a small civilian operation in Iraq.

These first operations can be seen to result from a need to show that the capabilities really are there, and that the EU can keep its promises. Giegerich and Wallace note that the EU countries' presence abroad in the form of peace support operations has been increasing, and more money has been spent: the number of troops abroad has doubled in 10 years. They explain this development by international crises and by pressure from the United States rather than by any ideational motivation as such.[11] Yet, the EU has also been responding to, in the case of Congo, an explicit request by the UN (see below). Overall, it is perhaps the growing expectations that best explain the growing presence: the EU's consenting to doing something, and having the capability to act, widens the realm for which the EU is seen to be in some sense responsible.

One could argue that a mechanism of growing expectations is built in the process of integration. Ernst B. Haas defined 'integration' in his book *The Uniting of Europe* (originally from 1958) as the formation of a new political community, a process in which national political actors are persuaded to shift their loyalties, *expectations* and political activities from the old political communities, the nation states, to a new centre whose institutions possess or demand jurisdiction over the national states.[12] The range of national political actors involved thus also broadens; foreign affairs actors are now joined by defence administrations. The first informal EU defence ministers' meeting was organised in 1998. With the onset of military crisis management, even national armed forces are increasingly linked to the process and a shift of expectations can be assumed to take place there as well.

Towards a clear affirmation of a global role and international responsibilities

Following the EU's definition as an international agent that 'plays its full role' and the collection of specific capabilities for this agent, the next question would logically be what kind of an agent the EU is going to be, and for what its capabilities are to be used. The EU now states with increasing clarity the aims that it has as an international actor. Already in the preamble of the Single European Act, the member states declared themselves

> AWARE of the responsibility incumbent upon Europe to aim at speaking ever increasingly with one voice and to act with consistency and solidarity in order more effectively to protect its common interests and independence, in particular to display the principles of democracy and compliance with the law and with human rights to which they are attached, so that together

they may make their own contribution to the preservation of international peace and security in accordance with the undertaking entered into by them within the framework of the United Nations Charter

(Single European Act, 17 February 1986).

Subsequently, the notion of the EU's responsibility for security has become an increasingly relevant justification for the EU's presence outside its own borders and its readiness to send troops in a crisis. However, 'responsibility' has not been given any legally binding format. In a formal sense, the EU cannot have responsibility of realms where it is not competent, and in the division of competencies between the Union and its members, security and defence still belong to the latter.[13]

In the Constitutional Treaty (formally adopted on 29 October 2004, not entered into force), the division of competences seems to follow the traditional path. The treaty distinguishes between exclusive competence and shared competence (articles 11–15). Foreign and security policy figures in neither of these. According to article 11:4, 'the Union shall have competence to define and implement a common foreign and security policy, including the progressive framing of a common defence policy', while article 15 states that '[t]he Union's competence in matters of common foreign and security policy shall cover all areas of foreign policy and all questions relating to the Union's security, including the progressive framing of a common defence policy, which might lead to a common defence.' Furthermore,

> Member States shall actively and unreservedly support the Union's common foreign and security policy in a spirit of loyalty and mutual solidarity and shall comply with the acts adopted by the Union in this area. They shall refrain from action contrary to the Union's interests or likely to impair its effectiveness.

While not recognising any specific legal competences of the Union over the member states, the treaty underlines the EU's competence to form a security policy of its own. It also considerably widens the scope of security- and defence-related tasks of the Union, and explicitly refers to the Common Security and Defence Policy (CSDP, more commonly called ESDP). The treaty introduces a solidarity clause covering the cases of terrorism and natural disasters, a common defence clause (for state aggression against a member country), and broadens the Petersberg tasks to include joint disarmament operations, military advice and assistance, conflict prevention and post-conflict stabilisation. It also sets the principles of permanent structured cooperation whereby more demanding tasks in crisis management can be undertaken by smaller groups and establishes the already mentioned battle groups as well as the European Defence Agency (EDA). The tasks of the EDA include crisis management capacity-building, cooperation in purchasing and developing weapons systems, and contributing to a shift from the traditional logic of national markets and national defence industries to European autonomy but also interoperability with the United States.[14]

The stipulations of the Constitutional Treaty thus give some ideas about the EU's international profile, but it is above all the EU Security Strategy (ESS)[15] of December 2003 that most clearly outlines the Union's external role and also explicitly tackles the issue of responsibility.

The ESS contains three direct references to the notion of responsibility. On its first page, the strategy states that 'Europe should be ready to share in the responsibility for global security and in building a better world.' The immediate reason seems to be self-interest: the strategy affirms that 'A European Union which takes greater responsibility and which is more active will be one which carries greater political weight.' Yet, it is also acknowledged that '[T]he United Nations Security Council has the primary responsibility for the maintenance of international peace and security'.

Alongside international peace and security, other more precisely defined – yet broad – fields of responsibility emerge. The Strategy lists the EU's strategic objectives, and thus the tasks it commits itself to doing – which implies that the EU can also be held, by virtue of an explicit consent, responsible for them. These include, first, addressing what are perceived as the key threats: terrorism, proliferation of weapons of mass destruction, regional conflicts, state failure and organised crime. Further, they comprise such issues as preventing crises, building security and stability in the neighbourhood, and upholding and developing international law and an international order based on effective multilateralism. Thus, the EES might be seen as implying EU responsibility not only for security, but also for existing international norms. The EU almost assumes a role of a watchdog that sees to it that all obey international norms: 'We (. . .) must therefore be ready to act when their rules are broken.'

Taken together, the Constitutional Treaty and the security strategy seem to imply a Union responsible not only for the security of its member states or citizens, but also for the international order. Signs of an emerging EU profile, be that 'civilian', 'normative' or 'positive',[16] can be distinguished, but military elements are also attached to it. This profile does not develop in a vacuum, however. Through the development into a security political agent, the European Union has come into increasingly close contact with particularly NATO and the UN, triggering a new kind of process in which the organisations mutually shape each others' roles and powers.

Sharing capabilities with NATO, or taking over NATO's functions?

Through NATO, the EU can get access to such military assets and capabilities that it needs but does not itself possess. This is indeed the basic content of the cooperation agreements between the two, called 'Berlin Plus'. Such an arrangement was needed after the decision at the end of 2000 that WEU had 'fulfilled its purpose': direct relations between the EU and NATO had to be organised once WEU no longer was a mediating entity between them. Under the agreement, the EU has presumed access to NATO's military capabilities and to the necessary structural and personnel assets. The agreement also guarantees the EU the possibility to make use of NATO's operational planning. Such assets can be seen to increase the EU's credibility: it has means to deliver what it promises, and does not need to spend resources in developing something that can be borrowed from another organisation. Still, one cannot speak about systematic cooperation or a clear division of labour between the two. 'Berlin Plus' was not put to use in the EU's crisis management operation in Congo, for instance. The need to borrow NATO's assets can also be perceived as a problem: it can reduce the EU's autonomy.

The need to be able to cooperate with other agents while retaining independence is expressed in the overall principles of EU relations with other organisations that were outlined at the Gothenburg European Council in 2001. They are: added value, interoperability, visibility and decision-making autonomy.[17] The December 2002 declaration of EU–NATO relations reflects these and confirms on paper the equality of the two organisations. It lists the following principles as the basis of the relations: partnership; ensuring that the crisis management activities of the two organisations are mutually reinforcing, while recognising that the organisations are of different nature; effective mutual consultation, dialogue, cooperation and transparency; equality and due regard for the decision-making autonomy and interests of both; respecting the interests of the member countries of both organisations; respect for the principles of the UN charter; and coherent, transparent and mutually reinforcing development of military capability requirements common to the two organisations. To this end, the EU ensures the fullest possible involvement of non-EU European members of NATO within the ESDP, while NATO supports the ESDP, and pledges to give the EU assured access to its planning capabilities.[18]

The complexity of the EU–NATO relationship is reflected in the different images that different documents give of it. The EU treaties, including the Constitutional Treaty, strongly reflect NATO's traditional position and role as Europe's only real defence organisation: NATO obligations have primacy over any EU arrangements. But when looking at the European Security Strategy, even though NATO is praised as an 'important expression' of the transatlantic relationship, in more concrete terms the document mentions a mere 'strategic partnership between the two organisations in crisis management'.

The increasing interaction to which the two organisations have been pushed by the EU's development into a security political agent makes the EU become somewhat like NATO. Cooperation requires interoperability. Many practices and organisational arrangements are copied from NATO.[19] The need to stress the importance of cooperation, avoidance of duplication and division of labour may also be an indication of increased competition. There is also another reason for increasing overlap: the change in the role of NATO which, in turn, has to do with the change in how security is understood. Traditional territorial defence has left space for the defence of the alliance's interests outside the territory, notably fight against terrorism. It would seem that the EU takes over from NATO at least the operations in Europe (Macedonia, Bosnia), if not also security functions in Europe in general.

When assessing what responsibilities NATO has had and what might thus be awaited from the EU, should these responsibilities spill over to the Union, NATO appears first and foremost as a framework in which the member states share responsibility or assume a collective responsibility for each others' defence, understood increasingly not in territorial but in interest-based terms ('out-of-area', 'non-article 5'). NATO is responsible for the integration of military command, and the preconditions for interoperability of member states' armed forces. NATO is also a forum for transatlantic security policy. With the introduction of the constitutional treaty, the EU comes to share the first function: its members also commit themselves to the defence of others. The other two are not far-fetched, either. The EU does not only focus on its own crisis management operations, but has also an impact on how the member countries plan for defence and invest in it, and it has a stake in defence industry. The goal is the strengthening of European armaments industry, and efficiency gained through, for instance, specialisation and common planning. The EU thus assumes an increasingly important role in questions related to defence planning, to armaments industry and arms trade. Even the responsibility for transatlantic relations in this field might be transferred to the EU, if NATO's importance as a forum declines.

Worries rightly arise about the Union's capacity to handle all these tasks, given its lack of traditions in military cooperation. There has also been concern for the change of identity this development is seen to entail. The means that the EU decides to deploy determine its image as an actor. While not discarding civilian means, the ESS has also been read as calling for more investment in armaments and defence, and it has therefore evoked negative responses from the academic community that endorses the EU's image as a civilian actor. Whether this civilian identity has been a deliberate choice or imposed upon the Union by the absence of other options has puzzled the analysts. For Sjursen, the civilian identity might be well anchored in the EU, and it can be a real choice: the EU would act in that way [as a normative rather than military power] 'because it thinks it ought to do so'.[20]

While there is pressure to become NATO-like, there is also pressure to develop an approach of its own to international security rather than merely imitate existing security agents. One can argue that the EU cannot be in all respects similar to NATO in its security policy: it is not a one-field, intergovernmental and transatlantic organisation as NATO is. Its broad scope and deep integration make it different. It therefore also needs a better-defined legal basis for its interventions, comprising the questions of threshold, determining authority, accountability, amendments and review.[21]

It thus becomes timely also to address the question of whose security one means, that is, what the global responsibility for security means in practice and whose interests determine or should determine the action of the EU. Through a document such as the ESS, the EU intends to affect decisions taken on what are seen as threats, as appropriate responses to them, and as priorities. Thus, it also assumes greater responsibility for perceptions and definitions. Here, it might also make a difference, should it decidedly put forward a view of its own.

Sharing responsibility for security with the UN?

It is not only with NATO that the EU is drawn into closer contact by way of its new security vocation. The EU's global outlook and ambitions as well as its declarations about responsibility for security immediately evoke the United Nations. It is the UN that is recognised as being the organisation that is in the first place responsible for peace and security in the world – and this is obviously what the UN also underlines itself.

The EU and the UN increasingly interact as international agents. The relationship between the two is not new, but their links have been intensifying since the early 2000s as a result of the Union's development and its active role in strengthening them.[22] At the level of concrete action, cooperation has been increasing particularly since the two EU crisis management operations of Bosnia–Herzegovina and Congo in 2003.[23] Even the Union's battle group concept has been developed bearing in mind the needs of the UN.[24]

On the level of principles, the EU, notably through the ESS, clearly expresses its intention to share responsibility for security with the UN, and to strengthen the UN system. In the drafting process of the European Security Strategy, the UN's importance was even further highlighted from the first to the second and final draft.[25] As Toje puts it, the EU maintains a faith that is more commonly found in small states about the effectiveness of the UN in global governance.[26] In general terms, one can say that the UN serves as a legality and legitimacy provider for the EU when it operates outside Europe. The EU also needs the UN as both the main partner and the main arena for fostering global governance. Thus, the EU needs the UN, but the need is mutual: also the UN needs the EU. The Union is for the UN a burden-sharing partner (particularly in crisis management in demanding conditions), and is seen to help the UN to manage or counterbalance American power. The EU is becoming the 'UN's main Western partner' that provides the bulk of contributions to the UN.[27]

There could, thus, be ample opportunities for a fruitful division of labour. As for human rights, for instance, Jurado's chapter in this book shows that there is a need to distribute responsibility for their promotion, and a good way would be to let the EU contribute with material resources for, for example, sanctioning, while the UN and the Council of Europe would have the authority and the legitimacy and thus function as sources of identity-driven compliance. Consequently, the EU should leave space to these other organisations and actively refer to them.

There is another side to the EU–UN relationship, too. Eide notes that the EU represents a challenge to the UN that was originally set up as a state-based, 20th century organisation. Even if the Union recognises the primacy of the UN, it does not want to be bound too strongly to the UN by way of, for instance, an explicit mandate of the UN for each of its operations.[28] Novosseloff talks about the EU's dualism in its relations with the UN: it recognises the primacy of the UN but also lays down its own principles or conditions for cooperation.[29]

The EU's special nature[30] might be a reason for it having a special role within the UN system. The 2005 report of the UN Secretary General *In Larger Freedom*[31] points out three such roles. First, the EU *qua* regional organisation can help the UN in peacekeeping where the UN's capacity is stretched. It can also help sovereign states serve their peoples, and assist in capacity-building for the African Union. This role is particularly important as there has been a negative trend among the rich countries to contribute less to UN operations. They show a clear preference for NATO, EU or *ad hoc* coalition-led operations that are deployed in regions of strategic, political or economic interest to contributing nations. They send five times as many troops to non-UN operations as to UN-led operations.[32] If the EU was willing to commit its civilian and military capabilities for the use of UN operations, the negative trend might be reversed.

Second, *qua* watchdog, in the role that the EU is assuming in the ESS, the Union could work for international norms. There would be need for further regulatory work in particular on the use of force, alongside the Secretary-General's suggested principles that include the need to consider, *inter alia*, the proper purpose of the proposed military action, whether it is proportional to the threat at hand, and whether there is a reasonable chance of success.[33] There is, however, no consensus about such principles among the EU member states. Toje notes that one of the most serious limitations of the EU's security strategy is that it avoids references to the use of force, not offering even the roughest guideline: there is, instead, a profound lack of agreement on when, where and for what reasons the EU should resort to armed force.[34]

Other elements of the new UN-promoted understanding of security might be easier to digest for the EU. As delineated by the UN Secretary General, this new common understanding could be the following: threats do not only include terrorism, weapons of mass destruction or organised crime, but also poverty, deadly infectious disease and environmental degradation. Different countries perceive different threats as the most pressing. The crux is the realisation that one cannot afford to choose, but all these threats have to be

tackled equally seriously. Furthermore, one should understand that development, security and human rights reinforce each other, and that threats are
interconnected.[35]

The EU's global approach might not be at all very far from this. Its fields of
activity comprise all these issues, and it has also been seen as a good candidate
for promoting human security rather than traditional state security, strengthening the position of the individual, and of human rights. For an entity like
the Union, the answer to the question of *whose* security one is talking about
is no longer self-evidently the state.[36] In a report to the High Representative
of the CFSP, a group of researchers, led by Mary Kaldor, has proposed a human
security doctrine for the EU, arguing that the EU's security policy should be
build on human security and not only on state security. The Kaldor group
finds three motivations for such a new doctrine. The first reason is moral,
the universal norms. Second, there is a legal reason: if human security is considered as a narrower category of protection of human rights, then there is
not only a right but a legal obligation for states and institutions to concern
themselves with human security worldwide.[37] A third reason is that of
'enlightened self-interest': Europeans cannot be secure while others in the
world live in severe insecurity.[38]

Third, the EU could have a significant role in implementation. Accountability
and the need to ensure that states abide by the security treaties they have
signed as the bases of implementation were specifically stressed by the
Secretary General;[39] the Union could lead by example in this respect. The
European Commission echoes this line clearly when stating that

> 'Global governance' will remain weak if multilateral institutions are unable
> to ensure effective implementation of their decisions and norms – whether
> in the 'high politics' sphere of international peace and security, or in the
> practical implementation of commitments made at recent UN conferences
> in the social, economic and environmental fields. The EU has a particular
> responsibility in this regard. On the one hand, it has made multilateralism
> a constant principle of its external relations. On the other, it could and
> should serve as a model to others in implementing – and even going
> beyond – its international commitments.

The Commission sees here two aspects to be further developed: the EU's
ability to act as a 'front-runner' in developing and implementing multilateral instruments and commitments, and support, where necessary, for the
capacity of other countries to implement their multilateral commitments
effectively. It also recalls that the Union's voice has often been decisive in
ensuring the 'critical mass' to facilitate the entry into force of multilateral
legal instruments (notably the Kyoto Protocol and the International Criminal
Court, ICC).[40] Still, the EU does not always take this opportunity to lead
by example: Biscop notes that the fundamental norm of Security Council

authorisation for the use of force is not explicitly included in the Security Strategy.[41]

To sum up, the two organisations, UN and EU, might be able to strengthen one another. In concrete terms, they may together achieve a lot in crisis management, and the EU may also help the UN clarify and strengthen its rules and practices concerning regional organisations in general. At the same time, however, the partition of responsibility seems also to involve a delicate problem of the partition of decision-making rights and authority. The EU is challenging the UN if it, for instance, makes itself an interpreter of the UN principles as regards the use of force by starting military operations without a UN mandate. In underlining its own autonomy and the necessity to act on behalf of the 'international community', the EU might even come to undermine the international norms it claims to sustain. To use the terminology of Jakobsen, a single-minded EU seeking to maximise its own visibility and decision-making autonomy will lead to a state of zero-sum competition and a sub-optimal outcome for both the EU and the UN.[42] The central problem may indeed be that the EU and the UN are growing increasingly similar inasmuch as the EU takes on global responsibilities, and extends to all policy fields.

Conclusion: not primarily a security agent, yet primary in contemporary security?

For a long time, security policy was not on the Union's agenda. Some see that the absence of security and defence was a necessary condition for the EEC/EC/EU to proceed in realms *other* than defence. As Andréani *et al.* (2001) put it, with the commitment of the United States to the defence of Europe, and with NATO providing a 'security umbrella', the EU could develop as a 'peaceful' entity, focused on economic and political goals. The Union was spared the demanding and divisive dilemmas which defence would have entailed. Yet, there was a negative side to this as well. Developing an identity as a 'civilian power' may have had negative effects on the European mind-set: it narrowed strategic horizons, *weakened the sense of responsibility*, and resulted in the lack of experience that is now felt in foreign policy, particularly when it comes to power politics or use of force.[43]

The EU's development into an agent in security and defence policy has certainly been rather sudden. Pushed by reasons that often are not directly linked to security but rather to the EU's image, autonomy, and self-interest, as well as to growing expectations, changes in other organisations, and the overall logic of integration, the EU has come in a short span of time to assume responsibility for the full range of security policy. It has taken on the tasks of crisis management outside its own territory. To this end, it has collected both civilian and military means, and started finding ways to improve its reaction capabilities – in terms of both efficiency and speed – also by intensifying cooperation in armaments industry and finding ways to influence its member states' operational and defence-related planning. The constitutional treaty strengthens the member states' commitment to each other's security and to the security of the Union. The ESS, in turn, outlines the EU's aspirations as a global security actor that shares responsibility for peace and security with the UN, that aims at strengthening international norms and multilateralism, and that claims a strong role as a legitimate regional power in its immediate neighbourhood.

The links to NATO and the UN have influenced the EU's scope of responsibilities and definition of tasks: it is replicating both, NATO in the integration of the military, the UN in terms of global reach. This entails contradictions: NATOish independence, work for the interests of the alliance, and perfecting the military tools to ensure interoperability with other actors meet with a UNish concept of dependency on international norms and global interests. Moreover, the division of tasks between organisations in security matters might not be ideally clear. In a given crisis situation, several organisations might have the capacity to take care of the problem at hand. In that case the question of whether one of them has *unique* capabilities or is more capable than the others arises.

The EU might not possess anything unique in terms of capabilities. The particularity of the EU as an agent in security policy might lie elsewhere: First, placing itself voluntarily under the general rules; second, in that it is, or can act as, both a state and an organisation. Third, it seems to assume a specific view on security of its own. The EU appears to take regional responsibility for its own security and that of its neighbourhood, but it also assumes responsibility for the UN system. Its security outlook would be based on norms, prevention of conflicts, and the aim of well-functioning states, something that could be seen as a holistic, long-term approach, an overall strategy for providing global public goods that extends to all external action.[44]

This brings the discussion to the question of legitimacy. Is the EU welcomed as an agent? Whose interests is it promoting? The EU's image in the world can be coloured by a bitter view of Europeans as 'the master thieves of the world', as in the chapter by Vogt. The EU can also easily be perceived as too influential. The EU might get criticised for being both too small or weak and too strong or independent.[45]

Some would indeed ask whether 'assuming responsibility for security' actually only is a smokescreen for wanting to protect European interests abroad. Youngs argues that proactive external projection in the name of certain values is now central to the EU's identity formation. He sees that the Union is truly committed to values but, importantly, a security-based instrumental reasoning might prevail as to how and what human rights are protected and where. Youngs sees Western strategic interests behind drawing a link between human rights and international instability: human rights would be promoted where there is international instability, and in a way that promotes western values. Also commercial concerns can be seen in the background of goals such as promoting good governance. The EU and NATO may also have common interests in promoting military reform (including increasing accountability and civilian control) that may assist the maintenance of military alliances.[46]

The drafting of a constitution for the EU entails identity-building whereby it is important to show the existence of common Union interests. By the outsiders, this might be perceived negatively, as a sign of the Union's willingness to promote its interests over those of others. Such state-like features might render the appearance of the Union less benign. Being an organisation 'only' can be a value in itself.

Basically, the EU is pushed to assuming functions of both states and defence alliances at a pace which might temporarily worsen rather than improve overall security, but may in the long run be the only effective way to handle security policy. While assuming a greater role, it also faces increasing criticism. Biscop argues that paradoxically, for coercive action to be perceived as legitimate, the EU must intervene sufficiently often; if it is perceived to apply too much selectivity in deciding where and when to intervene, and act on self-interest, its legitimacy is at risk.[47]

A potential source of problems is the expectations that shift rapidly, and grow, while the EU is not sufficiently equipped to deal with them. There is a risk for overstretch of its capacities. Particularly long-term presence in a crisis area – something that in principle could be the EU's 'speciality' – might be difficult to guarantee in practice. Priority-setting would be necessary.[48] Moreover, the Union has had a tendency to concentrate on carefully limited operations in order not to fail. This might put the credibility of talking about 'global responsibility' at risk. Secondly, the EU might also end up in rivalry with other agents for reasons of autonomy. This applies notably to NATO and the UN. These learn from each other, and shape each other. The EU might, however, be tempted to take over NATO's role and functions without having the capacity to handle suddenly worsening crisis situations. It might also step on the UN's toes when profiling itself as co-responsible for global security.

In the long run, states are not enough for coping with the various security threats. It is unavoidable that the EU assumes functions in this field, and it may also be the only way of inserting new thinking about security into the national apparatuses. This change is more likely to materialise through the EU than through conventional, intergovernmental organisations such as the UN and NATO. The EU is taking an approach to security that is necessarily broad and variegated as it reflects both its own hybrid nature and its interaction with other organisations. The frequent allusions to assuming responsibility for global security, even though partly too self-reliant, may also turn out to be quite consequential. Security changes, and so do the ways of providing security. The EU, while not primarily a security agent, may well turn out to be the primary security agent in contemporary world.

Notes

1. See Nuttall 2000, 19–21.
2. Integrating these into the CFSP was also a step in integrating Western European Union into the EU.
3. Joint Declaration, British-French summit, St-Malo, 3–4 December 1998, at http://www.iss-eu.org/chaillot/chai47e.html#3. Italics added.
4. On the role of growing expectations, see notably Christopher Hill's notion of a capability-expectations gap; Hill 1993, 1998.
5. In addition to some 100,000 troops, 400 combat aircrafts and 100 vessels, various capabilities from submarines to aircraft carriers were committed in these conferences. See Schmitt 2004, 90–8.
6. Only Malta and Ireland (although considering ways to take part) abstained for reasons of neutrality, while Denmark is out because it has a special exemption from all defence cooperation.
7. To start with, two formations will be ready at a time to be sent in a crisis at a very short notice of even 5 days only. See Protocol on permanent structured cooperation established by article I-41 (6) and article III-312 of the constitution. Official Journal of the EU, 16.12.2004. C310/364.
8. See Jakobsen 2004.
9. See Lindstrom 2004.
10. Cf. Hanna Ojanen, 'Operation Althea: healing, testing, or testing the healing?' *CFSP Forum* vol. 3 no 1 January 2005. http://www.fornet.info/CFSPforum.html
11. Giegerich and Wallace 2004, 168.
12. Haas 1958, 4–5, 16; italics added.
13. In connection with the work of the International Law Commission (ICL) to codify norms regarding the responsibility of international organisations, the EU Commission published a non-paper tackling the issue of the specificity of the EU. The paper looks at international agreements of which the EC or its member states are signatories and ponders on the responsibility of member states for the actions of the EC and on the EC's responsibility for the actions of its member states, but without looking at security and defence. See 'Responsibility of international organisations: the case of the European Community'. Non-Paper for Discussion. European Commission, Brussels, 19 May 2003.
14. Brady and Tonra 2005, 1–4.
15. *A Secure Europe in a Better World.* European Security Strategy. Brussels, 12 December 2003. Here pp. 1, 9, 11.
16. See Manners 2002 and Biscop 2005.
17. European Council Gothenburg 2001, annex V. See Jakobsen 2004, 10.
18. European Union – NATO declaration on ESDP, Brussels, 16 December 2002. Reprinted in 'From Laeken to Copenhagen'. European defence: core documents'. Volume III. Compiled by Jean-Yves Haine. *Chaillot Papers* n. 57, February 2003. Paris: EU Institute for Security Studies. (pp. 178–9.)
19. On EU–NATO relations from the point of view of European autonomy, see Howorth and Keeler 2003.
20. Sjursen 2004, 69–70.
21. Chinkin points out that NATO has a very narrow legal basis for action: the Washington Treaty only provides for one type of action: collective self-defence under article 5. See Chinkin 2004, 10, 19.
22. Tardy 2005, 54.

23. Novosseloff 2004, 3–5. – Note that the Artemis operation can also be seen as a recognition by the UN of the EU's capacity to act.
24. Different practical models are outlined in the document by the European Council 'EU–UN Cooperation in military crisis management operations: elements of implementation of the September 2003 EU–UN joint declaration'; see Ortega 2004, 18–19.
25. Biscop 2005, 55.
26. Toje 2005, 131–2.
27. Novosseloff 2004, 7, 15; Eide 2004, 3.
28. Chinkin 2004, 1.
29. Novosseloff 2004, 7–8.
30. Also reflected in the complex manner the EU is represented in the EU, and in the ongoing talks for and against a single EU seat in the Security Council.
31. *In larger freedom: towards development, security and human rights for all.* Report of the Secretary-General. A/59/2005, 6, 31.
32. See Novosseloff 2004, 8; von Hippel 2004, 12.
33. *In larger freedom: towards development, security and human rights for all.* Report of the Secretary-General. A/59/2005, 58.
34. Toje 2005, 121–122.
35. *In larger freedom: towards development, security and human rights for all.* Report of the Secretary-General. A/59/2005. Pp. 7, 25.
36. Sjursen 2004, 67.
37. Articles 55 and 56 of UN Charter, EU constitutional treaty, article 4.
38. A Human Security Doctrine for Europe, pp. 9–10.
39. In larger freedom: towards development, security and human rights for all. Report of the Secretary-General. A/59/2005, 7, 25.
40. *The European Union and the United Nations: the choice of multilateralism.* Communication from the Commission to the Council and the European Parliament, Brussels 10.9.2003. COM(2003) 526 final. Here p. 5.
41. Biscop 2005, 61.
42. Jakobsen 2004, 11.
43. Andréani *et al.* 2001, 17–19, italics added.
44. Biscop 2005; Brady and Tonra 2005.
45. See Jørgensen and Laatikainen 2004.
46. Youngs 2004, 418, 421–3, 427.
47. Biscop 2005, 29.
48. See also *A Human Security Doctrine for Europe*, pp. 11–12.

Bibliography

Andréani, Gilles, Christoph Bertram and Charles Grant, *Europe's Military Revolution* (London: Centre for European Reform, 2001).

Biscop, Sven, *The European Security Strategy: A Global Agenda for Positive Power* (Adershot and Burlington, VT: Ashgate, 2005).

Brady, Hugo and Ben Tonra, 'The European Defence Agency: serious opportunity, daunting challenge', *CFSP Forum*, vol. 3, no. 1 (2005), 1–4. http://www.fornet.info/CFSPforum.html

Chinkin, Christine, *European Security Strategy: an International Law Framework with Respect to International Peace and Security.* Background paper for the Barcelona group. (London: The Centre for the Study of Global Governance, 2004). http://www.lse.ac.uk/Depts/global/StudyGroup/LegalPaper.htm

Duke, Simon, 'The European Security Strategy in a Comparative Framework: Does it Make for Secure Alliances in a Better World?', *European Foreign Affairs Review*, vol. 9, no. 4 (2004), 459–81.

Eide, Espen Barth, Introduction: the Role of the EU in Fostering 'Effective Multilateralism', in Eide, Espen Barth (ed.) *'Effective Multilateralism': Europe, Regional Security and a Revitalised UN*. Global Europe, Report 1 (The Foreign Policy Centre, British Council and the European Commission, in association with Wilton Park, 2004). http://fpc.org.uk

Erskine, Toni, 'Introduction: Making Sense of "Responsibility" in International Relations – Key Questions and Concepts', in Toni Erskine (ed.), *Can Institutions Have Responsibilities? Collective Moral Agency and International Relations* (Basingstoke and New York: Palgrave Macmillan, 2004).

Giegerich, Bastian and William Wallace, 'Not Such a Soft Power: the External Deployment of European Forces', *Survival*, vol. 46, no. 2 (2004), 163–82.

Gnesotto, Nicole (ed.), *EU Security and Defence Policy. The First Five Years (1999–2004)* (Paris: EU Institute for Security Studies, 2004).

Haas, Ernst B., *The Uniting of Europe. Political, Social, and Economic Forces 1950–1957* (Stanford, California: Stanford University Press 1968). (Originally published by Stevens & Sons Limited, London 1958).

Hill, Christopher, 'The Capability–Expectations Gap, or Conceptualizing Europe's International Role', *Journal of Common Market Studies*, vol. 31, no. 3 (1993), 305–28.

Hill, Christopher, 'Closing the Capabilities-Expectations Gap?' in John Peterson and Helene Sjursen (eds), *A Common Foreign Policy for Europe? Competing Visions of the CFSP* (London and New York: Routledge, 1998).

von Hippel, Karin, 'NATO, EU and Ad Hoc Coalition-Led Peace Support Operations: The End of UN Peacekeeping or Pragmatic Subcontracting?', *Sicherheit und Frieden/ Security and Peace*, vol. 22, no. 1 (2004), 12–18.

Howorth, Jolyon and John T.S. Keeler (eds), *Defending Europe: The EU, NATO and the Quest for European Autonomy* (New York and Houndmills, Basingstoke: Palgrave Macmillan, 2003).

Jakobsen, Peter Viggo, 'The Emerging EU Civilian Crisis Management Capacity – A "real added value" for the UN?'. Background paper for the Copenhagen Seminar on Civilian Crisis Management arranged by the Royal Danish Ministry of Foreign Affairs, 8–9 June 2004, at http://www.um.dk/NR/rdonlyres/5BC4E781-AEC8-4A5D-BBAB-8780ED673EA5/0/TheEmergingEUCivilianCrisisManagementCapacityArealaddedvaluefortheUN.pdf.

Jørgensen, Knud Erik and Katie Verlin Laatikainen, *The EU @ the UN: Multilateralism a New Key?*, Paper prepared for presentation at panel 154, Second Pan-European Conference on EU Politics, Bologna 24–26 June 2004.

Lindstrom, Gustav, 'On the ground: ESDP operations', in Gnesotto, Nicole (ed.), *EU Security and Defence Policy. The first five years (1999–2004)* (Paris: EU Institute for Security Studies, 2004).

Nuttall, Simon J., *European Foreign Policy* (Oxford and New York: Oxford University Press, 2000).

Ortega, Martin, 'The EU and the UN: Strengthening Global Security', in Eide, Espen Barth (ed.), *'Effective Multilateralism': Europe, Regional Security and a Revitalised UN*. Global Europe, Report 1, (The Foreign Policy Centre, British Council and the European Commission, in association with Wilton Park, 2004). http://fpc.org.uk.

Manners, Ian, 'Normative Power Europe: A Contradiction in Terms?', *Journal of Common Market Studies*, vol. 40, no. 2 (2002), 235–58.

Novosseloff, Alexandra, *EU–UN Partnership in Crisis Management: Development and Prospects* (New York: International Peace Academy, 2004). www.ipacademy.org.

Petman, Jarna, 'Alueellisten järjestelmien uusi rooli globaalissa turvallisuus-järjestelmässä', *Ulkopolitiikka*, vol. 37, no. 3 (2000), 41–57.

Schmitt, Burkard, 'European Capabilities: How Many Divisions?', in Gnesotto, Nicole (ed.), *EU Security and Defence Policy. The first five years (1999–2004)* (Paris: EU Institute for Security Studies, 2004).

Sjursen, Helene, 'Security and Defence', in Walter Carlsnaes, Helene Sjursen and Brian White (eds.), *Contemporary European Foreign Policy* (London, Thousand Oaks and New Delhi: SAGE Publishers, 2004).

Tardy, Thierry, 'EU-UN cooperation in peacekeeping: a promising relationship in a constrained environment', in Martin Ortega (ed.), *The European Union and the United Nations. Partners in effective multilateralism*, Chaillot Paper n. 78 (Paris: EU Institute for Security Studies, 2005).

Toje, Asle, 'The 2003 European Union Security Strategy: A Critical Appraisal', *European Foreign Affairs Review*, vol. 10, no. 1 (2005), 117–33.

Youngs, Richard, 'Normative Dynamics and Strategic Interests in the EU's External Identity', *Journal of Common Market Studies*, vol. 42, no. 2 (2004), 415–35.

3
The 'Mutual', 'Shared' and 'Dual' Responsibility of the West: The EU and the US in a Sustainable Transatlantic Alliance

Hartmut Mayer

If there was a prize for the most enduring topic in post-war European International Relations scholarship, the ups and downs of the transatlantic alliance would be a serious contender. Ever since the 1950s, thinking about the past, present and future relations between Europe and the United States has been, at the same time, an old hat as well as a blossoming evergreen. In particular after 9/11 and the Iraq crisis, publications about transatlantic relations have been produced in a staggering rate by academics, journalists and think tanks alike. The general tone has become louder, clichés more pronounced, judgements more radical, anxieties more concrete and policy recommendations more impulsive. On the whole, the debate, attention seeking and headline driven, has become less 'responsible', less accountable, than what we were used to in the past.[1]

Is it worth writing yet another chapter on the theme? The answers are obvious: First, a book on the external relations of the EU would be hollow without reflections on the transatlantic alliance. Relations with the United States are far too central for the EU and each of its member states to be left out here. Second, there is a clear need to identify the deeper necessities and conditions for a responsible transatlantic partnership at the beginning of the 21st century.

The chapter is both ambitious and humble. It is ambitious as it tries to take the EU and the US seriously by their own words. At a time when both entities increasingly refer to morality, ethics, and categories of responsibility to justify their foreign policy actions, the following analysis aims to identify deeper and longer-term principles for a functioning transatlantic alliance by asking how the EU and the US can jointly fulfil the exact moral duties that each side claims to have set for itself in global politics. The chapter tries to define what constitutes a responsible transatlantic relationship, assuming, perhaps naively, that the EU as well as the US still wish to sustain what, to my mind, remains a central axis of the global order.

At the same time, the chapter is humble as it avoids all those categorical conclusions that have dominated the debate over the last few years: no Mars or Venus, old or new, no empire, no end of history, in fact, no real 'you name it'. It simply tries to provide a guideline for a more responsible treatment of a necessarily and continuously changing relationship between the United States and the European Union and its member states. Admittedly, the chapter also makes a somewhat passionate plea for keeping the West together despite, or maybe because of, the increasingly diverging interests. The central message is: undermining the transatlantic partnership further is irresponsible; holding it together is a moral duty regardless of which of this book's six sources of responsibility one would apply – community, beneficiary, legitimate expectations, contribution, consent and capacity principles. This normative claim will be substantiated further in the first part of the chapter.

The latter part of the chapter distinguishes between 'mutual', 'shared' and 'dual' responsibilities in transatlantic relations. A clearer understanding of these three dimensions of transatlantic responsibility allows us to provide a better justification for policy decisions whenever conflicts of interests or strategies between the US and the EU might arise.

A functioning transatlantic partnership as a moral duty

The central claim or point of departure of the chapter is that a functioning global governance system in the 21st century requires a cooperative transatlantic alliance. Maintaining the notion and unity of the West should therefore be a priority for the global role of the EU as well as for any US administration. Trying to preserve a co-operative West should become one of the first commandments for both sides whenever a divergence of priorities in world affairs is about to emerge. As will be shown below, the US or Europe calling for a reorganisation of the world order against one another cannot be justified when tested against our six principles of responsibility. Two prerequisites of this analysis need to be mentioned. The international and global responsibilities must, by definition, be given priority over internal responsibilities whenever assessing the EU's global role and responsibility. The second key prerequisite is that we need to place the EU within the emerging global order of the 21st century. It is not possible to define the EU's transatlantic responsibility without an idea of what a global order should look like.

Taking the six principles of responsibility alone, there seems to be a convincing case for a long-term functioning transatlantic alliance, as well as for short-term reconciliation after the fall out over Iraq. Both are reasonable normative claims. The *contribution principle*, meaning that agents have a duty to mitigate harmful consequences of action that they have contributed to, first springs to mind. Understood in broad terms, one could argue that the current global order, the international institutions, norms, rules and laws of engagement, state and individual rights, have largely been designed by American and

European action and ideas over roughly the last 200 years. While the origins are ancient, the traditions of American and European enlightenment from the late 18th century onwards still provide the foundation of the international system. The point is *not*, however, that this order would be good or desirable in itself, but that those who built it up do incur special responsibilities towards it.

The *capacity principle* – essentially stating that if there is a valid duty to be fulfilled, all actors who are capable of doing that should act – is an evenly uncontested moral category. In the context of the transatlantic partnership it is self-evident that some economic, military and legal requirements of the current and future global order can only be achieved through close cooperation between the United States and Europe. Examples are countless: the rules within the WTO and the World Bank system, regulation of economic globalisation, resources to and for the UN, the implementation of environmental treaties, the principles of international law, post-conflict nation-building and the promotion of democracy can hardly be imagined without the joined support and capacities of the US and the EU. Cooperation rather than conflict between these central players are obvious requirements of responsible action in these areas.

The *beneficiary principle*, that is, the obligation to alleviate harm or reduce loss once you have benefited from a situation where others suffered harm or loss, is closely related. If the current global order is indeed the historical product of joined Western design and if other states, cultures and individuals have a legitimate claim that they suffer from the system, it remains the obligation of the joined West to alleviate the harm. If, for example, as O'Shaughnessy and Vogt in their respective chapters point out, the EU and the US have jointly created a development agenda where fair and free trade are supposed to be the name of the game while both, the EU and the US, impose harm on the system by undermining the very same agenda, then they are also jointly responsible for mitigating such harm. The rich world's rivalries, their tit for tat over tariffs and textiles, bananas and steel, possibly each justified by references to their domestic responsibilities, do not free them from joined responsibility for transatlantic governance in the global economy.

These and other necessities for cooperation can also be clearly justified by an application of the *consent principle*, that is, agents are obliged to do something once they have agreed to do so, and the *legitimate expectations principle*, that is, the duty to follow certain action once others legitimately expect you to do so. The clearest duty thus arises if an agent has repeatedly stated an intent of action. After the end of the Cold War and prior to the Iraq crisis there was a remarkable explosion of statements of intent by the US and the EU to foster an 'ever closer partnership'.[2] While there was a sense that the geo-strategic shifts after bi-polarity might lead to the US and the EU drifting apart, there was a unified response to prevent it by a new level of institutionalisation in EU–US relations. In addition to the reforms and co-ordination efforts through the EU's Common Foreign and Security Policy and NATO (see Chapter 2 by Ojanen), the 1990 Transatlantic Declaration made a mutual promise of consultation.[3]

The 1995 adoption of the so-called New Transatlantic Agenda (NTA) intended to move further to the practice of close international co-ordination and to joint action in global affairs.[4] Innovative frameworks and terms such as the New Atlantic Community, the New Transatlantic Business Dialog, New Transatlantic Marketplace and Transatlantic Commercial Diplomacy might have been hyped-up mechanisms and labels, but they are clear evidence of 'legitimising' expectations and consent on a functioning transatlantic partnership.[5]

The most difficult of our six principles for the transatlantic relations seems to be the *community principle*, the notion that once part of a community, you have the responsibility to obey the law, rules and customs of this community. As Szigeti shows in detail, there is always a potential conflict between overlapping communities or, possibly, belonging to different communities with different contexts and changing values. Indeed, at the very heart of the recent transatlantic rifts lay questions of community: Is there still a transatlantic community? Are there overriding values which hold the community together? Are there in fact different interpretations in the US and the EU of which values constitute this community? Which rules and customs are to be obeyed? Is the transatlantic alliance still part of *Pax Americana* with Washington claiming primacy? Are America and Europe in fact fighting for primacy in the global community? Is Europe a part within or an obstacle to US hegemonic aspirations? As always in the context of the EU, the question also arises as to whether there should be one transatlantic alliance or in fact 27. Do different national foreign policy traditions, roles and special ties with America define the primary reference community? Do national foreign policy makers have to give priority to domestic, European, Western or global responsibilities all derived from different references to different communities?

At least five of the six principles thus indicate that a functioning transatlantic alliance can indeed be regarded as a moral duty; the principles provide a theoretical justification for the chapter's normative claim that the EU's and the US's global responsibility requires a functioning transatlantic alliance. The dimensions of transatlantic responsibility have to be further differentiated, however, and they also have to be applied to the challenges of real world politics. What follows is an attempt to do so. The distinction between mutual, shared and dual responsibility provides the analytical framework.

Mutual responsibility: reality and respect

Mutual responsibility is defined here as the obligation of the EU and the US to appreciate their common heritage and set of values and use this common understanding as a reference point for the treatment of one another. It is based on a realistic assessment of the state of transatlantic relations and global politics and respect for each others shifting priorities in the world. It also acknowledges that the current situation is unique in a wider historical perspective.

Much of what has been said on both sides of the Atlantic since 9/11 reflects an exception rather than a new rule. A lot of the rhetoric that led to the transatlantic rift was media-driven and often addressed to domestic rather than transatlantic audiences. Responsible foreign policy makers must distinguish between exaggerated crisis rhetoric and a cool-headed, realistic acknowledgement of the structural changes that have undoubtedly occurred in US–EU relations since 1989 and 2001. The Iraq crisis, which cannot be analysed in detail here, was an unmitigated disaster for transatlantic cooperation with what could be seen as irresponsible behaviour on both sides.[6] Regardless of where the blame lies – and analysts disagree sharply over this – there is hardly any disagreement that the post-Iraq state of affairs in transatlantic relations has been regrettable and unrepresentative.

Mutual responsibility also requires a historical appreciation of the relationship between the US and Europe. Most policy-makers and commentators seem to have been socialised during the Cold War; their definitions of normality are thus determined by the specific international relations of that period. As a result, they take 1945, 1989 or 2001 as their point of departure when defining the essence of transatlantic relations and marking the key turning points within the Atlantic Community. This is misleading. If the new security environment and economic globalisation at the beginning of the 21st century are indeed, as many analysts argue, epochal changes, then neither a 5 nor a 15 nor a 60 years perspective are sufficient in evaluating the Atlantic Community. Mutual responsibility requires a deeper historical understanding.

America and Europe: the ambivalent alliance

A vastly popular but possibly irresponsible feature of the current transatlantic tensions is the simplistic juxtaposition of European with American values at the societal level. This misleading debate currently absorbs too much intellectual energy in transatlantic discussions, energy which should better be spent on defining shared tasks of global governance.

Historically, the relations between Europe and the US have always been an 'ambivalent alliance'.[7] The current phase is the most recent expression of this very long-term trend. Ever since American independence in the late 18th century, political, social, cultural and economic developments in Europe and America have been mutually constitutive and often inseparable. One does not have to repeat and review the great narrative of Western civilisation so often dubbed 'From Plato to NATO'.[8] The narrative usually includes ancient Greece and Rome, the spread of Christianity, the Renaissance, the Reformation, the Enlightenment, the English, American and French Revolutions, capitalism, modernity, two World Wars, the Cold War and the Velvet Revolution in 1989 to make the case for one united West. What is more interesting is that what are nowadays widely portrayed as 'European values' hardly pass a strict historical test.

Take, for example, Peter Pulzer's convincing critique of the by now famous May 2003 'rebirth of Europe' manifesto by European intellectuals led by

Jürgen Habermas and the late Jacques Derrida. The intellectuals called for a cultural autonomy of Europe, a declaration of independence and the need of Europe to emancipate itself from the unilateralist and hegemonic ambitions of the US. The distinctiveness of Europe was defined by the European Union's supra-nationality, by the social justice of the welfare state, by outlawing the death penalty and by preserving the inviolability of the dignity of the individual.[9] Pulzer traces back the American as well as European origins of the above-mentioned values. He identifies a distinctly patchy record of those 'European' values. In history, he argues, the dividing line between the dominant political values ran, not through the Atlantic, but along the Rhine and later, during the Cold War, along the Elbe.[10]

Similarly, the German social scientist Claus Offe concludes that ever since Tocqueville there have been four constant and overlapping images in European and American thinking about the other: America was ahead for the good, ahead for the worse, backwards for the good, and backwards for the worse.[11] Despite the inseparable and mutually constitutive values of the West, there has always been admiration and rejection of the other by both Americans and Europeans. Even during the Cold War, nowadays seen as the 'golden age' of the transatlantic alliance,[12] there were always conceptual debates about '*Abendland* versus West'[13] and, in more policy-oriented European circles, between Atlanticist and Gaullist directions in European foreign policy. The historical precedents of the current Europe-is-not-America rhetoric thus put 'Mars and Venus', military and civilian power into context, and show that the current antagonisms are by no means unique. They undermine the simple juxtapositions between Europe and America.

This is not to say that there are no significant differences. As far as the societal level is concerned, there is a broad difference between the more brash and inegalitarian capitalist model of the United States and the more welfare-oriented, more state-managed (social) market economies of Europe. However, the varieties within Europe are almost as broad as between the old and the new continent.

The European Commission itself gives an illustrative example of this. In a recent document on 'European values in a globalised world' the Commission points out that Europeans have 'greater expectations of the state than their equivalents in Asia or America'. Europe's core values are seen to be: social solidarity and cohesion, a strong tradition of social dialogue and partnership, equal opportunities, the fight against all discrimination, universal access to education and healthcare, quality of life and quality in work, sustainable development and the involvement of civil society. Accordingly, the 'public sector tends to play a big role, either through regulation or government spending, in the organisation and financing of national systems' and states are decisive 'in the delivery of high quality services of general interest which have been a key feature of economic and social development' in Europe.[14]

One wonders how representative this Brussels view nowadays is. Their own figures tell a more complex story. It is true that, on average, the 25 EU members devote 27 per cent of their GDP to public spending on social protection, compared to 15 per cent in the United States and 17 per cent in Japan. At the same time, the variations within the EU are considerable. Ireland, Latvia and Lithuania spend about 15 per cent on social protection (similar to the US and Japan), the UK and Belgium 27 per cent, France and Sweden about 30 per cent. Furthermore, the results are so different that one wonders whether one can translate such figures into a set of core European values. For example, the level of public pensions within the apparent 'European Social Model' vary from between 31 and 37 per cent of average earnings in Ireland, the UK and Belgium to over 70 per cent in Austria, Finland, Hungary, Italy, Luxembourg, Portugal and Spain.[15] One wonders whether there are now at least three dividing lines with regard to those Western/European values: one across the English channel, the second a North-South demarcation within the Baltic Sea and the third one along the Oder river.

Whatever the geographic and mental borders might be, from a non-western perspective, the heated debates over European versus American values look provincial and self-absorbed. Is it therefore responsible to fight so vigorously over what amounts to marginal differences? Would Americans oppose the values mentioned above or would they just have different political and economic means to achieve (most of) them? And is this really all the West nowadays would have to say?

Mutual responsibility would simply mean to acknowledge the differences and to understand the long history of transatlantic identity formation against or, most of the time, together with one another. It would mean preserving the remarkable common achievements while adjusting it to new strategic realities.

Acknowledging the post-Cold War and post-Iraq realities

Mutual responsibility furthermore requires a fair and respectful acknowledgement of the post-Cold War and post-Iraq realities as perceived by the US and the European Union. No doubt the strategic and domestic environment for the transatlantic community has altered significantly over the last 15 years. A series of watersheds includes the end of the Cold War; the Maastricht Treaty and the EU's increased ambitions that came with it; the introduction of the euro; the establishment of the WTO; the new American threat perceptions after 9/11; the rise of terrorism and asymmetrical warfare, and, most recently, the transatlantic fallout over Iraq. All these factors make a readjustment of the balance between the US and Europe unavoidable.

At the beginning of the 21st century there indeed seems to be a widening gap between the US and the EU in their global outlooks and threat perceptions, and the coherence of strategic thinking on both sides of the Atlantic seems to have disintegrated. The necessary adjustments would include the recognition of the shifts of the domestic contexts for policy makers. The changing ethnic composition of the United States and increased trade links with Asia and Latin America inevitably reduce the relative weight of Europe in US domestic discourses. At the same time, European leaders, during the Cold War fixed on America, will have to develop a more global perspective as a result of EU's enlargement and its increased integration into the world economy. The new neighbourhoods in Eastern Europe, the Mediterranean and the Middle East as well as the increased global competition from Asia will no doubt open and, possibly, re-focus European foreign policy makers minds. Those shifts have to be accepted as realities on both sides of the Atlantic, but they should never lead us to ignore the overriding notion of a common responsibility of the West.

This mutual responsibility is the prerequisite for a larger and more important shared responsibility.

Shared responsibility: creating and sustaining global order

While mutual responsibility – Europe's and America's undeniable duties towards each other – is the first condition, sustaining global order remains the most important shared responsibility of these two actors – and this refers to something different from simple, traditional Western dominance or 'imperialism'. Throughout the book, we argue that the global community and the requirements of global governance must have priority over European or transatlantic duties. Both sides, Europe and the US, must learn to see our times as a transition period in which the parameters of the global order will evolve anew. In the context of the war on terrorism and the Iraq episode it has been difficult to see the larger picture.

In fact, 15 years after the end of the Cold War, the big questions posed today resemble those of the year 1990. They are still unanswered: Will the old bipolar order be replaced by a unipolar or a multipolar world? Do we expect the new world order to rely on regional and integrated economic blocks, and if so, will relations between such regions be of a cooperative or antagonistic nature? Given economic globalisation, will the necessary process of governing beyond the nation-state be achieved by supranational institutions or will the strongest nation-states continue to dominate the course of events? Will multi-lateral organisations be strengthened so that they will be able to maintain global order or will they merely become toys of the strongest nation-states? Will rising powers such as China, India or Brazil fully exhaust their economic and power potential, thereby challenging the West's leadership? Will the West remain the fixed point of the world order? And finally, will Europe and the United States become rivals or will they continue to act, and be perceived, as a united force?

In all these questions, even if the answers vary, the future of the transatlantic alliance plays a decisive role. Considering the influence and capacity of Europe and America in global affairs, a functioning transatlantic alliance must be a very high priority for the EU and each of its member states. As far as the preferred global order is concerned, the EU and most Europeans would probably aim for a multipolar world of co-operative regions with a united West as its anchor, but propagating either a 'purely' European or a 'purely' American attitude would be a dangerous idea – for both sides. Two questions need to be borne in mind, however: How integrated, ready to act and strong Europe must become to pull its natural weight in this very partnership?[16] And does Europe have to give priority to the transatlantic partnership over other global concerns?

As argued in detail in this book's conclusion, a functioning transatlantic relationship with a strong European component is the EU's second most important overall duty globally, just after what we call internal consolidation.[17] But transatlantic cooperation is also a prerequisite for the EU's power and ability with regard to inter-institutional cooperation. If Europe and the US fundamentally disagree on key issues within NATO, the UN, the WTO or any other multilateral framework, the room of manoeuvre for the EU is significantly diminished. As will be discussed later under the heading of 'dual responsibility', this does not mean that the EU should simply avoid conflict with the US at any cost or at the expense of its own cherished values. It means, however, that transatlantic rifts have to be restricted by both sides as Europe and the US have, whether they want it or not, a joined role in global leadership.

The contributions of the EU and the US to global governance

The contributions that the EU and the US can and should make to the processes of economic, political, social, cultural, environmental and security globalisation differ significantly.[18] Both the US and the EU have to contribute to sustaining and recreating global order and they have to recognise their different strengths and weaknesses in contributing to the emerging system of global governance. Both sides seem to agree that, ideally, global order should rest on liberal economic principles and democracy, cultural diversity, environmental sustainability, human rights and the principle of non-violent conflict resolution. Domestically, both sides agree that capitalism has to be civilised in one form or the other and that power has to be tamed, checked and balanced. If these shared values apply domestically, they should, at least this is the understanding in Europe, apply internationally. Based on the unifying values of the West, differences in strategies should be seen as simply as such and should always be subsumed under the shared leadership in global governance.

Having recognised that, policy makers must also be aware of three natural roles and essentials which should determine the distribution of responsibility of the US and the EU in world politics. The three essentials are: first, the US clearly leads in the field of global security; second, responsibility for global economic governance is evenly distributed; and third, the EU is the leader in global political governance. Together, these three principles form the essence of what is called 'shared responsibility' here.

Shared responsibility for *global security* starts with an acknowledgement of the realities in power capabilities. Despite the progress made by the EU in becoming a credible security actor,[19] there is still a yawning military gap between the US and the EU. The US leadership in this field will remain undisputed for decades to come; the US alone currently accounts for almost 40 per cent of the world's military expenditure. In fact, a comparison of the defence spending of individual European countries and the US even suggests that the gap will further widen. The US is already far ahead in the application of new weaponry technology and war-fighting, in fact concerning all the advances usually dubbed as the 'Revolution in Military Affairs'.[20] Furthermore, there is considerable doubt as to whether the Europeans and the US will in the future be able to fight together at all due to the increasing technology incompatibility. The messages of experts in this field are contradictory. While some emphasise the divergence in this area, others insist that convergence is still possible, and, most of all, desirable.

Shared responsibility for global security requires transatlantic co-ordination and dialogue over threat perceptions. As stated above, regional priorities are shifting after the demise of the Soviet Union as the common threat. However, there is and there should be agreement that asymmetrical warfare, terrorism and weapons of mass destruction in the hands of rogue states and/or non-state actors are the most important classical global security threats. As a response, the strengthening of the EU as a credible security player is in the US as well as in the European interest as it equips the transatlantic security community with a more comprehensive set of tools and institutions.

The EU's potential as a security actor should not be underestimated. Measured by defence spending alone, the Europeans are collectively the second largest military power (more than 150 billion dollars in 2002), roughly three times bigger than the third power, Russia.[21] The problem remains a lack of co-ordination, a fully developed strategic vision and appropriate capabilities[22] – even after the formulation of the European Security Strategy (ESS). However, the EU is uniquely equipped to combine military, economic and civilian means to deter and reduce the new common security threats and help to solve some of its underlying causes. Shared transatlantic responsibility for global security means combining the respective strengths of each player and trusting each other far more than what has been seen over the Iraq incident.

Many commentators support a natural division of labour for addressing global security, that is, the famous triplet 'the US fights, the UN feeds, the EU funds'. It would be irresponsible to assume that such a tacit division of labour exists and that it could be the basis for a sustainable and effective security partnership. Instead of neatly dividing the tasks, intelligently combining them would be the essence of the shared responsibility of the US, the EU and the UN for global security.

*   *   *

While US leadership in the field of security is undisputed, in the area of *global economic governance* the power relationship between the US and the EU is far more balanced. The US is clearly the more dynamic and innovative economic player, but the EU is the bigger one, in fact, the world's largest trading bloc. That size alone gives it uncontested influence in international trade. The European voice, whether it is a single one or not,[23] remains crucial for EU–US trade as well as for the functioning of the global trade institutions (see O'Shaugnessy chapter). Traditionally, the EC/EU's *raison d'être* was internal and external trade liberalisation. In the history of international economic governance, the Treaty of Rome was a revolution. It not only made unusually bold steps towards internal trade liberalisation, but also turned the EEC/EC/EU into an external authority to negotiate and implement all dimensions of European trade relations with the rest of the world. Ever since its inception, the development of European economic integration and global economic governance were intertwined.[24] The special status of the EU in trade affairs determines the essentials of the shared transatlantic responsibility for the global economy.

Baldwin, Petersen and Stokes have identified three basic paradoxes which lie at the centre of transatlantic economic relations, supposedly the 'world's most complex trade and economic relationship'.[25] The first paradox is that the underlying fundamentals of trade relations are immune to political changes in either the US or Europe, but that trade relations seem to have become highly politicised in recent years. While the sheer amount of bilateral economic exchange and interdependence condemns the US and the EU to co-operate,[26] tensions over trade following the election of George Bush have become bizarrely pronounced. Furthermore, public fears have been expressed that the US and the EU were in danger of divorce or that they were at least seriously heading towards an economic collision.[27] Actual economic data have never supported these political battles.

The second paradox is that although America and Europe are the most integrated and comprehensively inter-twined inter-regional economic blocs the world has ever seen, this interdependence does not prevent mutual fighting. Disagreements overshadow the fact that mutual trade and investment have reached an unprecedented level. A few figures illustrate the point: In 2000, the US accounted for more than 22 per cent of EU trade, the EU for 19 per cent of US trade. US investors provided more than 75 per cent of foreign direct investment in Europe, while the US accounted for about 65 per cent of all European foreign direct investment. In that same year, Europe invested more in Texas alone than all Japanese investors in the rest of the 50 states together.[28] Europe and America are not only each other's most significant trade and investment areas, they are also the most important trading regions for basically any country in the world. The shared responsibility for global economic well-being could not be clearer.

This leads to the third paradox: while so much intellectual and economic energy goes to redefining bilateral ties, the real question is what the EU and the US, both individually and together, can and should do to steer the increasingly global economy. There is no doubt that any sense of shared responsibility cries for joined leadership and action in agreeing, defining and implementing the rules of global economic governance. However, with emerging challenges from China, India, Brazil, Russia and Africa and with more than 140 members of the WTO, the days are over when the US and the EU alone could dominate all aspects of international trade. The new economic realities do not erase the old responsibilities, even though both Europe and America have to adjust to them.

To summarise, the central role that both regions play in world wealth creation, their equal weight and their common challenges bind the EU and the US together. Shared responsibility in an equal and benign partnership is more evident in the field of global economic governance than in any other policy area.

* * *

Global political governance seems to be an even harder challenge than economic governance. If one takes the concept of global political governance seriously, it is hardly imaginable without strong elements of supra-nationality. The key question is: how do we establish modes of governance beyond the nation-state and existing international organisations that can work efficiently in policy areas such as poverty, warfare, migration, health, epidemics, shortages in raw materials and environmental degradation? All of these areas have become global. Politicians in all nations should not limit themselves to the question of how to make their countries and economies fit for global competition. They should also ask how the global social question will be dealt with and how to strengthen global public goods and distribute them more fairly. Here, the EU is clearly in the lead. Despite all its recognised shortcomings, the EU is the world's only functioning system of democratic governance beyond and above the nation-state. It is therefore not presumptuous to identify Europe as a global model. Europe has created clear supranational decision-making structures, has shown in the 1989 revolutions how to overcome authoritarian rule peacefully and has, on the whole, devoted itself more than any other region to the sustainability of its economic and social development.

The open question is to what extent the European model can be extended to and copied by other regions and in which direction the EU should lead. A '50 year apprenticeship in structured multilateralism'[29] constitute a seriously good advantage, but it is not sufficient for being a superior model in all policy areas. It would go too far, for example, to see the EU as the leader towards what Held and McGrew have called 'cosmopolitan social democracy'. The term is defined as seeking 'to nurture some of the most important values of social democracy – the rule of law, political equality, democratic politics, social justice, social solidarity and economic effectiveness – while applying them to the new global constellation of economics and politics'.[30] While one would not stretch such ideas too far, some of these values are nevertheless what the EU ultimately stands for and what it could offer to the process of global political governance. The EU's post-modern, supranational governance is the most important independent asset that the EU can bring to the global political order.

To sum up, what is called shared transatlantic responsibility in this chapter has three dimensions: security, economic and political governance at a global scale. In each of these fields, with US leadership with regard to security, equal partnership in the global economy and EU leadership in multilateral governance, transatlantic cooperation can be seen in terms of a moral duty towards the global community.

Dual responsibility: softly balancing naivety and narcissism

Whilst 'mutual responsibility' calls for respect for the common heritage of the West and a realistic assessment of different interests within the same family and community, and whilst 'shared responsibility' defines the common duties in relation to the global community, 'dual responsibility' provides the necessary and collective safeguard against each other if and when either the US or the EU are in danger of behaving irresponsibly. It means that the US and the EU must somehow seek to balance each other whenever one of them undermines the common objectives derived from mutual and shared responsibilities. Nothing could be more American or European than providing checks and balances against each other's uncontrolled power, headless egotisms or self-absorbed naivety. In other words, dual responsibility simply says: if one player violates the principles of responsibility, the other must bring it back into line.

Dual responsibility lies at the heart of the recent transatlantic disputes. From a European perspective, the EU has the 'dual responsibility' of joined leadership with the US as well as the duty to 'softly' balance the unrestricted American unipolar moment.[31] The widespread notion in the United States that the US can afford to go alone in foreign affairs and that US primacy is as beneficial for the US as it is for the rest of the world is, of course, highly disputable. It will discussed below. However, the unmitigated belief that turning 'America First into America's Fist' would serve the global community is naïve, possibly ignorant and arrogant. It is certainly dangerous and irresponsible.

As said before, the Iraq episode cannot be discussed in detail here, but some basic assumptions should be drawn out. In essence, only Washington and Berlin were the really exceptional players during the Iraq crisis – not Paris, London, the UN, Moscow, China or the East Europeans.[32] Berlin's unilateral declaration in August 2002 not to support either militarily or financially any American 'adventure' in Iraq even if the UN Security Council blessed it, was a unique break with transatlantic traditions. The Schröder government, sailing on critical domestic sentiments against the American stance towards Iraq during an important election campaign, thereby broke the previous promise made to the US that Berlin would not turn Iraq into an election issue. In addition, Schröder's clumsy call for the 'German Way', a term never really defined and loosely used for both domestic as well as foreign policy, did not help either. Last but not least, the justice minister Herta Däubler-Gmelin's stupid remark that both Hitler and Bush concentrated on foreign wars in order to divert attention from domestic problems, seriously poisoned German-American relations at the time.[33] Berlin behaved irresponsibly, no doubt. Despite various attempts since 2003 the relations between Schröder and Bush remained strained. Rebuilding German-American trust is a major task for any post-Schröder German government.

However, despite such clear European mistakes, the key explanation for the transatlantic fallout lies in Washington. In order to substantiate this claim, one has to distinguish between three general themes. Firstly, there is the older and greater debate on how to tame US power and how to accommodate US hegemonic ambitions since the end of bi-polarity in 1990.[34] Secondly, there is the question of the appropriate response to the new American strategic thinking after 9/11 that seems to make the country's own security fears and concerns the only relevant consideration for its foreign policy. Third, and possibly the easiest of the three, we need to contemplate how to cater for the often incomprehensible attitude, outlook and rhetoric of the Bush administration.

The last point should be taken first as it is a temporary phenomenon. It is remarkable how insensitive the administration has been even before the attack on the Twin Towers in New York in September 2001. The roots of European mistrust were laid already in the early months of Bush's presidency. The unilateral pulling out of the Kyoto Protocol set the tone. Casually mentioned at a NATO meeting in March 2001, the US did not even make an effort to explain the reasons for the shift or to offer an alternative to the treaty – a treaty that admittedly has its deficiencies. More than its substance, it was the non-cooperative and arrogant rhetoric and lack of any consultation which broke with all previous traditions in transatlantic relations. Francis Fukuyama very rightly recalls the Kyoto episode in unequivocal terms: 'The damage that the Bush Administration did to itself by this single act – four months before September 11 – was as enormous as it was unnecessary and set the stage for much of the bad blood to come, blood brought to a boil a little less than two years later with the Iraq war.'[35]

The same policy of non-cooperation by the Bush administration then peaked in the beginning of 2002 with the famous 'axis-of-evil' State of the Union Address in January and Deputy Secretary of Defense Wolfowitz's conduct in the Munich security conference in February. What was undoubtedly puzzling for many Europeans was the fact that Europe had been downgraded in the State of the Union address by not even being mentioned. In Munich Wolfowitz's claim that from now on 'the mission would determine the coalition' and that the traditional NATO links were replaced by ad hoc assemblies of US subordinates provoked European outcry.[36] Again, the Bush administration could not have handled the transatlantic concerns in a more insensitive way.

When assessing the longer-term needs in transatlantic relations, the Bush factor, clearly a favourite for journalistic hyperbole, becomes less significant. The two larger questions, US unilateralism and hegemonic ambitions as well as the changed US threat perceptions which makes security fears the sole guideline for US foreign policy, provide a more serious and long-term concern for EU–US relations.[37] Over the past decade, Americans have debated how to yield US power while the rest of the world discussed how to best deal with it. Whatever one's position on the perceived American need for hegemonic stability might be, nobody could reasonably deny that US power makes the whole world feel uncomfortable.[38]

The EU and European national leaders must constantly remind all future US administrations that, as many Americans in fact understand themselves, the US's global responsibility can only be achieved if American power and sovereignty is dedicated to causes larger than its own security. The American interest must be made to coincide with the global interest.[39] Admittedly, the US is currently the only power that can afford to consider multilateral agreements and international law as non-binding. While one has to recognise this as a legitimate interpretation of US national interest, it can never become a general principle in global governance. How could it? Furthermore, the rosy view so often heard in America that US predominance is central for the world's future of freedom, for democracy and international order, is not shared outside America. Whether right or wrong, perceptions are realities in international relations. And America must care about its image abroad – which it increasingly seems to realise. The March 2005 National Defense Strategy at least recognises that 'our leading position in the world will continue to breed unease, a degree of resentment, and resistance'.[40]

Dual responsibility for the EU means lowering this resentment and reducing the global resistance against American power by softly balancing it. There is an irony here. While Americans might perceive any balance as part of the resistance, it is in fact a contribution to reducing possibly much stronger global resentment. To say it even more clearly: it is in the American interest not to offend the rest of the world while – for the time being – leading it. American power must not be balanced by hard power (which is impossible anyway), but through means of soft power. Europe has the duty to jointly lead with the US, but it also has the duty to balance it whenever Washington is perceived by others to go bananas. Because it is America's closest ally, it is also America's best moderate counterweight.

In an era of global governance the EU is best equipped to defend multilateralism. It has a moral duty to play its normative role as the most vocal advocate of the rule of law. It probably also has the duty to promote 'co-operative regionalism' and 'co-operative multipolarity' as the basis of global order. As a consequence, the EU must give priority to global norms and the rule of law over transatlantic solidarity whenever a 'conflict' of such values arises. Softly balancing US unilateralism is part of the mutual and shared responsibility and should be groomed through constant dialogue and mutually enriching joined leadership.

Conclusion

In one of the best and most balanced volumes on the current crisis in transatlantic alliance, David M. Andrews concludes that official attitudes and essential questions regarding the future of the Atlantic community are so unclear 'because leaders at the highest levels have permitted them to become so. This neglect does their collective publics a disservice. The Alliance is a patrimony; citizens should hold their governments responsible if this legacy is squandered'.[41] One can hardly say it better. Transforming the Atlantic partnership and adjusting it to new circumstances while essentially keeping it together is not a question of political will or strategic ambition, it is a matter of moral responsibility. Leaders across the Atlantic, confused and uncertain as they may be, might actually use some of the concepts and arguments developed here as a checklist against which they can judge their decisions and behaviour. In this respect this contribution and the book as a whole are a citizens' intervention to hold governments responsible.

In addition to holding them accountable, the chapter also tries to help. The six sources of responsibility, community, beneficiary, legitimate expectations, contribution, consent and capacity principles, establish a clear moral obligation for the continued leadership of the West. We can further break down this moral duty into three dimensions of transatlantic responsibility: the 'mutual responsibility' is the prerequisite, the 'shared responsibility' the main objective, and the 'dual responsibility' the ultimate safety net of the transatlantic alliance in the 21st century. As a responsible global actor the EU and its member states have to contribute to all three dimensions of the overall responsibility. The moral foundation and the linkage between the principles of moral philosophy and the tasks of everyday policy are the main objective of this citizens' intervention. It is hoped to be a compass for all those shipping in the wild and often eruptive ocean of literature which calls on us to reflect upon, improve, manage, bury or revitalise transatlantic relations and to put it onto a new footing.

The simple and more timeless message is: there is a moral obligation to keep the West together. US leadership and EU advocacy for the rule of law and multilateralism are two aspects of the same responsibility for global governance. They are inseparable. If the rest of the world is pressured to choose, America and Europe are doomed to lose.

Notes

1. E.g. Cooper 2004; Kagan 2003; Krauthammer 2002; Leonard 2005; Halper and Clarke 2005 represent some of the more extreme views of this debate.
2. Phillipart and Winand 2001.
3. Declaration on US–EC Relations, 23 November 1990, US Deparment of State Dispatch, 26 November 1990.
4. NTA of 3 December 1995, published in Agence Europe, 12 January 1996.
5. See the discussion of all these frameworks in Philippart and Winand 2001.
6. There is already a vast amount of literature on the transatlantic relations after Iraq. See e.g. Andrews 2005 and Cornish 2004.
7. Granieri 2003.
8. Garton Ash 2004, 5.

9. The most important contributions of the Habermas–Derrida debate have been published in Levy *et al.* 2005.
10. Pulzer 2005.
11. 'Self-reflection from afar: considerations on Europe from the American travels of Tocqueville, Weber, and Adorno', lecture by Claus Offe, 24 February 2005, All Souls College, Oxford.
12. Lundestadt 2005, 9.
13. See e.g. Garton Ash 2004; Granieri 2003.
14. Commission of the European Communities, *European values in the globalised world: Communication from the Commission to the European Parliament*, Brussels, 20 October 2005.
15. Ibid.
16. See also Mayer and Stehling 2005, 277.
17. My list of the EU's priorities of duties in and for global politics, derived from an application of the six sources of responsibility, is the following: 1. Internal Consolidation; 2. Transatlantic Relations; 3. Russia; 4. New Neighbourhood Policy; 5. Institutional Burden Sharing, that is, cooperation with NATO, UN, WTO, OSCE and Council of Europe; 6. Middle East; 7. Africa; 8. Larger Sustainable Development Strategy; 9. Larger and Independent Asia Strategy.
18. The author's view is rooted in what Held and McGrew (2002) call the transformationalist school of thought within the different camps of the globalisation debate.
19. See, in addition to Ojanen's chapter, e.g. Howorth and Keeler 2003.
20. Peterson and Pollack 2003, 128.
21. Howorth 2003, 26.
22. Brimmer 2002; Hagan 2002.
23. Meunier 2005.
24. See e.g. Meunier and Nicolaïdis 2005; Tsoukalis 2005.
25. Baldwin *et al.* 2003, 29.
26. Wallace 2002, 283.
27. Dalder 2001.
28. Data from European–American Business Council (EABC) cited in Baldwin *et al.* 2003, 30.
29. Howorth 2003, 14.
30. Held and McGrew 2002, 131.
31. Krauthammer 2003.
32. Andrews 2005, 71.
33. See for a detailed account, Pond 2005; Szabo 2004, 36–38.
34. See e.g. Buzan 2004; Cooper 2004.
35. Fukuyama 2005, 8.
36. Pond 2005, 33–6.
37. Allin 2004; Cox 2005; Jones 2004a; Jones 2004b; Moravcsik 2003; Wallace 2001 and 2003; Walls and Kühnhardt 2005.
38. Walt 2005; Nye 2002.
39. Brezinski 2005, 46.
40. Cited in Walt 2005, 108.
41. Andrews 2005, 266.

Bibliography

Allin, Dana, 'The Atlantic Crisis of Confidence', *International Affairs*, vol. 80, no. 4 (2004), 649–63.

Andrews, David M. (ed.), *The Atlantic Alliance Under Stress. US–European Relations After Iraq* (Cambridge: Cambridge University Press, 2005).

Baldwin, Matthew, John Peterson and Bruce Stokes, 'Trade and economic relations', in John Peterson and Mark A. Pollack (eds), *Europe, America, Bush. Transatlantic Relations in the Twenty-first Century* (London and New York: Routledge 2003).

Brzezinski, Zbigniew, 'The Dilemma of The Last Sovereign', *The American Interest*, vol. 1, no. 1 (2005), pp. 37–46.

Brimmer, Esther (ed.), *The EU's Search for a Strategic Role. ESDP and Its Implications for Transatlantic Relations* (Washington: Centre for Transatlantic Relations, 2002).

Buzan, Barry, *The United States and the Great Powers: World Politics in the Twenty-first Century* (Cambridge: Polity Press, 2004).

Cooper, Robert, *The Breaking of Nations. Order and Chaos in the Twenty-first Century* (London: Atlantic Books, 2004).

Cornish, Paul (ed.), *The Conflict in Iraq, 2003* (Basingstoke: Palgrave 2004).

Cox, Michael, 'Beyond the West: Terrors in Transatlantia', *European Journal of International Relations*, vol. 11, no. 2 (2005), pp. 202–33.

Daalder, Ivo, 'Are the United States and Europe heading for divorce?', *International Affairs*, vol. 77, no.3 (2001), pp. 553–67.

Fukuyama, Francis a.o., 'Symposium. The Sources of American Conduct', *The American Interest*, vol. 1, no. 1 (2005), pp. 7–36.

Garton Ash, Timothy, *Free World: Why a Crisis of the West reveals the Opportunity of Our Time* (London: Alan Lane, 2004).

Granieri, Ronald J., *The Ambivalent Alliance: Konrad Adenauer, the CDU/CSU, and the West, 1949–1966* (New York and Oxford: Berghahn Books, 2003).

Hagman, Hans-Christian, *European Crisis Management and Defence: The Search for Capabilities*, Adelphi-Paper 353 (London: IISS, 2002).

Halper, Stefan and Jonathan Clarke, *America Alone: The Neo-Conservatives and the Global Order* (Cambridge: Cambridge University Press, 2005).

Held, David and Anthony McGrew, *Globalization/Anti-Globalization* (Cambridge: Polity Press, 2002).

Howorth, Jolyon, 'Foreign and Defence Policy cooperation', in John Petersen and Mark A. Pollack (eds), *Europe, America, Bush. Transatlantic Relations in the Twenty-first Century* (London and New York: Routledge, 2003).

Howorth, Jolyon and J.T.S. Keeler (eds), *Defending Europe: The EU, NATO and the Quest for Autonomy* (New York: Palgrave, 2003).

Jones, Erik, 'Introduction', *International Affairs*, vol. 80, no. 4 (2004a), pp. 587–93.

Jones, Erik, 'Debating the transatlantic relationship: rhetoric and reality', *International Affairs*, vol. 80, no. 4 (2004b), pp. 595–612.

Kagan, Robert, *Paradise and Power: America and Europe in the New World Order* (London: Atlantic Books, 2003).

Krauthammer, Charles, 'The Unipolar Moment Revisited', *The National Interest* 70 (2003), pp. 5–17.

Leonard, Mark, *Why Europe Will Run The 21st Century* (London and New York: Fourth Estate 2005).

Levy, Daniel, Max Pensky and John Torpey (eds), *Old Europe, New Europe, Core Europe: Transatlantic Relations After The Iraq War* (London and New York: Verso, 2005).

Lieber, Robert J., *The American Era: Power and Strategy for the 21st Century* (Cambridge: Cambridge University Press, 2005).

Lundestad, Geir, *The United States and Western Europe Since 1945: From 'Empire' by Invitation to Transatlantic Drift* (Oxford: Oxford University Press, 2003).

Lundestad, Geir, 'Towards a Transatlantic Rift', in David M. Andrews (ed.), *The Atlantic Alliance under Stress: US–European Relations After Iraq* (Cambridge: Cambridge University Press, 2005).

Mayer, Hartmut and Thomas Bernd Stehling, 'Conclusion', in Hartmut Mayer and Thomas Bernd Stehling, *German–British Relations and 'the Spirit of Cadenabbia'* (Berlin: KAS, 2005).

Meunier, Sophie, *Trading Voices: The European Union in International Commercial Negotiations* (Princeton: Princeton University Press, 2005).

Meunier, Sophie and Kalypso Nicolaïdis, 'The European Union as a Trade Power', in Christopher Hill and Michael Smith (eds), *International Relations and the European Union* (Oxford: Oxford University Press, 2005).

Moravcsik, Andrew, 'Striking a New Transatlantic Bargain', *Foreign Affairs*, vol. 82, no. 4 (2003), pp. 74–89.

Nicolaïdis, Kalypso and Robert Howse, 'This is my EUtopia': The EU, the WTO, global governance and global justice', *Journal of Common Market Studies*, vol. 40, no. 4 (2002), pp. 767–89.

Nye, Joseph, *The Paradox of American Power: Why the World's Only Superpower Can't Go It Alone* (Oxford and New York: Oxford University Press, 2002).

Peterson, John and Mark A. Pollack (eds), *Europe, America, Bush: Transatlantic Relations in the Twenty-first Century* (London and New York: Routledge, 2003).

Philippart, Eric and Pascaline Winand (eds), *Ever Closer Partnership: Policy-Making in US–EU Relations*, (Brussels: Peter Lang 2001).

Pond, Elizabeth, 'The dynamics of the feud over Iraq', in David M. Andrews, *The Atlantic Alliance Under Stress: US–European Relations After Iraq* (Cambridge: Cambridge University Press 2005).

Pulzer, Peter, 'Europese warden of westerse warden?', *Nexus*, vol. 41 (2005), pp. 5–18.

Szabo, Stephen, *Parting Ways: The Crisis in German–American Relations* (Washington: Brookings Institution Press, 2004).

Trachtenberg, Mark, 'The Iraq crisis and the future of the Western Alliance', in David M. Andrews (ed.), *The Atlantic Alliance Under Stress: US–European Relations After Iraq* (Cambridge: Cambridge University Press, 2005).

Tsoukalis, Loukas, 'Managing Interdependence: The EU in the World Economy', in Christopher Hill and Michael Smith, *International Relations and the European Union* (Oxford: Oxford University Press, 2005).

Wallace, William, 'Europe: the necessary partner', *Foreign Affairs*, vol. 80, no. 2 (2001), pp. 16–34.

Wallace, William, 'As viewed from Europe: transatlantic sympathies, transatlantic fear', *International Relations*, vol. 16, no. 2 (2002), pp. 281–6.

Walls, Samuel and Ludger Kühnhardt (eds), 'The Crisis in Transatlantic Relations', *ZEI Discussion, Paper C143* (Bonn: Zentrum für Europäische Integrationsforschung 2005).

Walt, Stephen. M., 'Taming American Power', *Foreign Affairs*, vol. 84, no. 5 (2005), pp. 105–20.

4
The EU as a Regional Power: Extended Governance and Historical Responsibility

Kristi Raik

One of the most consensual issues in the field of EU foreign policy is the special importance of neighbouring areas or 'wider Europe'. Regardless of its capability to become an ever stronger global actor, the EU is a regional power and is expected by many to enhance its role in the broader European region. This is often framed as a matter of responsibility – a responsibility that primarily stems from the history and nature of the Union.

The predecessors of the current EU were established on the ruins of the Second World War with the aim of creating lasting peace among democratic European states. According to the Schuman declaration of May 1950, the European Coal and Steel Community was to create 'a European federation indispensable to the preservation of peace', which should be 'open to the participation of the other countries of Europe'.[1] The establishment of the European Economic Community in 1958 was carried by the same spirit, calling for an 'ever closer union among the peoples of Europe'[2] sharing the same ideals. According to Frank Schimmelfennig, these historical goals lay down the 'founding myth' of European integration. Making a similar point, Barry Buzan and Ole Wæver identify a meta-narrative that defines the EU as a security community and the institution responsible for not allowing Europe's past to become Europe's future.[3]

The historic origin of integration thus creates a European identity that ties security to the core principles of democracy. The EU is both a security community and a value community, and these two are inseparable from each other. In assessing the EU's policies towards its new neighbours, we ought to be aware of these different types of communities, especially given that 'community' is one of the central principles incurring responsibilities (cf. Chapter 1 by Szigeti). A distinction between security and value communities may be useful analytically, but in terms of responsibility it is crucial that these two are inherently linked.

The EU's regional power is at its strongest in relation to countries that are treated as future members: Bulgaria and Romania expected to join the Union in 2007, Turkey and Croatia, as well as other Western Balkan countries that have not yet started accession negotiations. Besides these current and potential candidates, there are many neighbouring countries whose membership is not considered likely at least within the next 10 to 20 years, if ever, but that nevertheless seek closer integration with the EU. For these countries, the EU has launched a new instrument, the European Neighbourhood Policy (ENP), in order to develop new forms of integration that would be more than cooperation, but fall short of membership. We may thus distinguish between two groups of countries: 'semi-insiders' or 'pre-ins', that is, countries acknowledged by the EU as member candidates, and 'semi-outsiders' for whom membership is not on offer. In addition, there is a third category of 'outsiders' – neighbours that cannot be fully included in the ENP because they violate the basic values of democracy and human rights. At the moment that group consists of Belarus and Libya, the only two neighbours that do not have formal relations with the Union. One of the most difficult tasks of the EU on the regional scale is to find ways to enhance its relations with such 'outsiders'.

Enlargement has definitely been the most effective instrument of the EU for extending the sphere of peace and democracy. During the 1990s, most non-EU European states – in particular those that had regained sovereignty after having been under Soviet rule – set the aim of membership at the top of their foreign policy agendas. Enlargement was framed on both sides, the EU and candidates, as a way of ending the division of Europe and safeguarding stability, prosperity and common values. The 'founding myth' and appealing to common European values was effectively used by the leaders of Central and Eastern European countries in order to persuade the EU of the inevitability of accepting their countries as members.[4] A similar logic presses the EU to continue enlargement and to develop deeper institutionalised relations with those neighbouring countries that it is currently unable or unwilling to accept as members – in the words of José Manuel Barroso, President of the European Commission:

> The European Neighbourhood Policy is our offer to share the benefits of enlargement with a broad arc of neighbouring regions. . . . We have the opportunity and a historic responsibility to build on the successful experience of our Partnership and Cooperation Agreements to the East and the Barcelona Process in the Mediterranean.[5]

The purpose of this chapter is not to examine in detail the enlargement and neighbourhood policies of the EU, but to discuss the underlying principles and overall mechanisms of its relations with neighbouring countries, focusing on the specific aspects of power and responsibility. I will first discuss the sources of the EU's responsibility in wider Europe, and then study the power exercised by the EU over its neighbours, applying the concept of *extended governance*. This will lead me to argue that the EU does carry responsibility for extending (partly unintentionally) its norms to the neighbouring countries, and for drawing the limits of inclusion/exclusion in relation to its own system of governance. However, due to the nature of relations between the EU and its neighbours – which has a lot to do with the nature of the EU itself – it is difficult for the Union to pursue the tasks and duties that are implied by its regional role. My analysis will bring out some cases among neighbours that have been particularly difficult for the EU to deal with: Turkey, Ukraine and Belarus.[6] In conclusion, I will outline two approaches to responsible regional agency, one focusing on shared values and the other on dialogue and pragmatism. I will argue that in order to be a responsible regional agent, the EU should draw on both approaches. The central role of shared values implies that the Union should offer full integration to all countries in the neighbourhood that are committed to the European values. However, in relation to those neighbours that do not share the EU's basic values, dialogue and pragmatism are required in order to avoid neglect and isolation.

The founding myth as a source of the EU's regional responsibility

During the Cold War, the founding myth mostly played a minor role in the practical integration process. There was, however, one significant exception: the accession of Greece, Portugal and Spain in the 1980s, which was made possible by the democratisation of these countries after the mid-1970s. The southern enlargement tested the EU's ability to promote stability and democracy in the region,[7] and it later became an important reference point for eastern enlargement.[8] The founding myth and the metanarrative of European security were revived as the Cold War was coming to its end. The EU declared its commitment 'to overcome the division of our continent and to promote the Western values and principles' as early as in 1988.[9]

The transformation of the international system after the Cold War is significant for the EU's regional role in at least two ways. First, as we all know, it created the possibility to end the division of Europe and opened up a vast new area to be included in the integration project. Second, the relative importance and autonomy of regions have arguably increased since the end of the Cold War bipolarity.[10] Thus, the EU has become far more significant and influential as a regional power now that it is no longer overshadowed by the confrontation between the two superpowers of the Cold War. This has raised high expectations towards its regional role. The gravest indication of these expectations has been the Balkans, where the EU's incapability to fulfil its (self-assumed) responsibilities became painfully evident in the 1990s. Instability in the Balkans and elsewhere in the EU's neighbourhood are not only relevant for its regional role, but also its external agency in general. Regional activity tests the EU's credibility and capability as a global agent – after all, it is quite natural to expect the Union to start the promotion of European values and ideals from its own 'backyard'.

It is worth underlining here that the fundamental purpose of integration, as defined above, does not only apply to EU member states but the whole of Europe. The founding myth continues to define the *raison d'être* of the Union both internally and in a wider regional context. The importance of regional responsibility is clearly expressed in the ESS (2003) that states, under the subtitle 'Building Security in our Neighbourhood', that 'Our task is to promote a ring of well governed countries to the East of the European Union and on the borders of the Mediterranean with whom we can enjoy close and cooperative relations.'[11] The EU is to be held responsible because of its multiple links with neighbours and the vulnerability of the latter to its conduct: inclusion in the EU system is indeed a crucial matter for the neighbouring countries.

To be more precise, the founding myth of integration makes the EU responsible towards wider Europe in at least four significant ways. Firstly, it defines a European *community* with no fixed borders which is open to all European countries that share the common values. Secondly, it evokes the *consent* principle by expressing the EU's intention to care about the wellbeing of that community. Thirdly, the EU has the *capacity* to pursue the founding myth and to promote democracy, security and wellbeing beyond its borders. And fourthly, as a consequence of each of the three principles just mentioned, it creates more or less *legitimate expectations* among neighbours, in broader international community and inside the Union itself.[12] Most of the underlying sources of responsibility that form the spine of this book are thus observable in the context of the EU's new neighbourhood policy.

The Union's unique power and influence in a wider European region is based on both material and non-material elements. The combination of different types of resources and power means that the EU is undoubtedly the agent that is best equipped for promoting the wellbeing of Europeans. It has overwhelming economic resources, weak but strengthening military capacity (see Chapter 2 by Ojanen), and perhaps most importantly, 'normative' or 'ideological' power which is expressed by the strong appeal of its norms and values among a growing number of neighbouring countries.[13] The founding myth of the EU is indeed inseparable from the shared values of Europeans, and it is one of the key aims of the EU's extended governance to spread these values. Because of the original purpose of the EU, regional responsibility should be carried out in a way that defends and spreads European values. Moreover, shared values are as such a significant source of responsibility.[14]

Not all the EU's neighbours share its values, however, and the content of European values is subject to dispute even within the Union itself. One should thus remember that the very same values imply a responsibility to keep the values open to dialogue and to be responsive towards 'others' who do not belong to the community. As noted by Cederman, European values require continuous balancing between exclusion, which may be counterproductive to the values, and inclusion, which may lead to the dilution of values.[15]

Governance approach to the EU's regional role

In order to determine the EU's responsibility towards the neighbourhood we need to understand the nature of the EU's capacity and power in the region. As it is argued throughout this volume, capacity is a crucial determinant of institutional agency and responsibility. A 'governance approach', and especially the concept of extended governance, proves a useful means for illuminating how the Union affects developments in its nearby areas.

As a powerful regional agent, the EU projects its norms and values beyond its borders. To some extent, this takes place through policies designed explicitly for that purpose: the pre-accession framework for the candidate countries and the ENP for non-candidates. In addition, a lot of the EU's influence is transmitted in a more or less unintended manner, through a great number of various actors and contacts. It may therefore be difficult to pinpoint specific acts or sources of power or to identify the effects of the EU. However, the integration of a growing number of European countries into the EU during the time of its existence is an undeniable indication of its appeal and influence.

The concept of governance has been widely applied in political science and increasingly also in IR,[16] but there is a considerable amount of confusion and lack of precision in the use of the concept. Nonetheless, it has become a useful overall catchword for the dispersion of authority and the increased complexity of social regulation that characterise political and social life in the globalising world. Different uses of the concept – 'good governance', 'global governance' and 'European governance' being probably the most widely used in IR and EU studies – all highlight a plurality of actors and modes of governing. The concept may refer both to the *practice* of governance and to *systems* of governance; both of these meanings are used in this chapter. The distinction between these two meanings is a key to understanding many of the problems that appear in the EU's regional role: the fact that the Union practices governance over its neighbours without including the neighbours fully in the system of governance is a major source of tension. It is difficult to identify the borders of the EU system of governance, since the patterns of inclusion and exclusion fluctuate, and the practices and effects of governance are projected beyond the borders of that system.

Governance entails a lack of central authority and is thus analytically distinct from government and the state. Different types of governance resemble each other in being 'sharp departures from the model of the all-powerful central state'.[17] They involve various actors, including both public and private institutions and organisations, civil society, and individuals acting in the framework of institutions. States continue to be in many respects primary actors even within systems of governance, but their relative role has weakened. From an analytical perspective, it is essential that the notion of governance does not presume a dominant role of the state, although this may still be an empirical fact in many policy areas.[18] One of the aims of governance approaches is precisely to come to terms with the blurring boundaries between the international, national and sub-national levels, and between public and private spheres.

In addition to the distinguishing features identified above, governance is characterised by the special role of values and norms shared by the actors involved. The necessity of inter-subjective meanings is 'a logical consequence of the fact that governance is not dependent upon vertical authority'.[19] When hierarchy and central authority are missing, the only way to avoid anarchy is voluntary compliance to a set of common rules.[20] As distinct from the compulsory nature of domestic laws and formal international agreements, governance is exercised, to a considerable extent, through rules that are non-binding in a formal or legal sense. From a constructivist perspective, governance functions as an effective instrument of socialisation: taking part in the process of governance transforms the values and preferences of a social actor, making them 'community compatible'.[21] As a logical companion to the central role of common norms, many authors emphasise the structured, coordinated nature and purposefulness of governance.[22] The underlying aim is to maintain social order; the pursuit of specific collective goals through the governance process serves to achieve this aim. However, there is a great deal of unintended and unregulated dynamics built in the mechanism of governance – an aspect that will turn out to be particularly relevant for the type of extended governance examined below.

* * *

Since the 1990s, it has become a prominent approach in EU studies to analyse the Union as a system of governance.[23] The concept does indeed seem particularly well-suited to describe the functioning of the EU. Probably more distinctly than in any other political institution or organisation, the governing of the Union takes place without a single authority and in the framework of a complex and multi-layered set of rules and norms. The EU is void of central authority, and yet thickly institutionalised and norm-ridden. Its unique nature and departure from the Westphalian system of nation-states make it a post-sovereign entity, with a considerable proportion of formal authority being pooled on the supranational level and shared with a variety of public and private actors. Furthermore, the notion of governance is particularly appropriate for the EU because of the express emphasis on common values as the basis of its identity and activity.

The implications of this internal nature for external relations and policies are not obvious or straightforward. One of the contributions of the governance approach is that it guides us to study these effects. Differently from classical integration theory where the EU system is the dependent variable that is shaped by policies, the governance approach treats the shape of the EU system as an independent variable explaining its policies.[24] According to Karen Smith, the EU's unique nature does not as such explain its distinctive foreign policy agenda with an emphasis on the promotion of common values. However, she highlights regional cooperation as an area where the internal system does explain foreign policy: since the 1960s, the EU has actively encouraged regional cooperation among its partners in different parts of the world, seeking to export its model of security and welfare.[25]

An area where the effects of the internal nature on external policy are particularly distinct is enlargement. The candidate countries' relations with the EU are determined by their success in adopting the internal EU system. A similar logic, although in a weaker form, is also inherent in the ENP that can be viewed as an 'external dimension of internal politics'.[26] In wider Europe, the linkage between the internal model and external agenda has resulted in the projection and extension of the EU's system to neighbouring areas. The Union's regional role seems to derive from its internal characteristics, involving a strongly normative and socialising dimension: the EU's governance beyond boundaries has strongly shaped the values and identities of the neighbouring countries, particularly in Central and Eastern Europe.[27] The strong linkage between the internal and the external in the EU's relations with neighbouring countries speaks in favour of the application of the concept of governance to the study of enlargement and neighbourhood policy. The concept contributes to my analysis also by helping to problematise the nature of the EU's responsibility, power and agency in a wider Europe. Furthermore, through its emphasis on norms and values, the governance approach raises normative questions concerning the future of Europe's political order. It is also helpful in addressing the difficulties of border-drawing and institution-building in the EU's neighbourhood.

Enlargement: effective governance over 'pre-ins'

The key role of political criteria

So far, only a few attempts have been made to apply the concept of governance to the study of EU enlargement, but these attempts are promising. Friis and Murphy have provided a compelling analysis of how, in the process of Eastern enlargement, EU governance was extended to countries that aspired to membership well before their actual accession.[28] They identify two distinct varieties of EU governance, both of which were at work in the enlargement. The first, 'soft governance', refers to the EU as a value community where commitment to shared norms conditions the activities of the members. The role model of the EU encourages outsiders to adopt the same underlying values, including democracy and the rule of law. This contributes to an informal and largely unintended spread of the EU model. 'Hard governance', by contrast, refers to negotiations over both the shape of the system and over shared goals to be pursued through it. The concept thus accounts for formal and goal-oriented activity in the framework of the governance system.

In practical terms, extended governance over 'pre-ins' takes place through two main instruments: membership criteria and accession negotiations. The former include both soft and hard elements of EU governance, while the latter are first and foremost about hard governance, although the negotiations also involve unintended socialisation and adoption of EU norms. The conditions of membership were spelled out more clearly than ever before in the context of the Eastern enlargement. The Copenhagen criteria laid down by the European Council in 1993[29] provide general guidelines that identify the core values and norms. The criteria are vague, however, and leave plenty of space for interpretation and flexibility. This gives considerable power to the Commission that carries out the task of regular monitoring of the applicant countries and assesses their readiness for membership. In its yearly reports on the candidates, issued since 1997, the Commission has stressed that it follows clear criteria and produces objective assessments. For example, in 1998 the Report stated:

> Our assessment was conducted on the basis of the same Copenhagen criteria as the opinions last year. The goalposts have not been shifted. The work of our officials was expert, objective, impartial, and free of political prejudice.[30]

Although the Commission claims to simply move towards pre-given goalposts, it has in fact given a precise content to the ambiguous Copenhagen criteria. The Commission reports function as signposts in the accession process and the applicants' preparations for membership, defining what has been achieved and how to move forward. The regular monitoring has enabled the EU to apply strict conditionality: on the whole, the success of candidates in the accession process has been tied to the extent to which they satisfy the criteria.

The 'soft' aspect of common values is represented in the first, political criteria: the applicants have to show commitment to democracy, the rule of law, human rights, and respect for and protection of minorities. The other criteria have more to do with the adoption of EU legislation, most of which, as we know, is of a rather technical nature and primarily concerns the common market and agricultural policy. The application of these criteria takes place in two stages: a candidate country has to meet the political criteria before being allowed to start accession negotiations. The rest of the criteria are addressed in the negotiations and define the point of accession. Due to this division, the Copenhagen criteria serve a double purpose of border-drawing in Europe: first, they distinguish pre-ins from outsiders and semi-outsiders on the basis of the political criteria, and second, the pre-ins are separated from members according to the adoption of the whole set of EU legislation. The pre-ins that satisfy the political criteria are acknowledged as full members of the value community, whereas countries that are not allowed to start accession negotiations are excluded primarily because of shortcomings in the application of common values.

The key role of the Copenhagen political criteria as a precondition for starting accession negotiations highlights the non-negotiability of the common values. They are the main determinant of enlargement – in the words of Olli Rehn, the Commissioner responsible for enlargement, 'values define Europe'.[31] And yet, the precise content of these common values is more ambiguous than often suggested. They are constantly contested and renegotiated, and it can be very difficult to identify when exactly a country satisfies them well enough to become a member candidate. Eastern enlargement has forced the EU to specify the definition of European values and develop ways to measure the adherence of applicant countries. The emphasis on values in relation to the Eastern candidate countries also gave an impetus to strengthening the legal status of the same values in the EU's internal system.[32]

Turkey as a test case

The crucial role of common values in defining the EU's borders implies that the Union has a responsibility to include in the integration process any European country that shares its values and satisfies the Copenhagen political criteria – a claim that can be justified on the basis of at least the 'community', 'legitimate expectations' and 'consent' principles. The most difficult and disputed case in this respect is Turkey whose membership aspirations have raised doubts and outright resistance for a number of reasons, including historical, religious and cultural cleavages between Turkey and the current EU. The official position of the Union, however, has not acknowledged these differences as an argument against Turkey's accession. On the contrary, we should regard them as an additional impetus to integrate the country, since history and religion must not be allowed to determine dividing lines in today's Europe. The Copenhagen political criteria do not include either religion or ethnicity. To quote Chris Patten, the then commissioner for external relations of the EU: 'The proposition that Europe can be defined by religion is a false one, not to say dangerous. In many ways, the European Union is a reaction against the idea that we can define ourselves by religion or ethnicity, and thus define others as beyond consideration.'[33]

This view was confirmed by the decision taken by the European Council in December 2004 to start accession negotiations with Turkey. What made the decisive difference for the EU's position was precisely the broad-ranging reforms that Turkey had carried out in the field of democracy, human rights and the rule of law in 2001–2004. In December 2002, the European Council clearly defined the fulfilment of Copenhagen political criteria as the precondition for the start of accession negotiations.[34] With reference to that decision, the Commission concluded in its report of October 2004 that Turkey did satisfy the political criteria and therefore the negotiations should be opened.[35] It was seen as the EU's duty to give a strong positive reaction to the democratisation of Turkey. The primary goal of accepting Turkey as a candidate country was to 'ensure that her legal and political reforms are sustainable and irreversible'.[36]

However, there continues to be considerable opposition and scepticism with regard to membership of a large, relatively poor Muslim country. In addition to perceiving Turkey as Europe's 'other' in terms of religious and cultural identity, the opponents (and indeed also supporters) are worried about the implications of Turkey's membership on the institutions and budget of the Union.[37] None of these reasons justify exclusion if the founding myth and the values of the Union are to be given priority. The Turkish accession process tests the endurance of the foundations of integration – if the country is going to implement the membership criteria and will nevertheless be denied full membership, the credibility and identity of the EU as the safeguard of democracy and security in Europe will be demolished. Furthermore, the importance of Turkey goes far beyond the EU's regional role, and beyond the scope of this chapter, as it shapes relations between the EU and Islamic world.

Accession negotiations: ambiguous role of values and responsibility

Based on previous experience, once an applicant country starts membership negotiations, the central role of founding values will be overshadowed and pushed aside by the technical details of EU legislation and the requirement of administrative capacity. In other words, negotiations turn the pursuit of idealist goals into a bureaucratic exercise of adopting the complicated EU system of governance, which takes place through '*acquis* conditionality'.[38] As the amount and scope of EU legislation has been steadily growing, each negotiation is a more demanding undertaking than the previous ones. In the negotiations that started in 1998 with Central and Eastern European countries, this task was organised to 31 chapters covering virtually all areas of social life.

During accession negotiations, the linkage between the internal system and external relations of the Union is at its strongest. The specific characteristics of internal governance, such as lack of central authority and the multilayered system of common rules and norms, have problematic implications from the viewpoint of political responsibility. Since governance by definition refers to diffusion of authority, it easily obscures and dilutes agency and power. The sources of the EU's power over applicant countries are manifold and not easily located. Key decisions are taken by the highest leaders of the Union and the member states in the European Council and the Council of Ministers, but they rely heavily on the Commission recommendations. The Commission, however, is an essentially bureaucratic institution, not democratically accountable in the same sense as national governments. It applies a technical approach to assessing the applicants and claims to simply follow the *acquis* and 'objective criteria' of membership. As opposed to political institutions that make value judgements, the Commission is supposed to embody expertise and impartiality.

According to the logic of enlargement, applicants are bound to accept the pre-existing set of rules before getting a chance to take part in shaping them. The EU norms and values that constitute the foundation of the system of governance are 'non-negotiable with outsiders'.[39] This creates a form of extended governance which is centred around predetermined rules and the rhetoric of objectiveness and expertise. Crucial questions of inclusion and exclusion in the European community are solved by technical assessment. Responsibility is shifted from the Union to the countries that wish to become members: it is up to them to implement EU requirements and earn membership in the club. Moreover, the diffuse and multi-layered shape of the system makes it easier for the EU to 'hide' behind objective criteria. Meanwhile, politicians in applicant countries also use EU requirements as a convenient way to deny their political responsibility. Politics in countries that negotiate about membership is to a large extent reduced to the approval of ready-made EU laws.

The implications of extended governance for institution-building in the candidate countries have been illuminated by Antoaneta Dimitrova. In her analysis, governance by enlargement is about modelling the candidate states' institutions in accordance with EU conditions, with the purpose of preparing them for the implementation of the *acquis communautaire*. Dimitrova tracks considerable differences between internal EU governance and governance by enlargement, although the latter stems from the former, and they are based on the same values and norms. The most important difference is the asymmetric, hierarchical nature of relations between the 'ins' and 'pre-ins', as opposed to the (at least formally) non-hierarchical relations between member states. While internal governance entails the possibility to take an active role in changing the system, the 'pre-ins' can influence the rules that constitute the system only indirectly. Another crucial point highlighted by Dimitrova is that the reforms implemented by the candidate states according to EU conditions in many cases lack the basis of domestic consensus and fail to take into account the views of domestic actors.[40]

I would like to stress that despite the predominantly technical nature of preparations for membership, the work done in both the EU and the candidate countries is not and should not be a mere technocratic, non-political exercise. On the contrary, it involves political considerations that call for political responsibility on both sides. The EU carries responsibility for exercising governance over candidate countries and defining the rules and norms that condition the relationship. On the side of the latter, the scope of choice is narrow once the decision to pursue membership has been taken, and therefore the implementation of EU criteria imposes considerable restrictions to the very same value that underlies integration: democracy.[41] Indeed, the relationship between the EU and applicants displays a strong version of the unavoidable problem that conditionality policy, if effective, always implies restrictions on democracy in the target country.[42] Yet we should also note that candidate countries do not merely follow the EU's criteria, but have to make numerous choices as to how they appropriate EU norms to their domestic political context. This demands open and responsible decision-making and not just mechanical application of EU criteria.

It is also worth emphasising that the system of EU governance is in a constant flux while being applied and reproduced, although in the context of accession negotiations, the system is usually presented as given and fixed. Outsiders, especially member candidates, influence the internal functioning of the system both indirectly and directly. The main indirect impact is evidenced by the fact that enlargements have been major impulses to the internal reform of the Union. The common institutions have usually been reshaped before the accession of new members.[43] The latest enlargement offers a unique case of direct involvement of pre-ins in reforming the EU: candidate countries were included in the preparation of the new constitutional treaty, as they took part in the European Convention held in 2002–2003 and the subsequent intergovernmental conference that concluded its work in 2004. In addition to the 25 member states, the signatories to the Treaty establishing a Constitution for Europe included three candidate countries (Bulgaria, Romania and Turkey). The position of candidates in preparing the treaty was in practice not equal to that of the member states: they were constrained by their applicant status, as they had to be 'nice' to all member states in order for not to spoil their opportunities to 'join the club'. Even so, inclusion in the process did give them some influence and made them better prepared for membership. It was also a considerable indication of the EU's aim to develop an equal relation and dialogue with candidates and treat them as partners.

Neighbourhood policy as governance over 'semi-outs'

The ENP: nothing is imposed, but . . .

How, then, does extended governance work for neighbouring countries that are not, and possibly will not become, member candidates? The European Neighbourhood Policy has been motivated by a similar sense of responsibility as enlargement – as expressed, for example, by the Swedish Prime Minister Göran Persson:

> We who have had the chance to live and build up our countries in freedom have a moral responsibility to share what we have. We have a responsibility to take part in creating the conditions for growth and development in our neighbouring countries.[44]

The policies of enlargement and the ENP are also in many respects similar, although the most important element of enlargement – the goal of accession – is missing from the ENP. The main common feature is the extension of EU values and norms to neighbours through conditionality. The Union's position may be described as 'we do not impose anything, but if you want closer cooperation, do as we say'. On the other hand, the EU's commitment to the

ENP countries is considerably weaker than its commitment to candidate countries. The financial resources allocated for the neighbourhood policy are modest in comparison with EU support to the candidate countries.[45]

The EU started to prepare a European neighbourhood policy in 2001 when it realised the challenges related to the new post-enlargement neighbouring countries. A report by the Commission outlining the new neighbourhood policy was launched in March 2003, followed by a more detailed strategy paper in May 2004. The latter document defines the general principles and goals on the basis of which the Union, in cooperation with its neighbours, prepares tailor-made bilateral action plans in accordance with the specific conditions of each country. The EU's aim is to develop closer relations with the neighbours, including economic integration, but without offering the prospect of full membership. In all, the strategy covers 16 states.[46]

In the ENP, the task of ending the Cold War division, which motivated the eastern enlargement, has been replaced with the aim to prevent 'a new dividing line being drawn across Europe following enlargement'.[47] The keywords of relations established in the framework of ENP are partnership, mutual gains and mutually agreed goals, and joint ownership. The ENP appears to be more dialogical than the relationship between the EU and applicant countries (cf. Aalto's chapter). While the latter have no choice but to adopt the whole set of EU norms, each ENP country negotiates a 'tailor-made' plan with the Union.[48] The EU stresses 'ownership' on the side of partners and their freedom to choose how far they want to deepen their political and economic ties with the EU. Conditionality is explicitly denied: 'The EU does not seek to impose priorities or conditions on its partners', and 'There can be no question of asking partners to accept a pre-determined set of priorities'.[49]

This can hardly be called anything but dishonesty – the EU does set conditions, and the closeness and depth of relations often depends on the extent to which the neighbours adopt EU norms. The impression of the neighbours having freedom to choose is quite deceptive. Many of them would choose a far closer relationship if they were able to satisfy the EU's conditions and if the Union were ready to build a closer relationship. The EU is obviously far stronger economically and politically, which makes the relationship inherently unequal, but nevertheless the rhetoric of 'equal partnership' is commonly used. This can be seen merely as an attempt to evade responsibility and to mould the *community principle* so as to make it match with political preferences. All this is particularly relevant for countries that wish to step from the ring of semi-outs to pre-ins, as many of them do.

The core problem is that the Union practices extended governance over its neighbours, but is not willing to extend the system of governance and include them. Sandra Lavenex highlights this problem by making a distinction between the institutional and the legal boundary of the EU: the EU can transpose its legal order upon neighbouring countries without a parallel institutional integration.[50] Indeed, the ENP offers to the neighbours 'everything but institutions', with an aim to project stability and prosperity in a similar manner as through enlargement, but without the prospect of membership.[51] The neighbours are thus doomed to stay in the asymmetrical relationship, which hardly motivates them to adopt in full the EU's legal order.

Difficult borderline cases: Ukraine and Belarus

The EU has difficulties in dealing with two categories of borderline countries in particular: the ones on the border of 'pre-ins' and 'semi-outs' that aspire for membership but are denied that prospect, and those that do not even qualify as semi-outs but are rather simply outsiders. Ukraine is a case that belongs to the first category, while its neighbour Belarus has yet to cross the border from outsiders to semi-outs.

As for the first category, the border between 'pre-ins' and 'semi-outs' may be even more difficult to cross than the one between 'ins' and 'pre-ins'. In principle, as discussed above, the key question here is adherence to the Copenhagen political criteria. However, it is not certain whether this will be enough in the future. Turkey is the most recent case that crossed the border on this basis, but a view that the Union, because of its internal cohesion and ability to function, is simply reaching the ultimate limits of enlargement is currently widely shared in the EU. Ukraine will test the durability of this position in the coming years. The country has been asking for the prospect of EU membership for many years, but as long as it was far from meeting the political criteria, it was fairly easy and justifiable for the EU to say 'no'. The 'Orange Revolution' and victory of democratic forces in the presidential election in late 2004 changed the situation.[52] The strong expression of commitment to democracy and to the 'European choice' made by Ukrainians during the Orange Revolution came as a surprise to the EU and most outside observers.

The new president Viktor Yushchenko defined membership in the EU as a top priority of Ukraine under his leadership. The EU on its behalf welcomed the outcome of the Orange Revolution that 'confirmed the country's place on the European map'.[53] Nonetheless, the Union has so far refused to treat Ukraine as a potential member state. The crucial question for the near future is whether the EU will remain true to its founding principles and the key role of values in defining the EU's borders, or whether it will permanently set the final limits of enlargement in the name of internal coherence. If Ukraine will in the next years show similar determination in carrying out domestic reforms as Turkey did over the past years (which is of course not guaranteed), denial of membership prospect will not be justifiable from the viewpoint of the basic values of integration. A 'no' to a democratising European country that seeks membership would seriously undermine the credibility and identity of the EU.

The countries that are outsiders rather than semi-outs have been left in that position because of their non-democratic regimes that violate the basic values of the EU. Although firmly anchored to the 'common values', the ENP does not provide sufficient motivation for neighbours to pursue the principles of democracy, the rule of law, and human and minority rights. At the same time, the Union does expect neighbouring countries to apply its own norms and values, and makes relations with the neighbours conditional upon their compliance. Countries that do not share the values are in principle covered by the ENP, but in practice excluded from regular cooperation until possible regime change. The ENP does not therefore function as an instrument for actively promoting the EU's values in countries that are not already committed to these values, and it is not capable of providing a functioning basis for relations with such countries.

Belarus, a country known as the only dictatorship in Europe, is a sore example. The EU has expressed its willingness to develop closer relations with the country 'once the Belarusian authorities clearly demonstrate their willingness to respect democratic values and the rule of law'.[54] The policy of neglect and isolation followed by the EU since the authoritarian turnabout that took place in 1996 has in no way promoted European values, security or wellbeing of the people in Belarus. Europe's passive attitude has even indirectly supported the authoritarian president Lukashenko by enabling him to use the slogan 'Nobody waits us in Europe' and making many Belarusians believe that their country has no alternatives. On the positive side, the EU seems to be aware of its failure and has started to reformulate its policy towards Belarus in order to promote a peaceful change of the political system. The Belarusian pro-democratic opposition forces and civil society groups that exist outside the formal institutions have been encouraged by the Orange Revolution in Ukraine and the increase of Western attention. It is also notable that, in spite of anti-European official propaganda, more than half of the Belarusian people are in favour of close cooperation with the EU. All these factors reinforce the EU's responsibility to enhance contacts with Belarus and promote a change that would make possible full inclusion of the country in the ENP and possibly even membership in the distant future.[55]

The inclusion of outsiders in a common European order is one of the greatest challenges faced by the EU as a responsible regional agent. So far, extended governance only works for countries that share the values and wish to be integrated with the system of the Union. The current neighbourhood policy is unable to deal with outsiders who reject European values. Hence there is a paradox inherent in the EU's policies towards neighbours: the mechanism of extended governance works most effectively for those countries that need it least. There seems to be no way out of the dilemma, since the EU cannot compromise its values in order to promote them, and it also cannot force them on others. Greater flexibility in relation to non-democracies may dilute the values, whereas their forceful promotion would violate and undermine the very same values (as we can evidence in the case of the US). In any case, neglect of neighbouring countries is the least suitable option if we believe that the Union bears a responsibility towards its neighbours. Thus, the EU needs to be more innovative and flexible in order to find ways to engage with countries that are currently excluded from the European value community.

By way of conclusion

The above analysis shows that the specific features of the EU's regional agency and responsibility in wider Europe are closely linked with the nature of internal EU governance and the basic values of integration. Our focus has been on Eastern Europe and Turkey, but the logic would certainly not be that different in the Mediterranean area. The extension of the system beyond the EU's borders is essential for promoting European values, but it is problematic from the viewpoint of responsibility for a number of reasons: it establishes an unequal, asymmetric relation between the parties, obscures agency and power on the side of the EU, restricts democracy and self-determination of neighbours, favours countries that are the fittest to adopt the whole set of EU norms, and excludes countries that do not share the EU's values.

The EU's relations with neighbouring countries raise many broad, unanswered questions, most of which are not only relevant for the neighbourhood, but the Union's external relations in general. These are problems that can probably never get a final answer, but that we should definitely be aware of, such as:

- Values and the limits of responsibility: What is the role of the EU's founding values in defining the limits of its responsibility? The EU ties responsibility to common values and political conditions, but what is our ultimate responsibility towards those who do not share our values?
- How tight/how flexible should the conditions of inclusion be? How can the EU legitimately differentiate between member candidates on the one hand, and neighbours that should not be offered the prospect of membership on the other hand?
- Defending 'our' values *versus* open-ended dialogue: How to defend the EU's values and norms and yet at the same time be attentive to alternative views, which is also an important value?
- Idealism *versus* pragmatism: To the extent that these two are mutually exclusive, where do we draw the border? Under which conditions is it justified to compromise one's values in order to promote other goals?

All of these are ultimately moral and political dilemmas to which formal rules (such as membership criteria) do not and must not provide straightforward answers. After all, formal criteria are no more than tools for justifying and applying political decisions. The EU can only be a responsible regional agent if it is able to balance between the contradicting goals. It should continue to encourage, but not to impose the adoption of its system of governance outside its borders. It is also important to remember that dialogue and

Table 4.1 Two approaches to responsible regional agency of the EU

Emphasis on shared values	Emphasis on dialogue and pragmatism
Strict conditionality based on shared values;	Dialogue over the conditions of inclusion, including values;
Non-negotiability of values;	Openness towards the views of 'others' (neighbours that do not comply with EU norms);
Unconditional priority of values in relations with neighbours;	Other interests (e.g. related to stability, security and the economy) may override the promotion of values;
The same value-based conditions for both membership and the ENP;	More flexibility towards countries that do not seek membership;
Strict exclusion of neighbours that violate the EU's values;	Aim to develop alternative ways of (semi)-inclusion;
Limited responsibility towards neighbours that violate the EU's values	Responsibility towards neighbours even if they violate the EU's values

pragmatism may harm our values, but the lack of them may be even more harmful.

The two alternative approaches that the EU needs to combine in practice – one focused on shared values and the other on dialogue and pragmatism – are summarised in Table 4.1. Emphasis on shared values is a suitable approach for those neighbouring countries that seek closer integration on the basis of common values and norms. As it has been argued throughout the chapter, the special regional role of the EU entails responsibility to make integration and eventually membership available for all such countries. However, the EU has also neighbours that do not share its basic values. In relation to them a strict value-based approach fails to provide a basis for responsible EU policies, because it leads to the isolation and neglect of these countries, and therefore actually fails to promote European values and violates the principles of dialogue and pragmatism.

The prospect of membership is by far the EU's most effective instrument of extended governance. Countries that negotiate about accession are motivated to adopt the whole set of EU norms, as they have the 'golden carrot' of membership in reach. The ENP fails to create a similar motivation, but it is nonetheless a form of extended governance similar to enlargement and raises expectations among partner countries to be included in the system. Governance over neighbours inevitably brings pressures to enlarge, which the EU has difficulties to manage. This requires a further balancing act between, on the one hand, continuous extension (through enlargement and other means) that increases stability and spreads European values, but also leads to the fragmentation of the system and possibly dilution of the values; and on the other hand, fixing the borders in the name of unity, which would considerably decrease the EU's ability to project stability and act as a responsible regional power.

In spite of the threat of fragmentation and possibly even destruction of the Union, I would like to underline that the EU has to continue to use enlargement as the main (although definitely not the only) instrument of promoting democracy and security in the neighbourhood. Thus, it should include in the accession process all European countries that are committed to democratisation. The exclusion of democratising countries that seek membership would cause serious damage to the EU's credibility and identity which are to a large extent based on the promotion of peace and democracy. The EU can only remain viable if it remains true to its basic goals and values and, at the same time, reforms itself in a way that enables it to function with a growing number of member states.

Notes

1. Declaration of 9 May 1950, by Robert Schuman, the foreign minister of France. http://europa.eu.int/abc/symbols/9-may/decl_en.htm
2. Preamble of the Treaty establishing the EEC (1958).
3. Buzan and Wæver 2003, 361–64; Schimmelfennig 2003, 265–6.
4. Schimmelfennig 2003, 265–78.
5. José Manuel Barroso, President of the European Commission: 'The European Union and the Emerging World Order – Perceptions and Strategies', Speech held at the 7th ECSA (European Community Studies Association) World Conference, Brussels, 30 November 2004. http://www.europaworld.org/week203/speechbarroso31204.htm
6. The chapter does not look more closely at any of the southern neighbours (other than Turkey), but their relations with the EU are part of the same framework of neighbourhood policy and therefore face similar problems and challenges as relations with eastern neighbours.
7. According to Christopher Preston (1997, 63), southern enlargement was 'a critical test of the capability of the EC model to act as a stabilising influence in the region and to establish a framework for the development of pluralist political and economic structures and processes'.
8. E.g. Laurence Whitehead criticised the EU before the start of accession negotiations as follows: 'Since 1989 the European Community has proved less reliable as an agency of democratic promotion in East–Central Europe than might have been expected, given its record in southern Europe' (Whitehead 1997, 48).
9. The European Council, Rhodes 2–3 December 1988, Conclusions of the Presidency.
10. Buzan and Wæver 2003.
11. The Security Strategy also states the continued importance of geography 'even in an area of globalisation', and the special role of the Balkans.
12. See also Barry (2003) on the principles of connectedness and capacity.
13. Manners 2002.
14. Cf. Barry 2003, 231.
15. Cederman 2001, 3; see also Introduction.
16. See e.g. Pierre and Peters 2000; Rosenau and Czempiel 1992.

17. Hooghe and Marks 2001, 16.
18. Cf. Aalberts 2004.
19. Webber *et al.* 2004, 7.
20. Cf. Webber *et al.* 2004, 5.
21. Eberlein and Kerwer 2004, 129; see also Christiansen *et al.* 2001.
22. Webber *et al.* 2004, 8.
23. Jachtenfuchs 2001; Jachtenfuchs and Kohler-Koch 2004; Kohler-Koch and Eising 1999; Marks *et al.* 1996.
24. Jachtenfuchs 2001.
25. Smith 2003, 69–96, 196–7.
26. Lavenex 2004, 681.
27. See Schimmelfennig 2003.
28. Friis and Murphy 1999; Schimmelfennig and Sedelmeier 2004.
29. The Copenhagen European Council declared that 'the associated countries in Central and Eastern Europe that so desire shall become members of the Union', provided that they satisfy the following criteria: 1) stability of institutions guaranteeing democracy, the rule of law, human rights and respect for and protection of minorities; 2) the existence of a functioning market economy, as well as the capacity to cope with competitive pressure and market forces within the Union; 3) the ability to take on the obligations of membership, including adherence to the aims of political, economic and monetary union.
30. Hans van den Broek, Member of the European Commission, Speech to the European Parliament, Brussels, 4 November 1998, SPEECH/98/236.
31. Olli Rehn, Member of the European Commission responsible for Enlargement, 'Values define Europe, not borders', Belgrade, 24 January 2005, SPEECH/05/32.
32. See de Witte 2003, 227–241. This issue was taken on the agenda of internal reform in the IGC of 1996, and the process culminated in defining the EU's values in the new Consitutional Treaty, signed by the heads of member states in October 2004.
33. Chris Patten, 'Islam and the West – at the Crossroads', Oxford Centre for Islamic Studies, Oxford, 24 May 2004, SPEECH/04/256.
34. Copenhagen European Council, 12–13 December 2002, Presidency Conclusios.
35. According to Olli Rehn, the EU had 'no choice but to honour its related commitments', and thus 'we have the responsibility to accept the country as a member if it fulfils the criteria' (Rehn: 'No "Plan B" for Turkey', EurActiv, 7 December 2004, http://www.euractiv.com/Article?tcmuri=tcm:29-133179-16&type=News).
36. Olli Rehn, Member of the European Commission responsible for Enlargement, 'Turkey and the EU: a Common Future', Istanbul, 20 October 2004, SPEECH/04/466.
37. See 'Turkey in Europe'.
38. Schimmelfennig and Sedelmeier 2004.
39. Friis and Murphy 1999, 216.
40. Dimitrova 2002.
41. For critical accounts of the EU's impact on democracy in the candidate countries, see Crawford 2001, Kubicek 2003, Olsen 2002, Raik 2003, Youngs 2001.
42. See Smith 1998.
43. See Preston 1997, 175–91.
44. Speech by Prime Minister Göran Persson, at the Baltic Sea Festival, Thursday 21 August 2003. http://www.sweden.gov.se/sb/d/1159/a/7380
45. Total expenditures on eastern enlargement were 6.8 billion Euro in 1990–99; an estimate for 2000–2006 is 62.7 billion Euro (incl. over 40 billion of post-accession

expenditures). Estimated support for the ENP and Russia – altogether manifold number of countries and people in comparison with the eastern enlargement – totals 8.5 billion Euro in 2000–2006 and is expected to rise to 14.9 billion for 2007–2013.

46. Eastern neighbours: Belarus, Ukraine, and Moldova; the Southern Caucasus countries: Georgia, Armenia, and Azerbaijan; the Mediterranean countries: Morocco, Algeria, Tunisia, Libya, Egypt, Israel, Jordan, Lebanon, Syria, and the Palestinian Authority.

47. Benita Ferrero-Waldner, Commissioner for External Relations and European Neighbourhood Policy, at the Press Conference to launch first seven Action Plans under the European Neighbourhood Policy, 9 December 2004. SPEECH/04/529.

48. In December 2004, the Union launched the first seven Action Plans with Moldova, Ukraine, Morocco, Tunisia, Jordan, Israel and the Palestinian Authority, followed by additional five with Egypt, Lebanon, Armenia, Georgia and Azerbaijan in March 2005.

49. European Commission, European Neighbourhood Policy: Strategy Paper, May 2004.

50. Lavenex 2004, 683.

51. Romano Prodi, A Wider Europe: A Proximity Policy as the key to stability. SPEECH/02/619, Brussels, 5–6 December 2002.

52. See Kurth and Kempe 2005.

53. Benita Ferrero-Waldner, EU Commissioner for External Relations, Letter of congratulation to the new Ukrainian President, 12 January 2005.

54. General Affairs and External Relations Council, Council Conclusions, 22 November 2004.

55. On the situation in Belarus and its relations with the EU, see Gromadzki *et al.* 2005; *Belarus Catching up with Europe*, 2004; and Haukkala and Moshes 2004, 22–30.

Bibliography

Aalberts, Tanja E. 'The Future of Sovereignty in Multilevel Governance Europe – A Constructivist Reading', *Journal of Common Market Studies*, vol. 42, no. 1 (2004), 23–46.

Barry, Christian, 'Global Justice: Aims, Arrangements, and Responsibilites', in Toni Erskine (ed.), *Can Institutions have Responsibilities?* (Basingstoke and New York: Palgrave, 2003).

Belarus Catching up with Europe. Stefan Batory Foundation (Warsaw, 2004).

Buzan, Barry and Ole Wæver, *Regions and Powers: The Structure of International Security* (Cambridge: Cambridge University Press, 2003).

Cederman, Lars-Erik (ed.), *Constructing Europe's Identity: The External Dimension* (Boulder and London: Lynne Rienner Publishers, 2001).

Christiansen, Thomas, Knud Erik Jorgensen and Antje Wiener, *The Social Construction of Europe* (London – Thousand Oaks – New Delhi: Sage Publications, 2001).

Crawford, Gordon, *Foreign Aid and Political Reform: A Comparative Analysis of Democracy Assistance and Political Conditionality* (Basingstoke and New York: Palgrave, 2001).

De Witte, Bruno, 'The Impact of Enlargement on the Constitution of the European Union', in Marise Cremona (ed.), *The Enlargement of the European Union* (Oxford: Oxford University Press, 2003).

Dimitrova, Antoaneta, 'Enlargement, Institution-Building and the EU's Administrative Capacity Requirement', *West European Politics*, vol. 25, no. 4 (2002), 171–90.

Eberlein, Burkard and Dieter Kerwer, 'New Governance in the European Union: A Theoretical Perspective', *Journal of Common Market Studies*, vol. 42, no. 1 (2004), 121–42.

Emerson, Michael, 'European Neighbourhood Policy: Strategy or Placebo?' *CEPS Working Document* no. 215/November 2004, Centre for European Policy Studies, Brussels.

Friis, Lykke and Anna Murphy, 'The European Union and Central and Eastern Europe: Governance and Boundaries', *Journal of Common Market Studies*, vol. 37, no. 2 (1999), 211–32.

Gromadzki, Grzegorz, Raimundas Lopata and Kristi Raik, *Friends or Family? Finnish, Lithuanian and Polish perspectives on the EU's policy towards Ukraine, Belarus and Moldova.* FIIA Report 12/2005 (Helsinki: Finnish Institute of International Affairs).

Gromadzki, Grzegorz, Vitali Silitski and Lubos Vesely, 'Effective policy towards Belarus: A challenge for the enlarged EU', Policy brief, Stefan Batory Foundation (Warsaw, May 2005).

Haukkala, Hiski and Arkady Moshes, *Beyond 'Big Bang': The Challenges of the EU's Neighbourhood Policy in the East after Enlargement.* FIIA Report 9/2004 (Helsinki: The Finnish Institute of International Affairs).

Hooghe, Liesbet and Gary Marks, 'Types of Multi-level Governance', European Integration online Papers (EIoP) 5:11, http://eiop.or.at/eiop/texte/2001-011a.htm., (2001).

Kubicek, Paul J. (ed.), *The European Union and Democratization* (London and New York: Routledge, 2003).

Jachtenfuchs, Markus, 'The Governance Approach to European Integration', *Journal of Common Market Studies*, vol. 39, no. 2 (2001), 245–64.

Jachtenfuchs, Markus and Beate Kohler-Koch, 'Governance and Institutional Development', in Antje Wiener and Thomas Diez, *European Integration Theory* (Oxford: Oxford University Press, 2004).

Kohler-Koch, Beate and Rainer Eising (eds), *The Transformation of Governance in the European Union* (London: Routledge, 1999).

Kurth, Helmut and Iris Kempe (eds), *Presidential Election and Orange Revolution: Implications for Ukraine's Transition*, Friedrich-Ebert-Stiftung Regional office Ukraine, Kyiv, Belarus, Moldova (2005).

Kubicek, Paul J. (ed.), *The European Union and Democratisation* (London: Routledge, 2003).

Lavenex, Sandra, 'EU external governance in "wider Europe"', *Journal of European Public Policy*, vol. 11, no. 4, pp. 680–700 (2004).

Manners, Ian, 'Normative Power Europe: A Contradiction in Terms?', *Journal of Common Market Studies*, vol. 40, no. 2, pp. 235–58 (2002).

Marks, Gary, Francois Nielsen, Leonard Ray and Jane Salk, 'Competencies, Cracks and Conflicts: Regional Mobilization in the European Union', in Marks, Scharpf, Schmitter and Streeck, *Governance in the European Union* (London – Thousand Oaks – New Delhi: Sage Publications, 1996).

Marks, Gary, Fritz W. Scharpf, Philippe C. Schmitter and Wolfgang Streeck, *Governance in the European Union* (London – Thousand Oaks – New Delhi: Sage Publications, 1996).

Myrjord, Anne, 'Governance beyond the Union: EU boundaries in the Barents Euro-Arctic region', *European Foreign Affairs Review*, vol. 8, no. 2 (2003), 239–57.

Olsen, Gorm Rye, 'The European Union: An Ad Hoc Policy with a Low Priority', in Peter J. Schraeder (ed.), *Exporting Democracy. Rhetoric vs. Reality* (Boulder, London: Lynne Rienner Publishers, 2002).

Pierre, Jon and B.Guy Peters, *Governance, Politics and the State* (Basingstoke: Macmillan, 2000).

Preston, Christopher, *Enlargement and Integration in the European Union* (London and New York: Routledge 1997).

Raik, Kristi, *Democratic Politics or the Implementation of Inevitabilities? – Estonia's Democracy and Integration into the European Union* (Tartu: Tartu University Press, 2003).

Rosenau, James N. and Ernst-Otto Czempiel, *Governance without Government: Order and Change in World Politics* (Cambridge: Cambridge University Press, 1992).

Schimmelfennig, Frank, *The EU, NATO and the Integration of Europe: Rules and Rhetoric* (Cambridge: Cambridge University Press, 2003).

Schimmelfennig, Frank and Ulrich Sedelmeier, 'Governance by conditionality: EU rule transfer to the candidate countries of Central and Eastern Europe', *Journal of European Public Policy*, vol. 11, no. 4 (2004), 661–79.

Smith, Karen E., 'The Use of Political Conditionality in the EU's Relations with Third Countries: How Effective?', *European Foreign Affairs Review*, vol. 3, no. 2 (1998), 253–74.

Smith, Karen E., *European Union Foreign Policy in a Changing World* (Cambridge: Polity Press, 2003).

'Turkey in Europe: More than a Promise?' Report of the Independent Commission on Turkey, British Council Brussels, September 2004.

Webber, Mark, Stuart Croft, Jolyon Howorth, Terry Terriff and Elke Krahmann, 'The Governance of European Security', *Review of International Studies*, vol. 30 (2004), 3–26.

Whitehead, Laurence, 'East–Central Europe in Comparative Perspective', in Geoffrey Pridham, Eric Herring and George Sanford (eds), *Building Democracy? The International Dimension of Democratisation in Eastern Europe* (London and Washington: Leicester University Press, 1997).

Youngs, Robert, 'European Union Democracy Promotion Policies: Ten Years On', *European Foreign Affairs Review*, vol. 6, no. 3 (2001), 55–73.

5
The EU, Russia and the Problem of Community[1]

Pami Aalto

'European'–Russian relations have always been crucial for peace, welfare and stability both on the European peninsula and in Russia itself. While dealing with and balancing Russia was traditionally left to individual European states or superpower politics, with the enhanced global role of the EU, and the development of its foreign policy, the Union has increasingly assumed the responsibility for these tasks. It is now required to develop coherent and preferably ethical strategies for the relations with its huge Eastern neighbour. An essential question then is: to what extent should the EU pay attention to the consequences that its policies have, or may have, on Russia's political, economic or social development? In what ways – and ultimately why – is the EU responsible for developments in Russia?

As this chapter seeks to answer this question, it suggests that the Union's special responsibilities towards Russia are primarily tied to what will be called *the problem of community*. In other words, the responsibility the Union can be deemed to have in relation to Russia is reducible to the question of what sort of community we invoke as the reference point of our analysis. Of the six principles identified as sources of responsibility in this volume, predominance is thus given to the community principle.

If we take the *EU-25* as the reference community, as many may be prone to do, the Union's external responsibility towards Russia naturally appears limited.[2] With this reference community, the protection of the EU-zone from the perceived post-Soviet threats such as political instability, criminality, nuclear leakages, environmental problems, communicable diseases, and illegal migration might define our perceptions of responsible behaviour in relation to Russia.[3] On a more positive note, activities like securing the supply of vital energy resources from Russia into EU use would come into play, as would the maintenance of cordial diplomatic and neighbourly relations. All in all, selfish concerns would legitimise EU policies.

In contrast, when we opt for a more inclusive view and take the notion of *wider Europe* as the reference community, the Union's responsibility becomes cast in a completely different light. As Michael Emerson puts it, wider Europe can be taken to roughly correspond to the Council of Europe map. In this vision, wider Europe embraces Russia, and connotes a political space of voluntary 'europeanisation', albeit leaving its nature, degree and concrete manifestations open to interpretation. The EU would take the main responsibility for providing the standards of peaceful development and socio-economic progress within this space, whilst at the same time co-operating at the strategic level with Russia in order to meet the overall goal of an extended area of peace and stability.[4]

In practice, the vision of a wider Europe would include regional cooperation frameworks between the EU and Russia which currently consist of (i) the *Northern Dimension* (ND) along the EU–Russian border from northern Finland to the Baltic–Russian borderlands; and (ii) the western *Newly Independent States/Commonwealth of Independent States* (NIS/CIS), incorporating the westernmost members of the former Soviet Union except for the Baltic states, that is, the Union's new and soon-to-be neighbours Belarus, Moldova and Ukraine, and the Caucasian countries Armenia, Azerbaijan and Georgia.[5] Within this wider European community we can thus discern two levels on which the EU needs to engage Russia constructively: the EU–Russian strategic partnership with an aim of guaranteeing overall peace and stability, and the EU–Russian regional cooperation frameworks of the ND and western NIS/CIS (Figure 5.1).

The notion of community has a specific meaning in this context. It is essentially defined by issues of tradition, belonging and identity, instead of

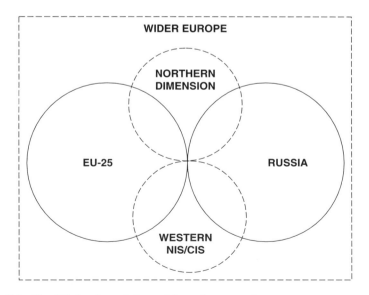

Figure 5.1   The EU, Russia and the problem of community

mere norms and rules of interaction that have traditionally determined the analyses of great power encounters. More precisely, a 'community perspective' privileges identity issues as the basis of international interaction, and expects normative questions on what agents can and should do to each other to be discernible in relations between powers.[6] What this chapter calls 'the problem of community' thus seems to have two dimensions: First, if one accepts the notion of community, the outcomes of EU–Russian encounters differ from those of the classical prism of great power politics. Second, there is still the problem of how – on the basis of which values and identities – either side defines this community and its own contribution to and place within it.

Proceeding from these premises, it is here argued that the problem of community overrides other principles by which responsibility can be assigned to the EU in relation to Russia. Such alternative principles include the *legitimate expectations principle* – the Union can be held responsible for raising its neighbours' expectations through its own successive enlargements and repeated references to the unification of 'Europe' since the early 1990s; the *contribution principle* – the Union can be held responsible for the effects of its own actions on third parties such as Russia; and the *capacity principle* – the Union can be deemed to possess unique capacities that induce it to act in occasions where others lack similar powers.

These principles do of course open up important aspects into the EU's responsibilities towards Russia, aspects that are relevant for the following analysis of the problem of community. However, as regards the legitimate expectations principle, we must assume at least some degree of community for any claims of legitimacy to be relevant in global politics. In the absence of community, various expectations may arise, but they are not necessarily legitimate, that is, accepted on the basis of shared norms. The contribution principle, for its part, is in danger of becoming reduced to a somewhat technical aspect of international law enforcement and dispute arbitration without any concomitant notion of community between the parties. The capacity principle is certainly a factor to be reckoned with in global politics, but again, its validity and applicability are very much tied to the notion of community interlinking the 'have' and 'have-not' parties.

The main normative argument advanced in this chapter is that the EU should try and engage Russia firmly into a dialogue in order to help construct a wider European community, both by means of the EU–Russian strategic partnership and the regional cooperation frameworks. Importantly, due to the centrality of Russia, such a policy guideline would also help the EU-25 to fulfil part of the responsibility it has elsewhere set *vis-à-vis* its new wider neighbourhood. In this chapter, it will be first suggested that there is a long-standing history to the problem of community in EU–Russian relations. This will be followed by a discussion of the emergence of community aspects at the strategic partnership level and the regional levels of the ND and the western NIS/CIS. As a conclusion, the normative content of the EU–Russian dialogue is somewhat paradoxically found to be shrinking, but the very continuance of the dialogue indicates that a much more responsible European power than might be expected on the basis of the history of great power encounters is in the making.

The 'problem of community' in Europe–Russia relations

In the eyes of many 'Europe-builders', Russia has – together with Turkey or the Ottoman empire – represented perhaps the most constant challenge with regard to the delimitation of Europe's borders. Already in the mid-seventeenth century, the French thinker Duc de Sully, Henri IV's protégé and Cardinal Richelieu's associate, suggested that Russia should have no place in the European order. According to de Sully, Russia should be excluded due to its Orthodox Christianity, which makes it a 'barbarous country . . . [that should be placed] in the same class as Turkey'.[7] Despite the fact that Peter the Great's reforms and expansionist politics lifted Russia to the group of European great powers by the early eighteenth century, for most of the time Russia has represented Europe's primary eastern 'Other'.[8] Arguably, this was also visible during the Cold War, when the EEC consistently blocked the Soviet Union's efforts to establish ties with it.

The EU–Russia relations as we know them today carry this historical baggage. The EC–Russian dialogue slowly began after the Italian Prime Minister Bettino Craxi visited Moscow in 1985 to meet the reform-minded Soviet leader Mikhail Gorbachev.[9] Thereafter, regardless of repeated failures to agree on EC–Russian economic relations, Gorbachev and other high-level European politicians started referring to an early version of a wider European community. The term used at the time was the 'Common European Home', embracing not only Western Europe, but also Russia. In 1993, then, the Union declared its Copenhagen criteria for EU membership. But this declaration famously did not define whom to include into the group of 'European countries' able to join upon fulfilment of the political, economic, judicial and practical criteria set by the EU (see Chapter 4 by Raik). Although Russia's interests *vis-à-vis* the EU were then still overshadowed by other political developments in Europe, particularly those pertaining to NATO, it is clear that such a fairly ambiguous politics of community by the EU only served to confuse Russian politicians over their prospects of European alignment after the end of the Cold War division. Consequently, the first Russian president Boris Yeltsin was during the late 1990s quoted as referring to the prospect of Russia's membership in the EU. His suggestion was not well received in most European capitals.

Apart from the Union's ill-preparedness to contemplate Russia's membership, its ability to respond to Russia's expectations has also been compromised by its own nature as a political entity. First, the EU acts both as a Union, and as the aggregate of its member states' own foreign policies. The Union introduced its Common Strategy on Russia (CSR) in June 1999. Russia replied with its Mid-Term Strategy towards the EU in December 1999. In addition, the Union has a Partnership and Cooperation Agreement (PCA) with Russia that entered into force in 1997. The Cooperation Council stipulated within the PCA was upgraded into a Permanent Partnership Council in 2004. Together with the senior official level cooperation committees, the Council provides the main institutional channel for the practical conduct of EU–Russia relations. However, big EU members like Germany, France and Italy continue a tradition of having their own *Ostpolitik* towards Russia. In Germany's case, this tradition dates back to the final decades of the Cold War. In France's case, ties between the two countries can even be sought from the geopolitical arrangements within the nineteenth century concert of Europe's great powers. The interests of big member states often appear to contradict the positions taken by the Union as part of its CFSP and ESDP. This serves to confuse Russia's expectations of its membership in the communities in which the EU plays a pivotal role.[10]

Second, the problem of community is exacerbated by the two-level nature of the Union's policies pertaining to Russia. The CFSP and ESDP relate to the EU–Russian *strategic partnership*, which was launched at the turn of the millennium. In the St Petersburg EU–Russia summit in 2003, the partnership was agreed to aim at creating a (i) Common European Economic Space (CEES, with a special reference to energy and environmental issues); (ii) Common Space of Freedom, Security and Justice; (iii) Common Space of Cooperation in the Field of External Security, and (iv) Common Space of Research and Education, Including Cultural Issues.[11] The Commission and large member states are the driving force at the strategic partnership level. In the EU–Russian *regional cooperation* within the ND, and prospectively, the western NIS/CIS, primarily the Commission together with the small member states located geographically close to Russia, Finland and Sweden in particular, advocate engaging the European parts of Russia into a privileged relationship with the EU.

The strategic partnership level is driven by a strong EU–Russian *interdependence* in the energy sector. Slowly, albeit somewhat painfully, *shared* EU–Russian policy projects are emerging as its defining characteristics, in opposition to unilaterally defined preferences of either side. Tied to this gradual and partial alleviation of the community problem are the already mentioned Russian expectations of ever closer relations with 'Europe'. They first surfaced in a general Euro-Atlanticist orientation of Russian foreign policy in the early 1990s, but then faded due to the disappointments in the degree of engagement by the 'west', and Russia's own identity political soul-searching, chaotic internal politics and, finally, economic collapse in 1998. They re-emerged after the turn of the millennium with renewed vigour, with President Vladimir Putin's rise to power. The new policy was well crystallised in Putin's state of the nation address in May 2003, where he asserted that '. . . real integration with Europe . . . of course is a complicated and long-term process. But this is our historical choice. It has been made'.[12]

This rapprochement notwithstanding, we have also seen Russian complaints regarding the manner in which the EU-15 enlarged into EU-25. The Kaliningrad region, already cut off geographically from mainland Russia with the independence of the three Baltic States, became psychologically even more distant from Moscow by the inclusion of these states into the legal framework of the European Union. This delivered a severe identity political blow to Russia. Russia's bilateral agreements with many new EU members were also abolished against Russian preferences. In this context, Russian foreign policy makers sought to influence the attitudes within the EU by pointing out how the problematic exclave status of Kaliningrad was harmfully exacerbated by the Union's enlargement to Lithuania and Poland and the planned establishment of a Schengen border regime around the region, and how Russia would suffer economically from EU enlargement. The Russian complaints also reflected identity (or 'community') concerns: Russia perceived itself to have earned the right to Kaliningrad by its heroic performance in protecting Europe from the Nazis in the Second World War. Likewise, losing the former bilateral treaties with the new EU members created an image of Russia being pushed away from its hard-fought access to Europe.

On the regional level we can find somewhat different, but complementary efforts to alleviate the community problem. The high initial expectations in the late 1990s of the capacity of the Northern Dimension to open up a new chapter in EU–Russian relations turned later into more sober assessments. The regional problems created by the encircling of Kaliningrad as well as the relatively small amounts of funding provided through the ND initiative also contributed to this. The *capacity principle* is thus also relevant in this context. It is of course quite clear that the Union cannot take responsibility for the modernisation of the whole of Russia to the degree some observers in Russia might wish for. But in the more limited context of the ND and northwest Russia, and even more so in the case of Kaliningrad, the Union is probably the only external agent that is both capable and suitable for providing substantial help. And crucially, the Union also has the capacity to direct resources to EU–Russian cooperation within the western NIS/CIS.

The strategic partnership level

The strategic partnership remains the main channel for coping with the problem of community in EU–Russian relations. It has, however, generated repeated criticism from outside observers. In their view, the partnership is portrayed as more 'strategic' and more coherently pursued than it actually is.[13] The alleged discrepancy between the strategic partnership discourse and its practical content can create one more unnecessary capability–expectations gap for the Union's foreign policy.[14] Christopher Hill famously applied the capability–expectations gap thesis in 1993, in the aftermath of the 1992 Maastricht treaty and as a result of the way in which the then European

Community was 'talked up' during the treaty-making process. According to Hill, the Union had been unable to formulate a clear strategy on questions like its eastern enlargement. In Hill's opinion, the gap had become a real danger. Non-EU members might be willing to take excessive risks in order to approach the EU, or the Union itself could adopt unrealistic policies towards them. To halt the widening of the gap, either the Union's capabilities would have to be increased, or expectations decreased.[15] By 1998, Roy Ginsberg argued that the gap was closing. Expectations were gradually becoming more modest and capabilities more efficient.[16]

The above-mentioned project on the four common spaces has also received at best a lukewarm reception among Russian observers regardless of its approval by the country's leadership, most recently in the form of agreeing new road maps for the project's further development in May 2005.[17] Let us now take a look at the degree to which each of the four spaces manages to contribute to the EU-Russian dialogue and the creation of a wider European community where Russia would have an integral role.

(i)   The CEES

The CEES is jointly defined by the EU and Russia to denote an 'open and integrated market between the EU and Russia, based on the implementation of common or compatible rules and regulations, including compatible administrative practices, as a basis for synergies and economies of scale associated with a higher degree of competition in bigger markets'.[18] The full implementation of the CEES includes the four freedoms of the EU's single market – goods, services, capital and labour. However, the extension of these freedoms to Russia would in practice mean Russia's partial inclusion into the EU's single market *acquis*. Some reports suggest, however, that the Russian *Duma* already takes into account EU legislation when it debates new draft laws; some others contend that the practical record remains meagre in this respect, proposing that in the short run the priority should be on conforming with WTO standards.[19] According to president Putin, his government constantly receives proposals from Russian business circles for further reforms directed at EU–Russian economic integration.[20]

The CEES is not a mere process of the EU trying to 'europeanise' Russia's economy. Economic interdependence between the EU and Russia is already on a relatively high level. The EU is partially dependent on Russia's energy resources, and this dependence is likely to increase in the future. The Union estimates that its overall dependence on energy imports will rise from 50 to 70 per cent by 2020 – Russian energy resources will provide a good alternative to those of the politically unstable Middle East. Several projects for additional gas and oil pipelines linking the EU and Russia are currently planned. Interconnection of the EU and Russian electricity networks is also a priority area, as is the materialisation of the already agreed on European transport corridors and telecommunications networks to facilitate energy and other trade. As Table 5.1 shows, Russia's economic dependence on the EU is even more extensive.

Table 5.1   Economic interdependence between the EU and Russia

EU	Russia
Oil imports from Russia (2003) 16%	Oil exports to the EU (2003) 56%
Gas imports from Russia (2003) 20%	Gas exports to the EU (2003) 62%
Exports to Russia (EU-15 + ten accession states, 2002) 4%	Exports to the EU (EU-15 + ten accession states, 2002) 62%
Imports from Russia (EU-15 + ten accession states, 2002) 7%	Imports from the EU (EU-15 + ten accession states, 2002) 61%
Foreign direct investment to Russia (2002) 2.2 billion euros	Accumulated foreign direct investment from the EU (as of the end of 2001) approximately 70% of total value

Sources: 'EC Commission Delegation . . .' 'The EU and Russia – Economic and Trade Indicators' http://www.delrus.cec.eu.int/en/images/pText_pict/216/Economic%20indicators.doc; 'E-Note: Foreign investments in Russia' http://www.delrus.cec.eu.int/en/images/pText_pict/222/Foreign%20investment_new%20data.doc, downloaded 27 September 2004.

So far it seems that, on balance, the CEES has not sufficiently improved the nature and outcome of the dialogue between the EU and Russia – possibly because mutual dependency also means mutual vulnerability. For example, the EU has required Russia to gradually reduce the gap in the energy prices for domestic industrial users and foreign energy buyers, with the argument that they violate the competition principles of an extended single market. Partly because of this the Union blocked Russia's admission into the WTO and hence also any large-scale implementation of the CEES until the energy pricing dispute was resolved in the EU–Russia summit of May 2004. Moreover, the EU expects Russia to make a choice between EU-linked and its own economic re-integration projects within the CIS framework. The most recent one of the latter was launched in September 2003 between Russia, Belarus, Kazakhstan and Ukraine.[21] The Russian president simply commented in late 2003 that the CEES should not restrict Russia's ability to take part in other regional integration processes, as Russia's 'geopolitical abilities' can help European businesses in the Central Asian and Asia-Pacific region.[22]

The May 2004 agreement on the long-term convergence of the Russian energy market to EU requirements signifies a promise of the transformation of the EU's individual concerns into shared ones. Although the EU side provides the standards of convergence here, the long transition period until 2010, reflecting Russia's concerns as expressed in its own energy strategy, represents a new and dialogic element.[23]

(ii)   Common space of freedom, security and justice

The main issue of debate within this sector is the long-term prospect of EU–Russia visa-free regime. The issue originally emerged as a result of Russian complaints about Kaliningrad's encirclement by the enlarging EU and its

Schengen borders. President Putin put forth the demand for a visa-free regime in order to prompt the EU to make concessions in the Kaliningrad transit problem during 2002, at a time when negotiations appeared deadlocked. Fearing the escalation of the dispute into other cooperation areas, the EU and Russia quickly came to a compromise and adopted what could be called a Schengen regime with some special exceptions for facilitating transit.[24]

The concrete steps so far include the signing of an agreement between Russia and Europol and the drafting of an Action Plan on organised crime. The list of issues to settle includes the slowly progressing EU–Russian readmission treaty. For the European Commission, a source of sheer frustration is also the way in which France, Germany and Italy agreed in 2003 with Russia on the easing of visa procedures for businessmen, politicians, athletes and academics. The Union was sidelined. Another problem of the implementation of this common space is the fact that, most likely, a visa-free regime would require the EU to help Russia in the massive task of closing its porous borders with the CIS countries to stop the smuggling of people and goods from Asia to the European continent. In a word, in this common space most EU concerns are still to translate into shared ones.

(iii)   Common space of cooperation in the field of external security

There are some promises but relatively little achievements in this sector so far. Russia is the only non-EU member country that has a good access, through monthly consultations, to the Union's Political and Security Committee, the main decision-making body of the ESDP. The EU–Russia summit in Moscow 2002 also announced the aim of working towards a common crisis management approach and the start of bilateral military contacts. However, rapid progress is not only blocked by the Union's doubts about Russia's peace-keeping and military operations in Chechnya and the CIS, but also by the vagueness of the ESDP, particularly in relation to NATO.[25] It is also notable that both parties underline their commitment to the central role of the UN in global questions. There have also been significant similarities in their declared positions on specific questions related to, for example, Iraq, the Middle East settlement, Cyprus, and Afghanistan, and the spread of weapons of mass destruction.[26] This relative security political convergence even prompted president Putin to refer, on an approving note, to the comprehensive character of EU–Russian relations that extend from a wide range of civilian to military issues.[27] Importantly, as will be explained below, the prospect of a joint EU–Russian perception of their shared responsibility in managing the numerous conflicts within the Caucasus and elsewhere in the western NIS/CIS looks fairly interesting.

(iv)   Common space of research and education, including cultural issues

The main element of this policy sector so far is an EU–Russian agreement on science and technology cooperation. A further issue is Russia's already agreed on entry to the Bologna process of harmonising higher education programmes across the wider European area. This is a sector where the EU's norms are already relatively well in place, and where the emergence of a shared responsibility seems unlikely in the short term only by means of the current, unidirectional 'europeanisation'. But it is also clear that the long-term effects of the progress within this space may be very dramatic for Russia's inclusion into the wider European community through the socialisation of its new elites into European-wide curricula.

*   *   *

The above analysis of developments within these common spaces leads us to conclude that there are indeed some signs of a shift towards a more dialogic approach at the strategic partnership level. This could also help alleviate the community problem. Although the dialogue is still in progress, it is clear that in some sectors the EU and Russia are slowly recognising and accommodating for each other's concerns.

Simultaneously, the Union's original community building project of promoting an area of democracy and human rights in Russia appears to be undergoing at least a partial transformation. Although many documents drafted by EU institutions continue to refer to the promotion of democracy and human rights in Russia, it is evident that the Union's leaders have grown disillusioned with Russia's (un)democratic development during Putin's reign. In place of flirting with democracy promotion as in the 1990s – with rather unimpressive overall results – the Union is introducing a new tone. We increasingly witness mere references to the more ambiguous term 'good governance', coupled with notions of shared responsibility, and materially and instrumentally defined common interests.[28] The dialogue is thus materialising at the expense of those explicitly normative considerations that are often attached to the EU.[29] In other words, the development of a more dialogic EU–Russian partnership does not necessarily strengthen the type of comprehensive normative agenda we are used to expect from the Union. Yet, the EU's promotion of a dialogue as such can in this case be seen as a powerful norm, and one which is not pre-defined and unidirectional in the same manner as is the EU's promotion of democracy.

The regional cooperation level of the Northern Dimension

The regional cooperation level as manifested within the Northern Dimension provides an additional forum within which the problem of community makes itself felt. Geographically the ND covers only the northern EU member countries around the Baltic Sea region, plus Norway and Iceland, and only the northwestern regions from the Russian side. It is within this geographical area where the only EU-Russian land borders can be found. Mutual relations around these borders vary a great deal, from the well-established neighbourly contacts between Finland and Russia, to the remaining mutual suspicions between the Balts and Russia. The ND covers all the themes and issues of the four spaces discussed above, except for cooperation in external security matters. In brief, compared to the strategic partnership level, there is a genuine perception of proximity.

Observers' opinions of the ND are divided. According to the positive views, the ND's inception created a more dialogic regional initiative than we have seen in the EU's other engagements with Russia. The ND (re)introduced the supposedly inclusive notion of the 'north' and offered Russia a place as a north European country, as opposed to the old debate on whether Russia belongs to the 'West' or 'East'. The ND also introduced a new horizontal approach as opposed to the Union's Maastricht-treaty-boosted, compartmentalised pillar organisation with little communication across policy sectors and competencies. But more critical observers refer to the initiative's failure to attract substance, special funds and tangible projects.[30]

The ND was suggested by Finland in 1997. It was first recognised EU-wide in the Luxembourg European Council of December the same year. The EU's first Action Plan for the ND covered several cooperation areas: the environment, energy, human and scientific resources, health, fight against crime, trade and investment and the special problems of Russia's Kaliningrad exclave. Funding was provided by the Union's existing programmes. The primary financial tool was Tacis and its Cross-Border Cooperation (CBC) programme. On the EU and accession country side of the border, for example Phare and Interreg funds were used for cross-border projects.

Although we might deem the EU capable of assisting considerably in the post-Soviet transformation of northwest Russia, the amounts actually committed by the EU have been fairly modest.[31] In 1995–2002, the total aid commitments of the EU to the whole of Russia were 1.1 billion euros. The seven euros that this figure makes per capita for the whole of Russia, compares rather unfavourably to the 71–465 euros per capita received by the states of the former Yugoslavia.[32] Moreover, 80 per cent of the Tacis funds went directly to European consultants simply visiting various Russian regions and then travelling away. These figures do not of course tell us precisely the amount of funds used for ND activities, as a large part of Tacis spending was directed outside the ND area, whilst additional ND funds were received from co-operating organisations and states. Yet, it is clear that the figures are in any case far from making such a decisive impact as seen in the accession states, which during 2000–2006 received altogether 22 billion euros.[33]

Russian policy makers have not always shared unambiguously the positive views of a strong dialogic element within the ND. In Russian eyes, the ND has been in an unfortunate manner dominated by the nexus of (energy supply) opportunities perceived by representatives of EU institutions, and concerns of northern member states in particular of the soft security threats allegedly resulting from the huge standard-of-living gap on the Finnish–Russian border.[34] Such apprehensions about the ND partly instructed Russia to seek dropping

Kaliningrad from the ND agenda and dealing with it at the strategic partnership level.[35] When the second Action Plan for the ND (for 2004–2006) was drafted in early 2003, Russian foreign policy makers made clear their unhappiness about the extent to which the ND process had so far involved dialogic elements. They referred to how in their opinion far too few items of the so-called Nida list jointly prepared by Russia and Lithuania in 2000 had ended up into the first ND Action Plan, and demanded that further steps should be taken on the basis of equal participation.[36]

On the whole, after its inception, the ND quickly started losing its character as an innovative, regionalising Russia policy of the Union and, at the time of writing, its future was only assured until the expiration of the second Action Plan by the end of 2006. At Russia's explicit request, Tacis funds started to be distributed directly to the Russian federal government in place of regional bodies. In this manner, the EU started inching the ND to become part of its centre-to-centre strategic partnership with Russia. The relative weight of exclusively EU-originated policy proposals lessened in this process, whilst Russian regional agents became sidelined as well. As president Putin puts it, 'we believe that interregional cooperation requires active support at state level'.[37] All in all, although the introduction of the ND failed to fulfil all of the optimistic expectations, it has helped sharpen the EU's and Russia's strategic partnership by providing a channel for Russia to express its concerns. In that way, the ND has helped to engage Russia into the wider Europe community.

A shared EU–Russian responsibility within the Western NIS/CIS?

In the 1990s, there were predictions of the EU and Russia possibly clashing over their self-defined spheres of influence in the case of the Baltic States. With Russia accepting the Baltic States' EU membership, and the extension of the Partnership and Cooperation Agreement provisions into Russo-Baltic relations agreed in April 2004, a possible new confrontation point emerged within the western NIS/CIS. These territories represent a new focus area for the EU as outlined in its neighbourhood policy. They also constitute the traditional backyard of imperial Russia.

The EU launched its European Neighbourhood Policy in 2003 (ENP; see Raik's chapter). The policy aims at providing a strategic gaze at the Union's new borders after the 2004 enlargement. The Commission issued a 'Communication' document to the Council in March 2003, which sets a clearly declared *responsibility* for the Union towards its new neighbours:

> The EU has a *duty*, not only towards its citizens and those of the new member states, but also towards its present and future neighbours to ensure continuing social cohesion and economic dynamism. The EU must act to promote the regional and sub-regional cooperation and integration that

are preconditions for political stability, economic development and the reduction of poverty and social divisions in our *shared* environment. The EU can and should work to spread the benefits of enlargement for political and economic stability in the neighbouring countries and to help reduce prosperity gaps where they exist. This should be reflected in a *clear vision* for the development of closer and more coherent relations with the Union's neighbours over the medium and long term.[38]

The Commission's document speaks of creating an area of *shared prosperity*. It also mentions explicitly *shared responsibilities for conflict prevention* between the EU and its neighbours. The overall aim is to 'develop a zone of prosperity and a friendly neighbourhood – a "ring of friends" – with whom the EU enjoys close, peaceful and co-operative relations'.[39] In practice, the neighbourhood policy has since then evolved into an effort of spreading the Union's peace project into the neighbourhood without offering the prospect of membership. The more ruthless motives include ensuring access to the rich natural resources to the east and south of the EU, and stabilising the markets opening up there. There are declarations of the neighbourhood policy being based on 'common values', including the rule of law, good governance, human rights and minority rights, good neighbourly relations, market economy and sustainable development.[40] However, the guiding principle of EU engagement will be case-by-case *differentiation* according to needs, capacities and common interests.[41] This allows, in reality, a departure from the declared value-based conditionality towards a more instrumental approach – an approach that better matches the preferences of those new neighbours who do not adhere to the whole set of the Union's values, as remains the case with Russia. There consequently is the possibility of the EU learning to pursue dialogue on a more limited agenda than it is used to in dealings with its neighbours and other powers.

The development of the neighbourhood policy is an open-ended process, but it is bound to effect EU–Russia relations and the political constellation of the wider European area in various ways.

First, the neighbourhood policy is capable of providing some linkages between the Union's strategic partnership and regional level policies. The neighbourhood policy is designed to interconnect the fragmented external assistance policies in various geographical directions. It will also function as an umbrella for the ND policy. Existing financial instruments will be merged into one Neighbourhood Instrument during 2004–2007. For 2004–2006, 255 million euros have been earmarked for external assistance and 700 million for Interreg funding on the EU side of the joint border. For 2007–2013, a substantial increase of funds is planned.[42]

What also distinguishes the new neighbourhood policy from previous instruments of engagement with nearby areas is its status as part of the Union's CFSP. The Union's High Representative for CFSP will be involved in the development and monitoring of the policy.[43] With reference to Russia, the policy is intended to 'enrich the work on the common spaces', as 'the EU and Russia need to work together, as neighbours, on common concerns'.[44] Potentially these factors could mean more coherent EU action in areas where both the Union and Russia share an interest.

Second, the ENP clearly makes Russia a special case. Russia insisted on not being lumped together with its former dominos, and therefore the country will not be part of the neighbourhood policy as will the western CIS/NIS states, despite the fact that some Russian regions will most likely benefit from the funds channelled through the Neighbourhood Instrument. The economic interdependence between the EU and Russia can be identified as the main reason for this special place of Russia in the Union's mental maps. The Commission says that in the western NIS, the EU should cooperate with Russia 'whenever possible'. As for the conflict-prone Caucasus, the EU was at first reluctant to include the region into the neighbourhood policy. However, it now speaks of a need for its inclusion and for a more coherent policy, pursued 'whenever possible, in cooperation with Russia'.[45]

Third, the ENP contributes to, and is affected by, changes within the NIS/CIS and between these states and Russia. The CIS started losing its initial supranational nature already a few years after its inception in 1991, and has since then taken the shape of bilateral arrangements between Russia and the other members.[46] Towards the late 1990s, many members started refusing to renew earlier commitments, preferring either national policies or forming competing groupings such as the so-called GUAM – Georgia, Ukraine, Azerbaijan and Moldova (Uzbekistan was member during 1999–2005) – to challenge the CIS. The GUAM officially aims at fighting separatism, establishing joint peace-keeping capabilities, developing the trade corridor from Central Asia through the Caucasus to the EU,[47] and facilitating the integration of its members into Euro-Atlantic and Atlantic structures. But it also aims at balancing against Russia.[48] It is remarkable, however, that even though the CIS is eroding and Russia's power generates vehement resistance in the region, the EU continues to speak of shared EU–Russian responsibility within and towards the western NIS/CIS. By contrast, the US clearly separates between Russian and CIS interests and formulates its policies towards the region irrespective of Moscow's concerns.

Fourth, the ENP may, in the middle to long term, overshadow or even side-line other regional cooperation forums where Russia is engaged, including the Council of Europe activities and the Black Sea Economic Cooperation. The way in which the ND gradually swallowed the previously established regional cooperation organisations in northern Europe like the Council of the Baltic Sea States and Barents Euro-Arctic Council provides an illustrative precedent. With the availability of EU funds in previously unseen amounts and the consequent introduction of EU practices into existing cooperation, these organisations gradually transformed into consultatory and implementation organs of the Union's ND policy.[49]

Fifth, the comprehensive nature of the European neighbourhood policy introduces a new dimension to the pattern of Russian and US involvement within the western NIS/CIS. This involvement has been predominantly security and military oriented. In addition, we find Russia's occasional economic coercion efforts towards, for example, Belarus, Ukraine and Georgia, as well as Russian and US economic interests related to the region's natural resources and its transport corridor function. The EU is just as interested in these same issues, but it arguably promotes a much more multi-sectoral policy than seen so far in the region. The consequence may well be that the EU may, if successful, make itself more attractive to the western NIS/CIS than it may actually wish to be.

Finally, on a conceptually slightly different note, some reservations must be aired regarding the extent to which the European neighbourhood policy is in fact dialogical. The EU speaks of 'joint ownership' of the policy, based on 'shared values and common interests'. It appears, however, that these are first and foremost EU and Council of Europe induced values that most partners have so far failed to embrace, at least on the evidence of practical policy and implementation. But the reference to common *interests* again provides an escape clause for the Union against accusations of imposing 'priorities or conditions on its partners'.[50] Be that as it may, it seems that with regard to the western NIS/CIS, the Union more pronouncedly suggests simple convergence with its own practices than it does in the case of Russia. In its Russian relations the Union seems more willing to promote openness and dialogue, with its character of an undetermined end result.[51]

Overall, the ENP may be seen as a significant step towards diminishing the 'community problem' in EU–Russian relations. In particular, it helps the Union to engage in a dialogue with Russia instead of just preaching about the 'common values' to deaf ears. Moreover, the western NIS/CIS provides potential for regional cooperation through which the EU–Russian strategic partnership can be sharpened and enhanced. So far, the lack of coordination and coherence between the strategic partnership and regional cooperation levels has been one of the major problems in the EU's relations with Russia. This incoherence and diverging policies have in the past allowed the EU to avoid confronting serious questions about what it is really responsible for and what it is not.

Conclusion

This chapter departed from the premise that the EU-25 is too narrow a community for thinking seriously about the normative aspects of the EU's engagement in its neighbourhood and particularly Russia. Instead, an approach taking the wider European community as the reference point of analysis was suggested. On the whole, the main normative argument advanced in the chapter has been that engaging and including Russia as a more integral part of a nascent wider European community is a basic condition for the EU to possess any quality of responsibility in relation to Russia. The EU should, in other words, respond to Russia's long-standing calls for a place in Europe. Addressing this basic question should form the basis of any further discussion of the EU's responsibility towards Russia.

The analyses above have conveyed a fairly mixed picture of how the EU has sought to cope with this normative challenge so far. We have seen that problems of constructive engagement by the EU in creating a wider European community exist both at the level of EU–Russian strategic partnership and the regional cooperation levels of the ND and western NIS/CIS. But we have also pointed out efforts to bridge the old European-Russian divide and thus gradually alleviate the problem of community. The main developments within this mixed picture can be summarised in three main points.

First, in the case of Russia, the EU is slowly re-defining its normative agenda. This is a result of the fading away of the overly ideological and idealistic Common European Home rhetoric of the early 1990s, and of the Union's weakened promotion of its common values in Russia after very meagre results during the previous decade. The Union has gradually become less vocal in its criticism of Russia's (un)democratic conduct. When criticism has been raised, it has not been allowed to slow down the promotion of the strategic partnership. Neither has regional cooperation been allowed to suffer extensively.

Second, on the face of the relatively short and not always entirely successful history, it is conceivable that normative considerations will continue to show up on a narrower scale than earlier. However, somewhat paradoxically, such a narrowing down of the Union's own, largely unilateral concerns is likely to promote dialogue. This in itself is a responsible thing to do. The more the EU's policies become dialogically defined and shared with Russia, the more they have a chance to evoke a positive response, even if their normative content narrows down in the process. EU–Russian cooperation is in this way likely to become more effective also from the normative point of view.

Third, even such a narrowed-down normative agenda represents for the Russian side a clear departure from the country's foreign relations elsewhere. Around its vast borders, Russia typically encounters fairly traditional power-political interaction with only a little explicit normative content. Thus, the EU–Russia relations could just as well be based on traditional great power rivalry and balancing. That such conflictual tendencies are nowhere near to be seen in EU–Russian relations, speaks strongly in favour of the fact that the Union is indeed an agent capable of promoting at least some sort of a normative agenda. The slow process of building a wider Europe community outlined here may not in all assessments be *the* responsible thing to do *vis-à-vis* Russia, but it is hardly possible to deem it a completely irresponsible project either.

Finally, what can we say about the normative character of the EU's global agency in general? It is very clear that the case of EU–Russian relations presents us with a much more responsible great power than we might expect on the basis of the history of great power encounters. Although this European great power in-the-making is certainly nowhere near ethical perfection, nor particularly effective in getting its normative message across, it is important to realise that normative issues are truly involved in its global and regional agency. And although the exact content and scope of these issues may vary as a result of the Union's internal politics and response from its partners, it is safe to assume that they will continue to be part of the EU's agenda. This is also, in all likelihood, what others will continue to expect from the Union.

Notes

1. This chapter is related to the author's project 'Russia, the Russians and Europe' (Academy of Finland decision no. 103049). Acknowledgements for useful discussions are due to all contributors to the present volume, and special thanks for detailed comments to Henri Vogt, Hartmut Mayer, Kristi Raik and Eiki Berg.
2. Cf. Webber 2000, 2–7.
3. See e.g. Pursiainen 2001, 3; 33.
4. See Emerson 2003, 1–3.
5. Newly independent countries, or NIS, as the EU calls it; or the western CIS, as Russia might call it, referring to the western part of the Russian-led Commonwealth of Independent States (CIS).
6. Cf. Frost 1996, 35–40.
7. Quoted in Heffernan 1998, 23.
8. Neumann 1999, 207–8.
9. Herrberg 1998, 88–92.
10. Smaller countries' own Russian policies are largely limited to regional cooperation; see body text below.
11. There were references to joint EU–Russian spaces already much earlier. For example the CSR mentioned the notion of common European economic and social space. The more precise idea of the CEES was submitted by the October 2001 EU–Russia summit for further consideration at the Cooperation Council.
12. Putin, Vladimir, 'A State of the Nation Address to the Federal Assembly of the Russian Federation', *International Affairs* (Moscow) vol. 49, no. 4 (2003), 13–14.
13. Haukkala and Toivonen 2002; Khudoley 2003, 15.
14. Spiegelaire 2001, 95–6.
15. Hill 1993, 315.
16. Ginsberg 1998, 431–2.
17. Author interviews in Moscow and St Petersburg with Russian foreign policy makers and analysts, Spring 2005; see also e.g. Karaganov *et al.* 2005, 12–13.
18. 'The Common European Economic Space (CEES), Concept Paper, 13990/03 (Presse 313), Annex I'.
19. Khudoley 2003; Karaganov *et al.* 2005, 6; 10–11.
20. Putin, Vladimir, 'Speech at a meeting with Representatives of the European Round Table of Industrialists and the Round Table of Industrialists of Russia and the EU, 2 December 2003'.
21. Vahl 2003.
22. Putin, Vladimir, 'Speech at a meeting with Representatives of the European Round Table of Industrialists and the Round Table of Industrialists of Russia and the EU, 2 December 2003'.

23. The inapplicability of the beneficiary principle into EU–Russian relations is most evident in light of the CEES, and especially its energy content. At issue are mutual interdependencies where neither the EU nor Russia can clearly be deemed to be benefiting more than the other. The EU is increasingly dependent on Russian energy resources, and Russia needs huge investments into its energy complex – according to Russia's energy strategy, 450–600 bn euro by 2020 – something that the EU area is best placed to provide, in contrast to 'pure' energy buyers such as China; 'Energy Strategy of the Russian Federation to the Year 2020' <http://www.europa. eu.int/comm/energy_transport/russia/energy-strategy2020_en.pdf>, accessed 13 May 2003; EU Commission Delegation in Russia (2003), 'Energy' <www.eur.ru/ eng/neweur/user_eng.php?func=coopspec&id=39>, accessed 11 April 2003. The US is neither in a position to provide such an amount of investment alone.

24. Aalto 2004a; 2006.

25. Rontoyanni 2002; see also Chapter 2 by Ojanen in this volume.

26. They also share the concern of terrorism as enshrined for example in the EU's security strategy drafted by the High Representative Javier Solana. However, as said, the EU continues to voice reservations about Russia's methods in its alleged counter-terrorist military operations (war) in Chechnya; European Commission, 'Joint Statement, EU–Russia Summit, 13990/03 (Presse 3 13) 2'; Ministry of Foreign Affairs of the Russian Federation, 'Russia-European Union Permanent Partnership Council (PPC) Meeting in Luxembourg, 921-28-04-2004, 28 April 2004' (unofficial translation from Russian).

27. Putin, Vladimir, 'Vystyplenie na soveshchanii s tslenami pravitel'stva, 24 November 2003, Moscow'.

28. See e.g. 'Joint Statement, EU–Russia Summit, 13990/03 (Presse 3 13) 2'.

29. Cf. Manners 2002.

30. Aalto *et al.* 2003, 7–13; note also that there is the special fund for the Northern Dimension Environmental Partnership (NDEP). A similar fund is currently developed in the public health sector.

31. See also Prozorov 2004, 16.

32. Emerson 2003, 91.

33. A further problem in the empowerment of the ND has been the weak interest towards north European issues shown by the southern member states in comparison to northerners. Germany, Austria, the Netherlands, France and the UK may support the northerners in some questions although their main attention is always on the more universal concerns within the Union; see Bonvicini and Vaahtoranta 2000, 261–2.

34. Characteristic of such apprehensions is the book on the ND by Valery Shliamin (2002, 19), the former foreign relations minister of the Karelian Republic bordering Finland. According to him, the EU views Russia 'as a source of oil fuel energy and other natural resources, and in addition to that, as a possible source of an ecological catastrophe'.

35. Here it must be recalled how president Putin's tough demands on the free visa question and the resulting series of high-level EU–Russia meetings on the Kaliningrad issue during the course of 2002 finally resulted in a compromise solution. This learning exercise proved to Russia that at the strategic partnership level, Russia can arrive at agreements with the EU. This realisation is made more significant by the Russians' view of the EU as the best-placed power for assisting in Russia's modernisation. Aalto 2004a, 56, and 2006.

36. 'Non-Paper: EU Northern Dimension: Russian Approach', 14 January 2003; 'Non-Paper: Further Steps in Areas Covered by the Northern Dimension of the EU: Russian Proposals', 17 February 2003.

37. Putin, Vladimir, 'Opening Address and Answers to Questions at the Press Conference on Talks with Silvio Berlusconi, 5 November 2003'.
38. European Commission, 'Communication from the Commission to the Council and the European Parliament, "Wider Europe – Neighbourhood: A New Framework for Relations with Our Eastern and Southern Neighbours", Brussels, 11.3.2003 COM(2003) 104 final', 3; 9; emphasis added.
39. European Commission, 'Communication from the Commission to the Council and the European Parliament, "Wider Europe – Neighbourhood: A New Framework for Relations with Our Eastern and Southern Neighbours", Brussels, 11.3.2003 COM (2003) 104 final', 4; 9.
40. European Commission, 'Communication from the Commission, European Neighbourhood Policy, Strategy Paper, Brussels, 12.5.2004, COM(2004) 373 final'.
41. European Commission, 'Beyond Enlargement: Commission Shifts European Neighbourhood Policy into higher gear, IP/04/308, Brussels, 12 May 2004'; 'Communication from the Commission, European Neighbourhood Policy, Strategy Paper, Brussels, 12.5.2004, COM(2004) 373 final'.
42. European Commission, 'Communication from the Commission: Paving the Way for a New Neighbourhood Instrument, Brussels, 1 July 2003, COM(2003) 393 final'.
43. European Commission, 'Communication from the Commission, European Neighbourhood Policy, Strategy Paper, Brussels, 12.5.2004, COM(2004) 373 final', 6; 8; 10.
44. European Commission, 'Communication from the Commission, European Neighbourhood Policy, Strategy Paper, Brussels, 12.5.2004, COM(2004) 373 final', 6.
45. European Commission, 'Communication from Commission to the Council and the European Parliament on Relations with Russia, COM(2004) 106 09/02/04'; 'Beyond Enlargement: Commission Shifts European Neighbourhood Policy into Higher Gear, IP/04/308, Brussels, 12 May 2004'.
46. Sakwa and Webber 1999.
47. This transit corridor is linked to the EU's TRACECA corridor that excludes Russia and has recently shifted more towards oil and gas issues. In 2005, a new US-pushed gas pipeline from Azerbaijan and Georgia was opened to Turkey, surpassing the cheaper route through Iran.
48. Splidsboel-Hansen 2000.
49. Aalto 2004b.
50. European Commission, 'Communication from the Commission, European Neighbourhood Policy, Strategy Paper, Brussels, 12.5.2004, COM(2004) 373 final', 8.
51. See Emerson *et al.* 2005, 29–39; see also Chapter 4 by Raik in this volume.

Bibliography

Aalto, Pami, 'Kaliningrad pelilaudalla', *Ulkopolitiikka*, no. 1 (2004a), 53–6.
Aalto, Pami, 'European Integration and the Declining Project of Building a Baltic Sea Region', in J. Stampehl, D. Brekenfeld, A. Bannwart and U. Plath (eds), *Perceptions of Loss, Decline, and Doom in the Baltic Sea Area* (Berlin: Berliner Wissenschaftsverlag, 2004b), 167–84.
Aalto, Pami, *European Union and the Making of a Wider Northern Europe* (London: Routledge, 2006).
Aalto, Pami, S. Dalby and V. Harle, 'The Critical Geopolitics of Northern Europe: Identity Politics Unlimited', *Geopolitics*, vol. 8, no. 1 (2003), 1–19.
Bonvicini, Gianni and T. Vaahtoranta, 'Conclusions: The Northern Security Dimension', in G. Bonvicini, T. Vaahtoranta and W. Wessels (eds), *The Northern EU: National*

Views on the Emerging Security Dimension (Helsinki: UPI-FIIA and Institut für Europäische Politik, 2000), 259–67.

Bordachev, Timofei V., 'Strategy and Strategies', in A. Moshes (ed.), *Rethinking the Respective Strategies of Russia and the European Union* (Helsinki and Moscow: UPI-FIIA and Carnegie Moscow Center, 2003), 31–61.

Emerson, Michael, 'The Shaping of a Policy Framework for the Wider Europe', *CEPS Policy Brief* no. 39/2003.

Emerson, Michael, S. Aydin, G. Noutcheva, N. Tocci, M. Vahl and R. Youngs, 'The Reluctant Debutante: The European Union as a Promoter of Democracy in Its Neighbourhood', *CEPS Working Document* 223/July 2005.

Frost, Mervyn, *Ethics in International Relations: A Constitutive Theory* (Cambridge: Cambridge University Press, 1996).

Ginsberg, Roy H., 'Conceptualizing the European Union as an International Actor: Narrowing the Theoretical Capability-Expectations Gap', *Journal of Common Market Studies*, vol. 37, no. 3 (1998), 429–54.

Haukkala, Hiski, 'A Problematic "Strategic Partnership"', in D. Lynch (ed.), *EU–Russian Security Dimensions* (Paris: The European Union Institute for Security Studies, 2003), 8–19.

Haukkala, Hiski and A. Toivonen, 'The EU Common Strategy on Russia: In Search of the Foundations of European Foreign Policy', in T. Vaahtoranta (ed.), *Yearbook of Finnish Foreign Policy 2002* (Helsinki: UPI-FIIA, 2002), 54–65.

Heffernan, Michael, *The Meaning of Europe: Geography and Geopolitics* (London: Arnold 1998).

Herrberg, Antje, 'The European Union and Russia: Toward a New *Ostpolitik*?', in C. Rhodes (ed.), *The European Union in the World Community* (Boulder: Lynne Rienner, 1998), 83–104.

Hill, Christopher, 'The Capability–Expectations Gap, or Conceptualizing Europe's International Role', *Journal of Common Market Studies*, vol. 31, no. 3 (1993), 305–28.

Karaganov, Sergei, T. Bordachev, V. Guseinov, F. Lukyanov and D. Suslov, 'Russia–EU Relations: The Present Situation and Prospects', *CEPS Working Document* 225/July 2005.

Khudoley, Konstantin, 'Russia and the European Union: New Opportunities, New Challenges', in A. Moshes (ed.), *Rethinking the Respective Strategies of Russia and the European Union* (Helsinki and Moscow: UPI-FIIA and Carnegie Moscow Center, 2003), 8–30.

Manners, Ian, 'Normative Power Europe: A Contradiction in Terms', *Journal of Common Market Studies*, vol. 40, no. 2 (2002), 235–58.

Moisio, Sami, 'Back to Baltoscandia? European Union and Geo-Conceptual Remaking of the European North', *Geopolitics*, vol. 8, no. 1 (2003), 72–100.

Neumann, Iver, *Uses of the Other: The 'East' in European Identity Formation* (Minneapolis: Minneapolis University Press, 1999).

Pinder, John, 'The Union's Common Strategy on Russia', in J. Pinder and Yu. Shiskov, *The EU and Russia: The Promise of Partnership* (London: The Federal Trust, 2002), 105–34.

Prozorov, Sergei, 'Border Regions and the Politics of EU–Russian Relations: The Role of the EU in Tempering and Producing Border Conflicts', *Working Paper Series in EU Border Conflict Studies* 3/2004.

Pursiainen, Christer, with P. Haavisto and N. Lomagin, 'Soft Security Problems in Northwest Russia and Their Implications for the Outside World', *UPI-FIIA Working Papers* 31/2001.

Rontoyanni, Clelia, 'So Far, So Good? Russia and the ESDP', *International Affairs*, vol. 78, no. 4 (2002), 813–30.

Sakwa, Richard and M. Webber 'The Commonwealth of Independent States, 1991–1998: Stagnation and Survival', *Europe–Asia Studies*, vol. 51, no. 3 (1999), 379–415.

Shliamin, Valery A., *Rossiia v 'Severnom Izmerenii'* (Petrozavodsk: Petrozavodsk State University Press, 2002).

Spiegelaire, Stephan de, 'The Implementation of the EU's Common Strategy on Russia', in H. Haukkala and S. Medvedev (ed.), *The EU Common Strategy on Russia* (Helsinki and Berlin: UPI-FIIA and Institut für Europäische Politik 2001), 81–116.

Splidsboel-Hansen, Flemming, 'GUUAM and the Future of CIS Military Cooperation', *European Security*, vol. 9, no. 4 (2000), 92–110.

Vahl, Marius, 'Whither the Common European Economic Space? Political and Institutional Aspects of Closer Economic Integration between the EU and Russia', paper presented at the workshop 'A Laboratory in the Margins: The EU's and Russia's Policies in Northern Europe', Danish Institute of International Studies, Copenhagen, 26–27 September 2003.

Webber, Mark, 'Introduction: Russia and Europe – Conflict or Cooperation?'. In M. Webber (ed.), *Russia and Europe: Conflict or Cooperation?* (Basingstoke: Macmillan, 2000), 1–21.

6
Assigning Duties in the Global System of Human Rights: The Role of the European Union

Elena Jurado[1]

In December 1997, on the eve of the 50th anniversary of the Universal Declaration of Human Rights, the EU Heads of State commissioned a Committee of Experts to write a report analysing and suggesting ways of improving the EU's activities in the area of human rights. This was not the first attempt by the EU to take stock of its human rights record. The report, duly published in 1998, was the latest in a series of proposals, starting in 1978, aimed at enhancing the EU's capacity to promote human rights not only in third countries, but also within the EU.[2] As in previous cases, the authors of the report identified a host of problems, including the marginal position of human rights in the Union's activities; the inadequate information base upon which the Union constructs its human rights policies; and the policy incoherence produced by the Union's fragmented decision-making structure. However, the most serious shortcoming identified by the authors was the inconsistency between the Union's internal and external human rights policies. Echoing the title of their report, *Leading by Example*, the authors warned:

> A Union which is not prepared to embrace a strong human rights policy for itself is highly unlikely to develop a credible external policy, let alone to apply it with energy or consistency. As long as human rights in Europe are considered to be an area in which the Union has only a very limited role, their status in the Union's external policy will remain tenuous.[3]

More than five years on from the publication of *Leading by Example*, the EU's efforts to promote human rights in third countries are still being criticised as piecemeal and incoherent at best,[4] and guilty of double standards and hypocrisy at worst.[5] Implicit in these criticisms is the acceptance that the EU has a duty not only to protect the welfare of EU citizens, but also to

119

safeguard and promote the rights of individuals throughout the world. This tacit acceptance is not only evident in academic discussions and in the reports of human rights activists; it is also discernable in the speeches of EU policy-makers. In a speech delivered to the UN Human Rights Commission in 2002, Javier Solana, the High Representative for the EU's Common Foreign and Security Policy, explained that 'the EU is determined fully to assume its inter-national responsibilities [for the global protection of human rights].'[6] This chapter departs from existing accounts of the EU's human rights policy by subjecting the tacit acceptance of EU responsibility in this field to critical examination.

The notion of responsibility – understood here as the moral requirements imposed on the behaviour of those who assume certain functions, roles and offices – offers a useful framework for analysing the global system of human rights by raising an important question: namely, which agent, or set of agents, bears responsibility for ensuring the protection of human rights? Or, put differently, on what basis do agents incur particular roles (and thus duties) in the global system of human rights? Until recently the answer to this question was relatively straightforward (if not necessarily satisfactory): each sovereign state was deemed responsible for protecting the rights of its own citizens. With the end of the Cold War a confluence of factors has eroded this assumption so that today it is generally accepted that human rights vio-lations represent a legitimate subject of international concern.[7] Nevertheless, little has been done to assign duties amongst relevant international agents – be these governments, international institutions or non-governmental organisa-tions (NGOs) – in any systematic way.[8] Assigning duties is necessary, however, in order to ensure that action is taken – or, in the event of non-action, blame apportioned – when gross human rights violations occur. It is also necessary in order to avoid wasteful duplication of activities and, as this chapter shall explain, to minimise the risk of divergent standards.

The analysis in this chapter proceeds as follows. I first review a variety of principles for distributing duties in the field of human rights and make a case for highlighting the capacity principle: whichever agent can bring about change most efficiently and effectively should do so. In the second section, I draw on recent empirical studies and theoretical debates in International Relations to develop a conceptual framework of the processes and mechanisms through which states comply with international norms. I use this model to explain why the global system of human rights must rely on a combination of instruments, including material incentives, political dialogue and moral consciousness-raising. I then turn to reviewing the mechanisms developed by the EU for promoting human rights in third countries. I argue that, notwith-standing some notable innovations introduced in recent years, the EU relies primarily on the mechanism of conditionality: the attempt to change the human rights practices of states by offering them economic and political opportunities in exchange for compliance with international human rights norms. Whilst the response of most observers has been to call on the EU to develop a greater range of instruments to promote human rights, in the fourth part, I argue that it is neither feasible nor, in fact, advisable for the EU to do this. Instead I suggest that a responsible EU should seek to coordinate its activities with other institutions, in particular the Council of Europe and UN, which already have the additional instruments at their disposal. In the final part, then, I offer a preliminary exploration of what such a system of shared responsibility might look like.

The normative sources of EU responsibility

In spite of their eagerness to shoulder the EU with responsibility for promoting human rights, most commentators do not stop to think about where this responsibility comes from. For them it is sufficient that the EU has established the promotion of human rights as one of its core objectives; their attention focuses on how the EU should consequently improve its record in this field. In fact, it is the EU itself (or rather its 'supranational' representatives) who have done most to explain the EU's assumption of responsibility in this field – perhaps to convince the more sceptical member states of its merits.[9] The explanation which emerges from the speeches of EU representatives is that the Union's duty to promote human rights stems from its identity as a 'community of values'. Thus, in a 2001 communication to the European Council and European Parliament, the European Commission explained that the basis of the EU's external human rights policy is Article 6 of the Amsterdam Treaty, which establishes that the Union 'is founded on the principles of liberty, democracy, respect for human rights and fundamental freedoms'.[10]

However, this identity-driven explanation is not actually consistent with the EU's historical development. The EC was founded in 1957 with the aim of creating a zone of peace and prosperity in Western Europe by means of economic integration. As more and more economic activities became integrated, concern was voiced about the implications this would have for human rights. However, apart from a nod in this direction by the European Court of Justice (ECJ), no moves were taken to make safeguarding human rights an objective of the European Community. It was only in 1999, when the Amsterdam Treaty came into force, that human rights were brought into the EU's *acquis communautaire*. Besides Article 6, mentioned above, the new treaty established that respect for human rights was required by countries who apply for EU membership (Article 49) and introduced a mechanism to sanction serious and persistent breaches of human rights by the EU member states (Article 7).

The timing of these innovations, and their grudging acceptance by European governments, suggests that the EU's new commitment to promoting human rights was driven less by internal demands and more by external developments.[11] Events in Eastern Europe during the early 1990s and, in particular, the outbreak of ethnic-based conflict in Yugoslavia, convinced EC Heads of State of the broader security implications of human rights violations. By emphasising the *external* origins of the EU's growing interest in human rights, my purpose is not to question the EU's responsibility in this field. There are at least three ways in which the international system, and the EU's place within it, could be said to shoulder the EU with specific human rights duties.

Firstly, in light of the importance of world peace and stability for the security and prosperity of EU citizens, the EU can be said to have a moral duty, as an important beneficiary, to foster an environment in third states where human rights are guaranteed. Secondly, promoting trade, aid and economic development in countries where human rights safeguards are not in place can have serious consequences for individuals, particularly in terms of their economic and social rights. Insofar as the EU's economic engagement with third countries may be contributing to human rights abuses, the EU can be said to have a duty to ensure that human rights are protected in these states. Finally, the EU can be said to have a special duty to promote human rights in the countries on its Eastern border by virtue of their common history and geographical proximity. Whilst these *beneficiary*, *contribution* and *community principles* serve to highlight important normative sources of EU responsibility in the field of human rights, none of them help to solve what Szigeti in this volume calls 'the problem of salience', that is, how to unambiguously identify one agent (in this case the EU) as a bearer of duties as distinct from other agents.

The EU and its citizens are certainly not the only agents (arguably they are not even the main agents) who would benefit from improved human rights practices in third countries, nor from the international peace and stability which this would lead to. Similarly, the EU's contribution to the global economic structures which (arguably) perpetuate human rights abuses is considerably smaller than the responsibility shouldered by international financial institutions such as the World Bank and International Monetary Fund (IMF), whose economic penetration in developing countries is both greater and of longer duration. Even the connectedness principle is less straightforward than one might expect for the purpose of assigning duties amongst different agents. The rejection of Spanish, Polish and Italian proposals to include references to Europe's 'Christian heritage' in the Treaty establishing a European Constitution suggests that efforts to carve out an identity for the EU are eschewing particularism in any form. Instead, the EU's identity tends to be presented in broad, universalist terms, as the ultimate republican polity, founded on democratic principles, human rights, cultural diversity and a commitment to the peaceful resolution of disputes.

Unlike the other principles discussed above, the *capacity principle*, whereby duties are allocated on the basis of ability, enables us to distinguish the EU from other agents in the global system of human rights by directing our attention to the resources and mechanisms available to each. To the extent that the EU has some instruments needed to promote human rights, then the EU is not only justified but morally required to use them. In this chapter I argue that the EU's special duties in the field of human rights stem from its impressive economic resources, which give it enormous political leverage over third states that are dependent on aid, trade or economic cooperation with the EU. Although there are other agents, such as the World Bank and IMF, which also occupy privileged bargaining positions *vis-à-vis* national decision-makers, I argue that they are not in fact as well placed as the EU to influence the human rights practices of states.[12] Before illustrating this argument, in the following section I outline the processes and mechanisms through which states comply with international norms. This discussion has important implications for identifying (and delimiting) the specific duties of the EU by indicating that material incentives are necessary but insufficient instruments for ensuring meaningful and enduring compliance with international human rights norms.

Why do states comply with international norms?

Theoretical work in International Relations has tended to fall into two 'warring paradigms' – rationalism or constructivism – each making different assumptions about the motivations of states in the international arena. According to rationalists, states enter into relations with already established and stable preferences which they attempt to maximise. Since the preferences of states are not expected to change, rationalists argue that ensuring compliance with international norms requires the use of material power: states have to be offered material rewards that exceed the costs of compliance or they have to be deprived of material resources needed for their survival.[13] Constructivists, on the other hand, assume that the behaviour of states is conditioned by shared rules or understandings of appropriateness embedded in conceptions of identity. The task of ensuring compliance among states, therefore, requires conducting a dialogue that reminds states of their obligations as members of a normative community.[14] More recently, however, an increasing number of scholars have begun to recognise that, far from generating incommensurable views of the world, rationalism and constructivism each shed light on *different stages* of the compliance process.

According to this 'sequencing perspective', states enter into relationships for instrumental reasons but develop identities and adopt rule-consistent behaviour in the course of their engagement. The key task for norm-promoters is therefore to establish the conditions which encourage states to shift from one mode of behaviour to the other. During the first, instrumental stage, the norm-promoting agent must enjoy superior bargaining power over the target state. On the one hand, the norm-promoter must be able to issue credible threats and promises as sanctions for norm-violating and norm-compliant behaviour. On the other hand, the target state must be sufficiently sensitive or vulnerable to the actions of the norm-promoter to respond to the sanctions in the desired way.[15] In short, the 'sequencing perspective' suggests that, in order to trigger changes in the human rights practices of norm-violating states, the global system of human rights must include agents which have access to vast reserves of material (economic or military) power.

However, whilst vulnerable states have been found to respond to material incentives, they have tended to do so by introducing changes that are cosmetic and subject to reversal when incentive structures change. For instance, whilst dependence on Western economic assistance during the 1970s led the communist government in Poland to grant dissidents greater political space, it did not prevent the government from renewing repression in 1981 when it felt its survival to be at stake.[16] Similarly, the threat of international sanctions led the Indonesian government to tolerate (though not recognise) the formation of new political parties, a trade union and an independent alliance of journalists in 1992; but in 1997, when the government felt it was losing control, it unleashed a massive crack-down which only worsened Indonesia's human rights situation.[17] Only when international human rights norms become genuinely embedded in the belief systems of national decision-makers can we expect meaningful and lasting improvements in the human rights practices of states. A different set of conditions is necessary, however, to enable this development.

Above all, norm-internalisation requires that target states perceive the system of producing and disseminating human rights as *legitimate*. This legitimacy depends on the system's ability to develop substantive and procedural rules which apply to all.[18] On the one hand, every state must be able to contribute to the process of drafting international human rights conventions and monitoring compliance with them. On the other hand, the system must treat all states in a non-discriminatory manner, irrespective of their commercial ties or strategic importance. Under these conditions we can expect the global system of human rights to command moral authority not only amongst norm-promoters but also amongst its targets. Only this moral authority can encourage states to adopt rule-consistent or identity-driven behaviour, that is, to comply with human rights norms even if doing so involves material sacrifices.[19]

The EU: developing the capacity to promote human rights

Calls for the EC to take a proactive stance towards human rights began to be issued by the European Parliament during the 1980s, in response to revelations of massive human rights violations committed by States which were receiving development assistance from the EC, particularly Uganda, South Africa and Chile. However, as mentioned already, these calls were largely disregarded by the EC until events in Eastern Europe, particularly the stream of refugees fleeing the war in Yugoslavia, alerted EC Heads of State about the security implications of the massive human rights violations taking place in their own backyard.[20]

From the start, the vast material resources of the EC were taken as the basis for exerting pressure on the human rights policies of third countries. A strategy of conditionality was developed whereby economic and political opportunities offered by the EC would be linked to compliance with international standards of human rights. This was enshrined in the Maastricht Treaty, signed in 1992, which called for economic and other cooperation agreements reached between the EU and third-parties to be made conditional on the latter's respect for democratic principles and human rights, including the rights of individuals belonging to minorities.[21] The states of Eastern Europe were the first to be targeted by the EC's conditionality policy, first by making aid and trade agreements conditional on meeting certain criteria, including human rights, and later by making membership conditional too. By November 1991, the policy of conditionality was officially extended to the EU's relations with developing countries.[22]

The EU went out of its way to emphasise that its use of conditionality was based on 'positive' measures, whereby economic rewards were offered to states which respected human rights. However, negative measures – namely the suspension of aid, trade or cooperation agreements – were explicitly identified as appropriate responses 'in the event of grave and persistent human rights violations or serious interruptions of the democratic process'.[23] The development of the EU's conditionality mechanism culminated in 1995, when the Council of Ministers established a set of guidelines that 'standardised' the provisions of the human rights clauses to be used in all subsequent trade, aid and cooperation agreements. Since 1995, the EU has signed over twenty agreements containing these clauses, such that they apply to over 120 countries.[24]

The progressive institutionalisation of a 'human rights clause' in EU external agreements shoulders the EU with specific moral duties above and beyond those of other economically powerful agents. In contrast to the EU, the World Bank's 'Articles of Agreement' explicitly prohibit it from taking political considerations into account when designing aid programmes in developing countries. The same is implicitly the case for the IMF. Whilst calls have been made in recent years to amend the charters of the World Bank and IMF to include the promotion of human rights, these have so far been rejected. This fact highlights the connection between the capacity principle and another principle identified in this volume, the *principle of consent*, where an agent shoulders a duty to do *x* insofar as she has expressly stated her intention to do *x*. Until member states consent to using the World Bank and IMF as agents for promoting human rights, these institutions (whatever their *potential* power) will continue to lack the requisite capacity.[25]

In recent years the EU has begun to develop a wider range of instruments for promoting human rights, in addition to conditionality. These new instruments are diplomatic in nature and are mostly, although not exclusively, associated with the EU's 'second pillar' or intergovernmental organs, that is, the Council of Ministers and its subsidiary bodies.[26] They range from the issuing of joint declarations to undertaking public or confidential *démarches*, supporting or rejecting proposals in international organisations, and engaging in 'critical dialogue' – the regular, high-level meetings conducted between EU member states (and/or the EU 'Troika') and their counterparts in third countries, such as that established by the EU with China and Iran.[27] Since 1999, these activities have been serviced by human rights units within the Council which compile annual reports on the human rights situation throughout the world. The EU has even begun to ensure greater consistency between its internal and external human rights policies. In addition to the changes mentioned in the first part of the chapter, the Amsterdam Treaty also made the acts of the Council of Ministers, Commission and European Parliament reviewable for violations of human rights by the European Court of Justice (Article 6-2). Units have been set up within the Commission in charge of scrutinising the human rights practices of EU member states.[28] Finally, the European Charter on Fundamental Rights, which was officially proclaimed at the Nice Summit in December 2000, will acquire binding force if/when the Treaty establishing a Constitution for Europe comes into effect.

These institutional and policy innovations suggest a growing awareness on the part of the EU of the limitations of conditionality as a mechanism for inducing meaningful and enduring change in the human rights practices of third states. In keeping with the conceptual framework outlined at the start of the chapter, the EU is attempting to develop greater capacity to engage in political dialogue and moral consciousness-raising, not least by improving its own human rights record. Indeed references to the need for 'coherence', 'consistency', 'dialogue', 'mainstreaming', etc. are scattered throughout the Commission's proposals calling for the above-mentioned reforms, suggesting that the EU has taken seriously the recommendations issued by successive Committees of Experts.[29] However, in spite of the reforms introduced so far, two conspicuous shortcomings remain in the EU's approach to human rights which will continue to hamper efforts by EU representatives to inspire a voluntary and enduring form of compliance on the part of governments in third countries.

The first factor impeding the effective use of dialogue and moral consciousness-raising by the EU is its inadequate information base and fragmented administrative structure. The Union's joint declarations and public *démarches* tend to consist of vague generalities which cast doubt on the EU's commitment to the human rights principles it claims to stand for. The human rights units set up in the Commission and Council are simply too small to engage in the systematic monitoring needed for the results of this exercise to be credible in the eyes of target states.[30] Lacking their own fact-finding and monitoring capacities, the units rely on other organisations for obtaining information, a practice which has resulted in inconsistent assessments of the human rights situation in different parts of the world. This inconsistency is aggravated by the Commission's administrative fragmentation along geographical lines. Thus, African, Caribbean and Pacific (ACP) countries, non-ACP countries and EU applicant countries are dealt with by three different Directorate Generals (Development, External Affairs and Enlargement, respectively).

The second shortcoming in the EU's approach is the continuing discrepancy in its internal and external human rights policies, in spite of the above-mentioned efforts to reduce it. Recent studies of the EU's evolving asylum and immigration policy highlight the prioritisation of 'security' and 'order' issues at the expense of the human rights values that the EU claims to promote in its external relations.[31] The United Nations High Commissioner for Refugees (UNHCR) has repeatedly expressed concern that the common measures to fight illegal immigration developed by the EU will hamper effective access to protection for refugees and asylum-seekers. For instance, the decision to compile a list of countries from where asylum-seekers are automatically excluded from consideration (the 'safe country of origin' list), has been criticised by the UNHCR as contrary to the 'necessary individual determination of refugee status' provided for in the UN Refugee Convention, which all EU member states have signed. The UNHCR has also criticised the EU's decision to exclude non-state forms of persecution, such as civil wars or other forms of internal armed conflict, from its definition of what constitutes a 'refugee'.[32]

More does not always mean better

What should be done to tackle these shortcomings in the EU's human rights policy? One possibility (which appears to inform current thinking within the Commission)[33] is to refashion the EU into a proper human rights organisation. In this section I argue that it is neither necessary nor indeed advisable for the EU to develop a more ambitious human rights policy. It is not necessary because there are other international institutions, in particular the Council of Europe and UN, which already have at their disposal the political instruments and moral authority needed to supplement the EU's activities. Furthermore, attempts by the EU to develop a set of human rights mechanisms which parallels those of the Council of Europe and UN may end up undermining the very global system of international human rights that the EU and its member states are legally and morally bound to defend. Therefore, rather than try to out-do the Council of Europe and UN, a responsible EU should pay more attention to how it can cooperate with them in order to achieve the objectives which they share.

The first reason why we should be wary of too much human rights activism on the part of the EU is the policy incoherence which can result from the large and continuously expanding scope of EU activities. Article I-3 of the Treaty establishing a European Constitution says that 'in its relations with the outside world, the Union shall uphold and promote its values and inter-ests.'[34] By distinguishing between the 'values' and 'interests' of the EU, this Article reminds us that, at least in the EU's external relations, the two can easily be in tension. The EU is increasingly responsible for promoting the welfare of EU citizens, for trade, for protecting the environment, etc. and now for promoting the human rights of individuals in third states as well. If human rights were a top priority for the EU, then the increasing range of interests it is developing might not matter. However, the record so far is clear: when the EU's duty to maximise Europe's economic or strategic welfare comes into con-flict with its duty to promote human rights, the former too easily trumps the latter.[35] We need only look at the Union's 'appeasement' of Islamists in Syria, Iran, Algeria and Morocco, considered valuable strategic partners in the fight against irregular migrants, to question its commitment to promoting human rights throughout the world.[36]

In contrast, international institutions such as the Council of Europe or the specialised agencies of the UN, which are only devoted to human rights, do not have to confront these dilemmas of conflicting responsibilities, or at least not so starkly. This means we can expect them to promote human rights more consistently than the EU. Both the Council of Europe and UN have developed judicial or quasi-judicial mechanisms to monitor member state compliance with the standards enshrined in European and international human rights law. For instance, the Human Rights Committee of the UN, charged with supervising compliance with the International Covenant on Civil and Political Rights (ICCPR), is made up of 18 independent human rights experts, who must be 'persons of high moral character and recognised competence in the field of human rights'. Governments are required to sub-mit regular reports to this and other UN Treaty-based organs, outlining the measures they have taken to give effect to the rights enumerated in each Treaty.[37] The Council of Europe has similar monitoring mechanisms attached to its human rights Treaties, with the exception of the European Convention for the Protection of Human Rights and Fundamental Freedoms (ECHR), which is supervised by the European Court of Human Rights (ECtHR) – a Strasbourg-based Court, which is totally independent, can receive individual complaints, and produces decisions which are binding on state parties.

This is not to say that the human rights systems of the UN and Council of Europe are free of problems. Their complex monitoring mechanisms are slow and cumbersome, and thus ill-equipped to deal with mass human rights vio-lations that require immediate attention. Moreover, the European Court of Human Rights works by legal precedent rather than actual monitoring, and requires the exhaustion of domestic remedies before cases can come before it, all of which means that many human rights violations never get heard by the Court at all. Whilst the judicial nature of the European Court of Human Rights prevents it from being influenced by political considerations, this cannot be said of all the human rights organs of the UN. The UN Commission on Human

Rights is particularly vulnerable to political influence, frequently from states with questionable human rights records. This Commission is not a Treaty-based organ, but rather a political body, whose main function is to investigate countries that 'appear to reveal a consistent pattern of gross and reliably attested violations of human rights'.[38] Made up of 53 state representatives (rather than independent experts), the sessions of the Commission and the resolutions it produces have been criticised as 'unadulterated political horse-trading rather than a probing enquiry into the facts'.[39] However, as already explained, the situation is different in the UN Human Rights Committee and other Treaty-based organs, which are protected from such politicisation by their quasi-judicial nature, and which in fact do the lion's share of the UN monitoring work.[40]

The second danger associated with the EU's human rights activism derives from the institution's exclusive membership base. Whilst limiting EU membership to a small group of relatively prosperous, liberal-democratic states gives the institution enormous bargaining power *vis-à-vis* third countries – a necessary condition, as I have argued, to encourage the latter to embark on the first stage of compliance – the same characteristic could impair the effectiveness of the global human rights system, should the EU try to present itself as the system's *principal* agent. There are at least two dimensions to this problem. Firstly, the EU's exclusive membership means that the way it defines human rights will necessarily be partial, reflecting the liberal-democratic and market-oriented values of its member states. This partiality is reflected in the EU's tendency to lump together democracy and human rights, even though the relationship between the two is far from simple. It also results in the EU's excessive focus on civil and political rights at the expense of social, economic and cultural rights.[41] Secondly, the EU's superior bargaining power means that the human rights 'dialogue' that the EU conducts with third countries is strongly shaped by the preferences of EU member states. Recent analyses of EU–ACP negotiations have highlighted the minimal contribution of African, Pacific and Caribbean countries to the content of the 'human rights clauses' enshrined in EU–ACP trade and cooperation agreements, which are supposed to be binding on both sides. This negotiating style disguises rather than solves (and may even aggravate) what is often a gulf separating the values of the two or more sides, a gulf which breeds disagreement regarding the legitimate scope and prioritisation of specific human rights.[42]

In contrast to the EU's partiality, the Council of Europe and UN possess assets which serve to strengthen claims about the universality of human rights. For the global system of human rights to be legitimately spoken of as universal, it must neither suppress nor ignore the world's cultural diversity. Instead, it must recognise that different conceptions of 'rights' exist and try to accommodate them by fostering cross-cultural understanding and dialogue. It is not enough for this cross-cultural dialogue to take place in academic circles; it must be fostered in the very international institutions whose task it is to draft human rights conventions and promote compliance with them. Only this way can a 'common core' of human rights, which must nevertheless remain flexible and open to change, be acknowledged as legitimate by all the world's cultures – a necessary condition, as I have argued, for the voluntary (rule-consistent or identity-driven) stage of compliance with international human rights to come about.[43] The pan-European membership of the Council of Europe (it currently possesses 46 member states in contrast to the EU's 25) and especially the near-universal membership of the UN mean that these two institutions are in a better position to foster cross-cultural dialogue than the EU.

The third danger associated with the EU's efforts to develop a more ambitious human rights profile is the divergence of human rights standards which it can lead to. There is already some ambiguity in the respective competences of the ECJ, which supervises compliance with EU law, and the European Court of Human Rights, which supervises compliance with the Council of Europe's European Convention of Human Rights. For a long time, the lack of EU competence in human rights issues meant that the respective jurisdiction of each European Court was easy to distinguish. However, since the Amsterdam Treaty came into effect, in 1999, the incorporation of human rights-related concerns into the EU's *acquis communautaire* has complicated the picture considerably. As mentioned already, Amsterdam gave the ECJ competence to review the acts of the Council of Ministers, Commission and European Parliament for violations of human rights (Article 6-2). The ECJ's increasing competence in the field of human rights risks creating a divergence in the human rights case law produced by the two European Courts, which would undermine the coherence and legal certainty of the human rights standards applicable in Europe. This risk will increase if the Treaty establishing a European Constitution comes into effect, as this gives binding force to the European Charter of Fundamental Rights, which means it will be reviewable by the European Court of Justice.

Towards a system of shared responsibility

This chapter makes a case for promoting a cooperative rather than competitive relationship between the European Union, Council of Europe and UN by emphasising the complementary nature of their respective instruments for ensuring compliance with international human rights standards. In view of the complementary nature of the three organisations, the situation we find ourselves in today is very sad indeed. Although the secretariats of these organisations pay lip service to the idea of inter-institutional cooperation, few efforts have been made to translate this idea into practice, and their cooperation in the human rights field has thus remained rare and *ad hoc* in nature. What has been particularly problematic is that, on the one hand, the UN and (especially) the Council of Europe are anxiously 'defending their turf' from EU encroachment,[44] and, on the other hand, the EU's desire for protagonism has impaired whatever efforts there have been at inter-institutional cooperation. It is worth quoting at some length the assessment given by one observer of a recent EU/UN 'mixed operation' of human rights monitors in Rwanda, to illustrate the waste and, still worse, the damage to the credibility of the global human rights system, which can result from unchecked competition between the institutions:

> The EU team retained separate insignia [their vehicles carried both UN and EU logos], separate radio frequencies, and there were computer compatibility problems with the rest of [the operation]. In principle the EU observers were to be paid at UN rates, but they ended up being paid more than the UN monitors and this also caused some friction. In addition it sounds as if some of the EU contingent had felt superior to the UN team proper, and did not hide it very well. Also at times it appeared that the EU was retaining a degree of distance from the rest of [the operation] partly for European media profile. Positive publicity about EU efforts per se were perceived to be more likely if the EU component was distinct and almost separate.[45]

In this final section I return to the conceptual framework outlined at the start of the chapter to offer a preliminary exploration of how responsibility for promoting human rights could be distributed effectively amongst the three institutions.[46] My suggestions should not be taken to imply an outright rejection of 'functional doubling', the term coined by French professor Georges Scelle to refer to situations where institutions established for one purpose take on additional functions; nor should they be understood as implying a totally inflexible division of labour.[47] A degree of institutional overlap (and indeed competition) can be beneficial, firstly, by providing a greater number of agents, and coalitions of agents, with the capacity to respond to human rights violations whenever and wherever they occur; and, secondly, by encouraging each institution to improve its overall performance. Nevertheless, the thrust of my argument has been that too much competition can be injurious to the cause of human rights. The complementary assets of the EU, Council of Europe and UN, moreover, suggest that, whilst the participation of all three institutions is necessary in the global system of human rights, each can best contribute in a particular way and perhaps could even intensify their activities in different stages.

Given the abundant material resources at its disposal, the EU is best placed to act at the beginning of the compliance process: only the EU has the means to apply positive or negative sanctions upon a state that engages in human rights violations. Whilst these sanctions are necessary to encourage national decision-makers to embark on reforms of their own, material incentives cannot guarantee that the reforms will produce noticeable or lasting improvements in the rights enjoyed by individuals. For the latter to happen, the global system of human rights must acquire an 'aura of authority', which is where the strengths of the UN and Council of Europe lie. The judicial and quasi-judicial nature of the human rights mechanisms available to the Council of Europe and UN, combined with their inclusive membership, means their involvement will appear more legitimate to national decision-makers – a necessary condition for the second, identity-driven stage of compliance to 'kick in'.

Thus, once the EU has opened the door to policy reform in a country by applying positive or negative sanctions, it must recognise the limits of its influence and allow the other international institutions to take over. The precise division of labour between the EU, on the one hand, and the UN and Council of Europe, on the other, should depend on geographical criteria. If the norm-violating state is located in the 'wider Europe', that is, in any country that is a member of the Council of Europe, the EU should be the dominant agent in the first instance, with the human rights mechanisms of the Council of Europe gradually taking over. A similar arrangement between the EU and UN should be established to respond to human rights violations which occur in the rest of the world. There is no space here to discuss all the arrangements which could be set up between the EU, Council of Europe and UN in order to make such a division of labour possible. However, in the remainder of this chapter I identify three basic forms of cooperation, which, if established, would constitute useful starting points for more advanced forms of cooperation to develop in the future.

Firstly, the EU itself, and not only all EU member states as is currently the case, should, in the earliest possible instance, accede to the European Convention on Human Rights (ECHR) of the Council of Europe, and to the UN' six main human rights treaties, each of which establishes an independent committee charged with monitoring compliance: the ICCPR; the International Covenant on Economic, Social and Cultural Rights (ICESC); the International Convention on the Elimination of All Forms of Racial Discrimination (CERD); the Convention Against Torture and Other Cruel, Inhuman or Degrading Treatment or Punishment (CAT); the Convention on the Rights of the Child (CRC); and the Convention on the Elimination of All Forms of Discrimination Against Women (CEDAW).[48] By allowing EU officials to participate in the reporting mechanisms of the Council of Europe and UN, accession to these treaties would resolve the internal/external discrepancy which currently afflicts the EU's handling of human rights, and would serve to develop a human rights culture amongst EU decision-makers. The EU's accession to the ECHR would also prevent the risk of divergence in the case-law of the European Court of Human Rights and of the ECJ which, as I suggested in the previous section, threatens to undermine the coherence and legal certainty of the human rights standards applied in Europe.[49]

Secondly, in order to ensure greater credibility and efficiency, the EU should share responsibility with the Council of Europe and UN or managing the 'human rights clauses' which it includes in its Trade and Cooperation Agreements with third countries. The EU should define the rights that are at stake in these clauses by reference to Council of Europe and/or UN standards. Currently, the EU's human rights clauses are too vague: without clear benchmarks for assessing whether the governments in question meet the standards required, the threat or actual suspension of a Trade and Cooperation Agreement by the EU cannot but appear arbitrary to the affected states.[50] In addition, the independent human rights committees of the Council of Europe and UN should be made responsible for deciding when the human rights suspension clauses, enshrined in EU agreements, are invoked. The long-established human rights reporting mechanisms of the UN and Council of Europe constitute an invaluable resource for this purpose. The EC (or EU member states) could be given the right to veto decisions taken by Council of Europe and UN experts (this would seem fair given that EU trade and/or funding would be at stake); however, if suspension of EU aid, trade or cooperation is to carry legitimacy, the initial assessment must be done by bodies that are independent and experienced in human rights matters.

Thirdly, rather than engage in a separate 'critical dialogue' on human rights with individual states, the EU should consider financing missions of human rights rapporteurs sent by the Council of Europe and UN. There is already considerable experience of this type of cooperation between the EU and the Council of Europe in the Joint Programmes that have been established to assist the processes of democratic consolidation in Central and Eastern Europe.[51] This type of cooperation should be extended to other parts of the world by setting up similar arrangements between the EU and UN. Since the year 2000, the EU has begun to show some interest in financing UN operations, but the amount set aside by the EU for this purpose continues to be very unsatisfactory.[52] If the values enshrined in the global human rights system are to become a reality, an attempt must be made to reverse this pattern by raising awareness of the importance of inter-institutional cooperation.

Conclusion

Without denying the validity of other principles, I have argued in this chapter that the capacity principle is particularly helpful for assigning duties within the global system of human rights. In this concluding section, I would like to return to those critics, mentioned at the start of the chapter, who dismiss the EU's external human rights policy as incoherent, piecemeal and/or guilty of double standards. In view of the EU's grandiose statements about human rights and its repeated failure to live up to them, these criticisms, and the high expectations that they feed upon, are certainly understandable. This, however, brings me to the final principle of this volume's conceptual framework for assigning duties amongst relevant agents, the so-called *principle of legitimate expectations*. According to this principle, one has a duty to do *x* if others legitimately expect one to do *x*. By identifying the limits to the EU's 'institutional elasticity'[53] my chapter suggests that the criticisms which surround the EU's external human rights policy are grounded, in part, on unfounded expectations of what the EU can achieve. In order to avoid the creation of yet another 'capabilities–expectations gap', this time in the field of human rights,[54] it is necessary to ensure that governments and populations alike perceive the differences between international institutions. By identifying the respective strengths and limitations of the EU, UN and Council of Europe as global agents of human rights, this chapter will hopefully inspire a more realistic debate about what the EU can and ought to achieve in this field. It is the responsibility of European policy-makers and academics alike to carry this debate forward.

Notes

1. The views expressed in this chapter are solely those of the author and do not represent the views of the Council of Europe.
2. Alston and Weiler 1999, 10.
3. Leading by Example: A Human Rights Agenda for the European Union for the Year 2000 (Agenda of the Comité des Sages and Final Project Report, 1998).
4. Smith 2003, 116–20; Nicolaïdis and Lacroix 2003, 144–6.
5. According to Amnesty International, 'The EU is failing to set the right example as far as human rights at home are concerned, leaving itself open to accusations of double standards which affect its international credibility.' Amnesty International, *Human Rights Begin at Home: Recommendations to Ireland's EU Presidency* (A.I. EU Office: Belgium, 2004, p. 2).
6. Address by Mr Javier Solana, EU High Representative for the CFSP, to the 58th Session of the UN Commission on Human Rights (Geneva, 19 March, 2002). Ref: PRES02-035EN.
7. While the protection of human rights through international action began in 1948, with the United Nations Declaration of Human Rights, the need to render the system of international protection more effective gained widespread recognition during the 1990s (Robertson and Merrills 1996, 1–2).
8. There is a large literature on human rights in IR, but this has mostly focused on the tension between humanitarian principles ('the cosmopolitan morality') and considerations of power, security and interest ('the morality of states'), e.g. Vincent 1986; Donnelly 1998; Dunne and Wheeler 2000. Few efforts have been made to consider the relationship between different non-state agents within the global human rights system, perhaps owing to the obsession, amongst IR scholars, with the international v. state dichotomy. International Lawyers have given more attention to the competences of different international institutions (e.g. Bloed *et al.* 1993), although the notion of responsibility is not usually at the centre of their analyses. For an important exception, see Klabbers 2002.
9. The United Kingdom has been the most stubborn opponent of strengthening the role of the Commission, the European Court of Justice and the European Parliament in the social field, followed closely by Denmark. Geddes 2000, 115.

10. 'The European Union's Role', 2001.
11. Elgström 2000, 191.
12. Other candidates include economically powerful states such as the United States and Japan. Whilst my focus in this chapter is on the role and activities of international institutions, it is worth noting that it is likely to be more difficult for states to abandon their selfish interests when pursuing compliance in third countries, especially if we accept that the primary role of states is to exercise power on behalf of their own citizens.
13. See Keohane 1984 and Waltz 1979 for two variants of rationalist theory.
14. See especially Wendt 1992 and Finnemore 1996.
15. Schimmelfennig 2002, 14.
16. Thomas 1999, 218–21.
17. Jetschke 1999, 156–7.
18. See especially Franck 1990.
19. Attempts to illustrate this second, *socialisation* phase are, of course, beset by numerous methodological difficulties. The intangible nature of moral considerations, like ideas in general, means they are not amenable to direct observation. Empirical research has attempted to minimise these difficulties, if not solve them altogether, by analysing changes in the way national decision-makers talk about human rights. Klotz 1995; Risse *et al.* 1999; Jurado 2003.
20. The EC did respond to two cases of human rights violations prior to the 1990s, imposing limited sanctions on South Africa between 1985 and 1986 and even more limited sanctions on China after the events on Tienanmen Square in 1989. Smith 2003, 104.
21. Article 130U of the Treaty on European Union.
22. Simma *et al.* 1999, 575.
23. Resolution of the Council and of the Member States meeting in the Council of Human Rights, Democracy, and Development of 28 November 1991, *Bulletin of the European Communities* 11-1991.
24. Riedel and Will 1999, 732.
25. For contrasting viewpoints on the benefits and drawbacks of involving the World Bank and IMF in efforts to enforce compliance with international human rights norms, see Gianviti 2001 and Skogly 2001.
26. The conditionality instrument, on the other hand, is associated mostly (although again not exclusively) with the EU's 'first pillar' organs, the Commission and European Parliament. In reality the human rights activities of each pillar are not so clear-cut (Fouwels 1997).
27. For a generally positive appraisal of this development, see Struwe 1998.
28. Clapham 1999.
29. For examples of the language used by the Commission to justify the need for reforms, see 'The European Union's Role', 2001.
30. Clapham 1999.
31. Nicolaïdis and Lacroix 2003, 145.
32. Geddes 2000, 122; 148.
33. See the Commission's 'Proposal for a Council Regulation establishing a European Union Agency for Fundamental Rights', COM (2005) 280 final, Brussels, 30 June 2005.
34. See: Draft Treaty establishing a Constitution for Europe. *Official Journal* C 169, 18 July 2003, pp. 1–105.
35. For analysis of the double standards in EU trade and cooperation agreements, see Ward 1998.

36. Youngs 2001, 81; 193.
37. Whilst the recommendations delivered by these Treaty-based organs are not binding on State parties, their value lies in their ability to inspire a human rights culture amongst government representatives by immersing them in a discursive environment that attaches moral censure to their failure to live up to international human rights standards.
38. Donnelly 2003, 129.
39. Alston 1992. The sessions of the UN Commission on Human Rights are confidential until they have been concluded, whereupon a resolution may or may not be issued. So far, these resolutions have been expressed in extraordinarily mild language, regularly infuriating Amnesty International and other NGOs.
40. The problem, however, is that whilst all UN Member States can be the subject of investigation by the United Nations Commission on Human Rights, only those which are parties to the individual human rights treaties are investigated by the UN's Treaty-based organs.
41. Crawford 2000, 119.
42. Ibhawoh (2001) and Kausikan (1993) provide useful descriptions of the 'Africanist' and 'Asian' approaches to human rights.
43. I have borrowed the notion of a 'common core' of human rights, which allows for flexibility of application and is open to change, from Ibhawoh (2001). This argument, which tries to reconcile the claims of 'radical universalists' and 'cultural relativists', is consistent with Bikhu Parekh's theory of 'non-ethnocentric universalism' (1999, 139–50). For a similar but not identical argument about the need to 'temper' (rather than dismiss) universalist claims about human rights, see Donnelly 2003, 90–106.
44. The Council of Europe's nervousness is evident in the debates held in the Parliamentary Assembly of the Council of Europe (PACE) to discuss the implications for the Council of Europe of the Treaty establishing a Constitution for the EU. See for example Pangalos, 2003.
45. Paul LaRose-Edwards, author of a report commissioned for the Human Rights and Justice Division of the Canadian Department of Foreign Affairs, quoted by Clapham 1999, 650.
46. Other institutions should also be mentioned when considering responsibility for promoting human rights, including other European-based institutions (like the OSCE and NATO), but also regional institutions in other parts of the world, international and local NGOs, and of course States. Analysis of the respective duties of each of these agents in the global system of human rights goes beyond the scope of this chapter.
47. Reisman 1987, 392.
48. Farer and Gaer 2000, 264.
49. Pangalos 2003, III-18. It is worth noting that, in the past, some international lawyers and justices (including members of the ECJ itself) identified legal obstacles in the way of the EC's accession to international human rights treaties. (Weiler and Fries 1999, 150). Whilst their opinion was by no means uncontroversial, any remaining doubt will be dispelled if/when the Treaty establishing a European Constitution comes into force. Article I-7 paragraph 2 of the draft Treaty establishes that the EU 'shall seek accession to the European Convention for the Protection of Human Rights and Fundamental Freedoms'. Draft Treaty, 2003.
50. According to Tomaševski, many African leaders see the EU's human rights dialogue as a 'stick with which to beat them'. Tomaševski 1997, 43.

51. For recent examples of these Joint Programmes, financed by the European Commission and managed by experts at the Council of Europe, see 'Relations between the Council of Europe and the European Union', SG/Inf (2004) 11, 23 March 2004.
52. One recent – and so far rather exceptional – success story of EU/UN cooperation in the human rights field was the setting up of a Permanent Office of the UN High Commissioner for Human Rights in Colombia. The EU has paid the salaries of the human rights observers without trying to administer the operation. Clapham 1999, 651.
53. Reisman (1987, 395) uses this term to question 'the extent to which institutions created and still used for other purposes can be "stretched" in order to get them to perform human rights functions, especially when those functions are accomplished *at the expense* of their manifest functions.'
54. The EU's 'capabilities-expectations' gap was first identified in the area of defence (Hill 1993).

Bibliography

Alston, Philip, *The United Nations and Human Rights: A Critical Appraisal* (Oxford: Clarendon Press, 1992).

Alston, Philip and Joseph. H. H. Weiler, 'An "Ever Closer Union" in Need of a Human Rights Policy: The European Union and Human Rights', in Philip Alston *et al.* (eds), *The European Union and Human Rights* (Oxford: Oxford University Press, 1999).

Bloed, Arie, Liselotte Leicht, Manfred Nowak and Allan Rosas (eds), *Monitoring Human Rights in Europe: Comparing International Procedures and Mechanisms* (Dordrecht, Boston and London: Martinus Nijhoff, 1993).

Clapham, Andrew, 'Where is the European Union's Human Rights Common Foreign and Security Policy, and How is it Manifested in Multilateral Fora?', in Philip Alston *et al.* (eds), *The EU and Human Rights* (Oxford: Oxford University Press, 1999).

Crawford, Gordon, 'European Union Development Cooperation and the Promotion of Democracy', in Peter Burnell (ed.), *Democracy Assistance: International Cooperation for Democratization* (London: Frank Cass, 2000).

Donnelly, Jack, *International Human Rights*, 2nd edition (Boulder, Colorado and Oxford: Westview, 1998).

Donnelly, Jack, *Universal Human Rights in Theory and Practice*, 2nd edition (Ithaca and London: Cornell University Press, 2003).

Dunne, Tim and Nicholas J. Wheeler (eds), *Human Rights in Global Politics* (Cambridge: Cambridge University Press, 2000).

Elgström, Ole, 'Lomé and post-Lomé: asymmetric negotiation and the impact of norms', *European Foreign Affairs Review*, vol. 5, no. 2 (2000).

'The European Union's Role in Promoting Human Rights and Democratisation in Third Countries', COM (2001) 252 final, Brussels, 8 May 2001.

Farer, Tom and Felice Gaer, 'The UN and Human Rights: At the End of the Beginning', in Adam Roberts and Benedict Kingsbury (eds), *United Nations, Divided World: The UN's Roles in International Relations* (Oxford: Oxford University Press, 2000).

Finnemore, Martha, 'International Organizations as Teachers of Norms: The United Nations Educational, Scientific, and Cultural Organization and Science Policy', *International Organization*, vol. 47, no. 4 (1993).

Finnemore, Martha, *National Interests in International Society* (Ithaca and New York: Cornell University Press, 1996).

Fouwels, Martine, 'The European Union's Common Foreign and Security Policy and Human Rights', *Netherlands Quarterly of Human Rights*, vol. 15, no. 3 (1997).

Franck, Thomas, *The Power of Legitimacy Among Nations* (New York: Oxford University Press, 1990).

Geddes, Andrew, *Immigration and European Integration: Towards Fortress Europe?* (Manchester: Manchester University Press, 2000).

Gianviti, François, 'Economic, Social and Cultural Human Rights and the International Monetary Fund', United Nations Economic and Social Council, E/C.12/2001/WP.5, 7 May 2001.

Hill, Christopher, 'The Capability-Expectations Gap, or Conceptualizing Europe's International Role', *Journal of Common Market Studies*, vol. 31, no. 3 (1993).

Ibhawoh, Bonny, 'Cultural Relativism and Human Rights: Reconsidering the Africanist Discourse', *Netherlands Quarterly of Human Rights*, vol. 19, no. 1 (2001).

Jetschke, Anja, 'Linking the unlinkable? International norms and nationalism in Indonesia and the Philippines', in Thomas Risse *et al.* (eds), *The Power of Human Rights: International Norms and Domestic Change The Power of Human Rights* (Cambridge: Cambridge University Press, 1999).

Jurado, Elena, 'Complying with European Standards of Minority Education: Estonia's relations with the European Union, OSCE and Council of Europe', *Journal of Baltic Studies*, vol. 34, no. 4 (2003).

Kausikan, Bilahari, 'Asia's Different Standard', *Foreign Policy*, no. 92 (autumn 1993).

Keohane, Robert O., *After Hegemony: Cooperation and Discord in the World Political Economy* (Princeton, New Jersey: Princeton University Press, 1984).

Klabbers, Jan, *An Introduction to International Institutional Law* (Cambridge: Cambridge University Press, 2002).

Klotz, Audie, *Norms in International Relations: The Struggle Against Apartheid* (Ithaca and London: Cornell University Press, 1995).

Nicolaïdis, Kalypso and Justine Lacroix 'Order and Justice Beyond the Nation-State: Europe's Competing Paradigms', in Rosemary Foot *et al.* (eds), *Order and Justice in International Relations* (Oxford: Oxford University Press, 2003).

Pangalos, Theodoros, 'The Council of Europe and the Convention on the Future of Europe', report by the Political Affairs Committee of PACE, Doc. 9846, 24 June 2003.

Parekh, Bikhu, 'Non-ethnocentric universalism', in Tim Dunne and Nicholas J. Wheeler (eds), *Human Rights in Global Politics* (Cambridge: Cambridge University Press, 1999).

Reisman, W. Michael, 'Through or Despite Governments: Differentiated Responsibilities in Human Rights Programs', *Iowa Law Review*, vol. 72 (1987).

Riedel, Eibe and Martin Will, 'Human Rights Clauses in External Agreements of the European Community' in Alston *et al.* (eds), *The European Union and Human Rights* (Oxford: Oxford University Press, 1999).

Risse, Thomas, Stephen C. Ropp and Kathryn Sikkink (eds), *The Power of Human Rights: International Norms and Domestic Change The Power of Human Rights* (Cambridge: Cambridge University Press, 1999).

Robertson, Arthur Henry and J. G. Merrills, *Human Rights in the World: An Introduction to the Study of the International Protection of Human Rights* (Manchester and New York: Manchester University Press, 1996).

Schimmelfennig, Frank, 'Introduction: The Impact of International Organizations on the Central and Eastern European States – Conceptual and Theoretical Issues', in Linden, Ronald H. (ed.), *Norms and Nannies: The Impact of International Organizations on the Central and East European States* (Oxford: Rowman and Littlefield, 2002).

Simma, Bruno *et al.*, 'Human Rights Considerations in the Development Cooperation Activities of the EC', in Philip Alston *et al.* (eds), *The European Union and Human Rights* (Oxford: Oxford University Press, 1999).

Skogly, Sigrun, *The Human Rights Obligations of the World Bank and International Monetary Fund* (London and Sydney: Cavendish, 2001).

Smith, Karen, *European Union Foreign Policy in a Changing World* (Cambridge: Polity Press, 2003).

Struwe, Matthias, 'The Policy of "Critical Dialogue". An Analysis of the European Union's Human Rights Policy Towards Iran' (University of Durham: Durham Middle East Papers, 1998).

Thomas, Daniel C. 'The Helsinki Accords and Political Change in Eastern Europe', in Thomas Risse *et al.* (eds), *The Power of Human Rights: International Norms and Domestic Change The Power of Human Rights* (Cambridge: Cambridge University Press, 1999).

Tomaševski, Katarina, *Between Sanctions and Elections: Aid Donors and Their Human Rights Performance* (London: Pinter, 1997).

Vincent, R. J., *Human Rights and International Relations* (Cambridge: Cambridge University Press, 1986).

Waltz, Kenneth, *Theory of International Politics* (New York: Addison-Wesley, 1979).

Wendt, Alex, 'Anarchy is What States Make of It: The Social Construction of Power Politics', in *International Organization*, vol. 46, no. 2 (Spring 1992).

Ward, Angela, 'Frameworks for Cooperation between the European Union and Third States: A Variable Matrix for Uniform Human Rights Standards?' *European Foreign Affairs Review*, vol. 3, no. 3 (1998).

Weiler, Joseph H. H. and Sybilla C. Fries 'A Human Rights Policy for the European Union: The Question of Competences', in Philip Alston *et al.* (eds), *The European Union and Human Rights* (Oxford: Oxford University Press, 1999).

Youngs, Richard, *The European Union and the Promotion of Democracy: Europe's Mediterranean and Asian Policies* (Oxford: Oxford University Press, 2001).

7
A 'Responsible EU', Multinational Migration Control and the Case of ASEM

Rieko Karatani

The purpose of this chapter is to investigate the role of the EU in establishing a framework for multilateral migration control, and to ask to what extent the Union has acted in a 'responsible' manner in the context of the global migration regime – a regime that has become a hugely important building block of today's world politics. As an empirical case study, the chapter looks at recent attempts at the Asia–Europe Meeting (ASEM) to set up mechanisms of multinational migration control through inter-regional dialogue. The chapter thus also sheds some light on how inter-regional dialogues are assuming an increasingly important role globally, and on what the potential implications of this development might be.

The notion of responsibility is notorious for its confusing usages and wide range of different definitions. However, the six sources of responsibility that guide the empirical investigations of this book, appear highly useful in the context of migration issues. The community principle seems to explain, or even justify, the fact that governments tend to treat members and non-members of the state differently. The assumption is that the state owes more to its members and is required to prioritise them over non-members. What is important for the present chapter, however, is that due to people's current high mobility, it has become increasingly difficult to distinguish between 'internal' responsibility for the citizens and 'external' responsibility for the non-citizens; it is particularly difficult for such intergovernmental institutions as the EU. Migration redraws the borders of community.

The capacity principle is also relevant here: it may help us distribute duties between different levels and types of actors, very much in the same way as in the preceding chapter on human rights. Moreover, the EU's strong promotion of its core values – values that should also guide its migration policies – can be conceptualised in terms of the (legitimate) expectations and consent principles. The value rhetoric easily raises outsiders' expectations of the EU, makes them believe that the Union truly acts in a responsible manner towards its partners elsewhere in the world – even though this may not necessarily be the case.

The next section of the chapter takes up three conceptual perspectives for analysing multinational migration control and the EU's appropriate role in it. The second section shows that the emergence of multi-level migration control – multinational, localised, and privatised – represents one way of vertically distributing responsibilities. However, national, political and economic interests have tended to overshadow migrants and asylum seekers' human rights at each of these levels, and thus turn policies restrictive and exclusive. Multinational control can thus be harmful from the perspective of human rights. With that tendency in mind, the section reviews some aspects of the EU's common policy in the field of migration and asylum.

The third part focuses on the emerging inter-regional dialogues using the ASEM process as an example. It warns that the risk of human rights being sidelined is great at ASEM because no regional mechanisms exist in Asia for people's voices to be heard. The role of the EU is thus likely to be crucial in order to prevent the ASEM framework from turning overtly restrictive for migrants and to pay due respect to the protection of their rights. The concluding section further explores the EU's role as a 'responsible' actor over the building of multinational migration control. It emphasises the importance of the EU's persistence upon human rights protection. In the end, it is today's debate out of which inter-regional understanding of the purpose and methods of multinational migration control will develop in the future.

Three analytical perspectives

Migration control is one of the most widely debated issues within the current EU. One recent Commission paper, for example, described migration as 'a major strategic priority for the European Union'.[1] Since the Treaty of Amsterdam and the European Council in Tampere in 1999, the EU has been committed to developing a common policy on asylum and migration in order to 'ensure more efficient management of migratory flows at all their stages'.[2] This approach aims to integrate migration and asylum policy into the EU's relations with third countries. It also indicates that the Union wishes to use all appropriate external relations instruments to tackle the problems of migration and asylum. In consequence, migration and asylum policy has become an essential part of the EU's external policies and actions, duly developed through cooperation with the relevant third countries. What has begun with information exchanges and police cooperation may eventually turn into a regime with a more solid institutional basis.

Some experts warn, however, that this development – what this chapter calls the 'multinationalisation of migration control' – potentially represents a means of curbing human rights.[3] To avoid this, the premises and aims of EU policies are highly significant. The question is: in building up a multinational migration framework, to what extent does and will the EU seek to act from the perspective of *global* human rights protection, or are its actions primarily driven by notions of responsibility towards its own EU citizens? To provide at least tentative answers, it is essential to examine the EU's approach to migration control through three key areas: 'internal' versus 'external' responsibility, the vertical distribution of responsibilities through the subsidiarity principle, and human rights protection in relation to the society's other values.

First of all, and as already indicated in the introduction, the EU's attitude to multinational migration control brings forth the distinction between 'internal' and 'external' responsibilities. There is, in other words, an obvious discrepancy between an actor's responsibility towards its own members ('internal' responsibility) and towards outsiders ('external' responsibility); a responsible agency might then mean that the actor can accommodate this discrepancy in a constructive manner. In the terminology of this book, the question is of what kind of community (community principle) we invoke as our primary point of reference.

The way the EU defines its 'internal' and 'external' responsibility obviously has a significant global impact. The problem is that the distinction between 'internal' and 'external' has become increasingly murky. There are now approximately 13 million 'foreigners' (25 per cent of the world's migrants) living in Europe. The vast majority of these third-country nationals are long-term residents, but they are still often excluded from formal citizenship in Europe.[4] In this context, if the EU seeks to be a 'responsible' actor in a global sense, it may be liable for preventing the distance between the members and non-members from becoming too great. Furthermore, it is accountable for explaining how the distinction between 'internal' to 'external' responsibility relates to its core values, the 'principles of liberty, democracy, respect for human rights and fundamental freedoms, and rule of law'. There is indeed no self-evident way of doing this; democracy, for example, should by definition apply to everyone, but in reality it, of course, does not.[5]

This author does not intend to argue, however, that the EU countries should treat all individuals similarly, on the basis of some sort of universal values, regardless of their membership of the country.[6] With a limited amount of resources available, it may be legitimate, at least to a certain extent, that each polity claims a particular responsibility for its constituent members and prioritises them over non-members, and weighs 'internal' against 'external' responsibility. Also, we cannot expect one polity to bear the responsibility of migration control single-handedly; this would neither be efficient nor realistic. The distribution of responsibility internationally in accordance with the capacity and role of each polity is certainly beneficial to all of us. Nonetheless, when responsibility is assigned to it, the EU needs to be aware of these both aspects of responsibility, both because of its own welfare and of that of others: today's 'external' responsibility may easily turn into tomorrow's 'internal' responsibility and vice versa.

*   *   *

In an effort to distribute 'responsibility', one of the core institutional rules of the EU – that of subsidiarity – deserves special attention. This is the second main point that this section aims to make. A number of scholars have examined how (political) duties are being distributed between different actors, but they tend to focus on what can be called horizontal distribution among polities, say between Britain and France. Nonetheless, migration control is an example of a policy field in which not only a horizontal but a vertical framework has emerged. We thus need to consider how we distribute responsibilities between different levels, be they multinational, national or local, and also between the public and private sectors.

The notion of subsidiarity is notoriously malleable. It was written into the Treaty of the European Union, but the definition leaves a great deal to be hoped for in terms of clarity: 'decisions [are to be] taken as closely as possible to the citizen in accordance with the principle of subsidiarity'.[7] The problem of this definition is obviously the formulation 'as closely as possible'. It means, in reality – and this is the interpretation applied in this chapter – 'as effectively as possible'. The subsidiarity principle thus requests that the most effective level of authority, whatever that may be, should make the decisions. In a sense, therefore, we could understand subsidiarity in terms of a 'qualified capacity principle'.

The principle of subsidiarity, in all its complexity, is appropriate for considering what role a 'responsible' EU should play in multinational migration control. According to the principle of subsidiarity, the EU, before taking part in the process, has to answer the question which level – whether multinational rather than national or local – is the most 'effective' in conducting migration control. The problem is, of course, that it is far from self-evident how the EU should define 'effectiveness' in the case of multinational migration control. Our interpretations of 'effectiveness' vary, depending on what each of us is after. On the one hand, subsidiarity can be understood through the question 'What is best (that is, most effectively) done at each level?'; from this perspective, subsidiarity becomes 'constitutive of multilevel governance'.[8] On the other hand, the subsidiarity question can be discussed normatively: 'What should (best) be done at each level?' The point is that a 'responsible' EU needs to evaluate 'effectiveness' in relation to the latter question. Given that a multinational migration framework potentially leads to weaker protection of human rights, the EU should be able to take such compensatory measures that may appear harmful from the perspective of a straightforward principle of effectiveness.

Subsidiarity and effectiveness are also useful when we think about the relative power of each decision-making level. Human rights advocates tend to welcome international negotiations and dialogue which they think have contributed to the spread of international norms and the building of an international regime in the field after the Second World War. The development of international human rights instruments certainly helped improve the treatment of foreigners, migrants and asylum seekers in their countries of residence and employment. Those vulnerable people who are devoid of domestic support tend to rely upon the so-called 'boomerang effect' for their remedies, and thus appeal to the international arena in order to put external pressure on the government that is oppressing them. Yet, we ought to keep in mind that the 'boomerang effect' works only to the extent that each government takes international opinion seriously. Even under international treaties, treaty organisations cannot force the signatory countries to obey treaty obligations if they do not want to. Therefore, without a guarantee of implementation, efforts to draft and pass international treaties for the purpose of strengthening the 'boomerang effect' often fall short of initial expectations. In the end, in the face of the principle of national sovereignty, international norms and obligations evolve and influence national policies, but cannot with any certainty be domestically implemented against the wishes of governments.

*   *   *

This leads to the third point: there is a risk that human rights are compromised because of some other inherent values, national security in particular. Again, the balance between the 'internal' and the 'external' becomes an issue; 'internal' national security is weighed against protecting the rights of 'external' people like migrants and asylums seekers. The question is often to what extent governments and some sections of the media stir public anxiety over migration by stressing the alleged link between migration and transnational criminal activity and the subsequent risk to the national security of receiving countries. Some researchers even argue that public threat and security problems in relation to migration are 'constructed' by a 'community of security professionals'.[9] It is beyond the focus of this chapter to examine whether the public fear of migration is real or socially constructed. Nonetheless, it is hard to deny, first, that official policies and public debates often seem to conflate migrants and asylum seekers with criminals, and, second, that the current mechanisms of migration control tend to focus on the restriction of migration at the expense of protecting human rights.

The EU is not free from these criticisms. In the Treaty of the European Union (1992) both policing and migration policy were placed in Justice and Home Affairs (JHA), making the conflation of these policies possible. This is still a problem today, although the Amsterdam Treaty shifted competence for issues of asylum, admission, residence of third-country nationals and immigration to the Community level. Especially since 9/11, alleged risks to national security have led to significant limitations of migration flows under the banner of 'regulated openness'[10] – originally, concepts such as 'managed migration'[11] and 'regulated openness' were supposed to protect vulnerable migrants by ensuring routes for legal migration and eliminating human trafficking. For example, a Commission working document issued soon after

9/11 pledges to the international human rights obligations and protection of refugees and asylum seekers, while simultaneously emphasising the introduction and implementation of measures against the entry of terrorists under the guise of refugees or asylum seekers. Indeed, the official EU documents do promise that the Union complies with international obligations for human rights protection, but no concrete precautions are taken specifically to protect the rights of migrants and asylum seekers. As a result, the goal of protecting migrants' human rights seems to be overshadowed by that of restricting migratory movements.[12]

There are a number of concrete examples of this. In this author's view, it is not justifiable from a human rights perspective, for instance, to take the fingerprints of every applicant for asylum over the age of 14 and establish a database on them; fingerprints have historically been associated with the punishment of criminals and prevention of repeated offences.[13] Indeed, supposing we agree that some types of migration – that of terrorists – might damage national security, we still have to seek suitable means of singling these out without jeopardising other migrants.[14]

It is obvious that the problem discussed here is also dependent on how we understand the notion of 'security'. In the 1990s, 'security' gradually seemed to assume a fairly broad meaning, one closely related to the rights of the individual. For example the UNDP *Human Development Report of 1994* gave the concept two different definitions: 'safety from such chronic threats as hunger, disease and repression', and 'protection from sudden and hurtful disruptions in the patterns of daily life'.[15] The emerging consensus was thus that the protection of human rights is an important part of security; we feel safer without the fear of terrorist bombs, but that is not enough to create 'security'. Efforts to re-interpret the concept of 'security' were, however, quickly forgotten after 9/11. It is, again, primarily understood in terms of national security. Nonetheless, the distinction between 'internal' and 'external', national and non-national, is increasingly difficult to make even in terms of security.

A vertical migration regime

As was mentioned earlier, the pursuit of a common migration policy has been on the European Commission's agenda since the enactment of the Amsterdam Treaty in 1999. Initially, a common policy on asylum and migration was to be completed by 2004. However, according to a 2003 Commission communication, the legislative programme for harmonisation had been progressing but the pace had been slower than anticipated because of the 'need for a unanimous adoption of Community instrument' and the 'difficulty met by the member states in abandoning their national agenda'.[16] The Commission is currently targeting the establishment of a common asylum procedure and a uniform status for migrants as the second stage of harmonisation. The

Commission also continues to stress the importance of 'partnerships' with relevant third countries.

There seems to be two rather pragmatic reasons for the apparent 'success' of migration policy on EU level. Firstly, migration control is an easy way for governments to show that they are doing 'something' to solve the structural problems of society. It is also a traditional way: historically, as rates of unemployment and crime increased, so did attacks on migrants, especially illegal migrants. The real causes of economic depression and social deprivation are hard to pinpoint and tackle. Yet, if governments can convince the public that the inflow of migrants ought to be blamed, the solution becomes clear and simple: to regulate and restrict that inflow.[17] Secondly, for EU governments, migration control through a common policy on asylum and trafficking is easier to accept than that on qualified labour force migration, since its goal is generally straightforward: restriction. Any failure of a common policy can also be attributed to the incompetence of the Commission, leaving intact the authority of national governments.

This multinationalisation trend can be seen as part of the growing phenomenon of the 'vertical dimension of immigration policy-making'.[18] According to Guiraudon, who has published extensively on this phenomenon, there are three ways of delegating competence of migration policy to non-state actors (these are certainly valid in other policy sectors as well): upwards to the supranational, downwards to the local, and, less vertically, outwards to the private sector.[19] Both the downward and the outward shifting have been conspicuous in Europe since the 1980s. Successive British governments, for example, actively adopted both of them in order to strengthen their capacity to screen migrants and asylum seekers. A white paper issued by the Home Office in 1998 recommended that an integrated approach to asylum seekers and migrants be established, in which pre-entry, on-entry and after-entry control measures exist in a single framework.[20] As a result of recent developments in after-entry control, registrars are now required to inform the Home Office if they suspect marriages are taking place for purely immigration purposes. This is a typical example of policy devolution to the sub-national level. Civil servants who are not in theory engaged with migration-related matters are in reality taking part in control.

The most prevalent method of pre-entry control, carrier sanctions against illegal immigrants, represents outward shifting. The first carrier sanctions were enacted in Britain in 1987. Initially, only airlines and shipping companies were subject to the fines, yet now even lorry drivers are subject to legislation. Critics of this practice have long argued that staffs at private carrier companies are unlikely to be familiar with migration and asylum legislation, let alone human rights protection. As a result, while the costs of migration control are reduced and the number of passport and travel document inspections are doubled, due procedures and fair process for migration control are likely to be compromised.

The shifting upwards of migration control can take place through at least three different forms: multinational treaties, (inter-regional) political dialogue, and bilateral relations. First, the most explicit form of shifting upwards is the setting up of multinational migration control based on treaties and agreements. European countries currently enjoy the most advanced treaty-based cooperation in this field. The Schengen Treaty in particular confirmed the institutionalisation of multinational migration control, for example through the establishment of the Schengen visa. The harmonisation of legislation and procedures for migration and asylum aims to establish EU-wide common criteria for visa and asylum applications.

Second, as the next section of this chapter discusses in detail, multinational dialogue of cooperation is also well on track inter-regionally, and particularly within the framework of ASEM. Without a treaty basis, however, whatever is agreed on the inter-regional level is not legally binding on member countries; their cooperation in policing and information exchange progresses only through the mutual understanding that the dialogue possibly creates.

The third form of shifting upwards is the 'readmission' agreements, originally bilateral treaties signed with Eastern European countries in the 1980s. Under these, a signatory country would accept back its nationals found illegally in the territory of another signatory country. This practice now spreads outside Europe, and some Asian countries such as Hong Kong and Sri Lanka have already signed a readmission agreement with the EU, both in 2002. In further promoting readmission agreements with other countries, the Commission recommends that negotiations with third countries should include accompanying measures such as technical assistance and financial support for the repatriation of the person concerned.[21] In this way, it hopes to counter-balance the claim by partner governments who see these agreements as being solely in the interests of the European Union.

*   *   *

These categorisations of policy delegation well explain some aspects of the current emphasis on restrictive migration control. The strong vertical dimension of migration control indicates that national governments, especially those in industrial countries, diversify the range of potential control methods for the purpose of further migration restriction, more or less intentionally.[22] Indeed, as a result of the accumulated effect of downward, upward and outward delegation, the drive for restrictive migration control is strong, much stronger than usually expected, for example in the recent Commission reports on the issue. Moreover, the emerging division of labour – and the division of responsibilities – between each level is not necessarily 'effective', in the sense of giving due respect to the core values of the EU; this is the 'subsidiary question' that we posed earlier. With a great number of different actors with rather pragmatic interests along the vertical dimension, the common values are easily sidelined.

This is also closely related to the fact that the biggest danger of multinationalising migration control seems to lie in the absence of judicial scrutiny.[23] On the national level, court rulings generally work to protect the rights of migrants by securing their equality before the law and observing international rules and norms of human rights. Multinational and vertical migration control, in contrast, lacks judicial inspection, which makes it easy for the participating countries to act according to their own narrowly defined interests. Furthermore, when migrants' rights are threatened and abused under the multinational framework, it is next to impossible for individuals to seek amendment of the framework, let alone redeem compensation. Guiraudon and others explain the delegation of policy to different levels by governments' wishes to protect the status quo in this respect, to avoid judicial intervention. If this truly is the primary reason, the EU's involvement with the building of the multi-level form of migration control cannot be justified: it goes counter to the core values which the EU is supposed to embody and by which the 'effectiveness' of multinational framework is to be measured. All in all, the establishment of a vertical migration regime seems to blur the capacity that the Union and its member states have and thereby evade the responsibility they reasonably should bear, and that they have committed themselves to having, for the human rights protection.

Indeed, provided that the EU wishes to be 'responsible', it is under the obligation to take the initiative in retaining human rights standards. Moreover, a strong restrictive drive built into the multinationalisation of migration control should make the EU more emphatic about asserting human rights protection. In the case of the inter-regional negotiations, where the tendency for restriction is much stronger than in other forms of multinationalisation, the role of the EU becomes especially important in safeguarding human rights.

Migration control within ASEM: the danger of inter-regionalism

A brain-child of the 1994 Europe–East Asia Economic Summit organised by the World Economic Forum, ASEM materialised in 1996 with the first summit held in Bangkok. Since then, a summit meeting has been held every other year; the next one will take place in Finland in 2006. The main purpose of the ASEM process is to gradually foster consensus and to advance mutual understanding between the two regions. By the end of 2004, ASEM consisted of 13 Asian countries (China, Japan, South Korea, Brunei, Indonesia, Malaysia, the Philippines, Singapore, Thailand, Vietnam, Cambodia, Laos, and Myanmar) and 25 EU member states and the EC.[24]

Gradually, ASEM seems to be developing into a permanent structure, with a reasonably broad agenda. There are more and more frequent meetings at ministerial, official and expert levels in the three core fields of economic, political, and cultural and intellectual issues.[25] In addition, such areas as science and technology, environment and migration have entered the ASEM agenda. There are also 'track two' activities, still marginal as their impact may be upon the ASEM process. For example, the People's Forum (AEPF) of Asian and European non-governmental organisations is held concurrently with ASEM summits. The Council for Asia–Europe Cooperation (CAEC), initiated by the then prime minister of Japan, Hashimoto, provides a network for think tanks and sets up various expert committees around topical issues.

With its unique inter-regional membership, the ASEM process has never aimed at building a firm structural organisation; the ASEM process is meant to develop as an *informal* process without significant institutionalisation, and with the idea that its unique inter-regional perspective *complements* that of other regional organisations. The European Commission has compressed the rationale behind the ASEM process by pointing out six characteristics of it: informality, complementarity, multidimensionality, emphasis on equal partnership, and provision of a platform for meetings.[26] ASEM thus also lacks structural sophistication comparable to some other regional arrangements. For instance, it does not have a permanent secretariat, but is coordinated by four of the participants, two from the EU (Commission and the presidency) and two from Asia (one from the Southeast Asia sub-region and the other from the Northeast).

Issues of concern and interest to Asia and Europe are no longer confined to economic relations between the two regions, but cover *multidimensional* topics, both regions now respecting their *equal partnership* and organising a wide spectrum of meetings from high level summits to people-to-people contacts. One Japanese expert on Asia–EU relations has also depicted the process with the notion of the 'Asian Way', by which consensus rather than breakthrough, companionship rather than formality, and procedures rather than contents are valued and pursued.[27] In sum, through the ASEM process, it is hoped that constant manoeuvres and adjustments between two regions of different cultures and histories would eventually result in mutual understanding on the basis of which solid rules and agreements are later established elsewhere.

Possibly the main problem so far has been that the ASEM process remains dominated by elite politicians and bureaucrats, with little input from ordinary people in the two regions. The highly limited and apparently declining interest shown by the media – the media coverage that the latest ASEM summit in Hanoi in 2004 gained was minimal compared with earlier summits – may also contribute to this public indifference. We will return to this shortly.

*   *   *

Issues under discussion at the ASEM level were initially not as diverse as they are now. Particularly for the EU, the focus was clearly on the economic field. The Commission had become aware that its relationship with Asia was much weaker than with the United States, and its involvement in trade and investments in the area lagged behind its American competitors. In the face of the dramatic rise of the Asian economies in 1980s, the Commission issued, in 1994, a document – 'Towards a New Asia Strategy' – on future relations with Asia.[28] It made clear that the overall objective was 'to strengthen the Union's economic presence in Asia in order to maintain the Union's leading role in the world economy'.[29] For fear of losing access to markets in East and Southeast Asia, which, according to the World Bank estimates, would produce half of the growth in the global economy by 2000, the Commission paper urged the EU to accord Asia a higher priority than before.

Asian states also had economic interests in strengthening their ties with the EU. For countries in East and Southeast Asia, access to European markets, technology, and investments were deemed indispensable for their continued growth. Some Asian scholars have also emphasised that the political strategy of ASEAN, and especially that of Singapore, was crucial in realising ASEM. Soeya, for example, argues that ASEAN's enthusiasm for the establishment of ASEM was part of the overall plan to strengthen its international standing by diversifying the diplomatic tools.[30] Singaporean leaders, the then prime minister, Goh Chok Tong and Lee Kuan Yew in particular, were also concerned that within the triangle of the three engines of the world economy – North America, Western Europe and East Asia – the link between Europe and Asia was hardly visible in comparison to the transatlantic (US–EU) and transpacific (US–Asia) links. According to Yeo's analysis, they saw a balanced triangular partnership as the key to global peace and economic growth.[31] Three non-ASEAN countries, Japan, China and South Korea, were later persuaded by ASEAN to take part in ASEM in order to establish 'the first forum in history where political leaders of 10 Asian countries and 15 EU member countries regularly meet and discuss on the basis of equal partnership'.[32]

Including non-economic issues on the ASEM agenda was far from self-evident. Although economic interests prevailed in the EU side, it was willing to table issues like the promotion of democracy, human rights and the rule of law, whereas the Asian counterparts insisted on concentrating on economic cooperation. Wishing to prioritise the creation of ASEM and avoid a head-on clash between the two regions from the beginning, the European participants conceded and agreed to avoid particular issues of national importance.[33] Furthermore, some of the initiators of the ASEM process, especially on the EU-side, were keen on getting the non-governmental sectors more involved in order to avoid criticism about another 'democratic deficit'. This bore results in the ASEM 2 summit in London in 1998. Despite hesitation among some Asian members, the summit duly made the promotion of 'dialogue and cooperation between the business/private sectors of the two regions, and no less importantly, between the peoples of the two regions' an important element of the ASEM framework.[34]

Yet, as will be discussed below, inputs from the non-governmental sectors are still too small to hold ASEM accountable to peoples in both regions.

Given that the main role of ASEM is to prepare inter-regionally for a shared cognitive basis through social interaction and the exchange of opinion – what Gilson termed 'cognitive institutionalisation'[35] – it is more than essential to guarantee and expand the involvement of civil society. Otherwise, the 'results' of inter-regionalism between Europe and Asia will be far removed from the opinions and feelings of ordinary people. With democracy in some Asian participating countries still embryonic and fragile, the risk of inter-regionalism supporting oppressive political systems is in fact significant.

*   *   *

Migration is one of the most important current issues on the ASEM agenda. The Commission made it clear in its Communication published in 2001 that, as part of its new strategy for enhanced partnership with Asia, the EU should play a more pro-active role in regional fora, and enhance EU–Asia dialogue in the realms of justice and home affairs, including areas such as asylum and immigration.[36] After 9/11, the EU also began to hasten the establishment of common standards on issues such as external border controls and multinational cooperation for migration control. Asian leaders were as keen as their European counterparts on consolidating their own control mechanisms. As noted by the two UN protocols on the issue in 2001, both regional and inter-regional coordination after 2000 were part of the global attempt to tackle transnational crimes, including trafficking with people, within a multinational framework.[37]

At the ASEM 3 summit in Seoul (October 2000), both European and Asian leaders agreed to commit themselves to global issues of common concern, among which was the management of migratory flows. An expert seminar on migratory flows between Asia and Europe took place in Madrid (September 2001), and several symposiums and conferences on migration control were held concurrently both in Europe and Asia during that year, especially regarding human smuggling and trafficking. These led to what is possibly the most important event in this field so far, the ASEM Ministerial Conference on Cooperation for the Management of Migratory Flows between Asia and Europe, held in Lanzarote as part of the Spanish EU presidency, on 4 and 5 April 2002.[38]

The Lanzarote conference agenda included three plenary sessions in which the policies on admission, family reunion and the integration of immigrants were discussed, in addition to the causes and consequences of illegal immigration, the routes and means employed, and the need for cooperation in the fight against criminal organisations engaged in the trafficking of human beings. The main outcome of the conference, the Lanzarote declaration, identified the following five priorities for future cooperation in the field:

1. fight against illegal migration and human trafficking;
2. cooperation in the area of return and readmission;

3. increased sharing of information (concerning migration flows as well as detection of falsified and counterfeit documents) through the establishment of a network of contact points of officials and experts in charge of migration;
4. public awareness campaign on the adverse effects of illegal migration; and
5. the need to ensure the social integration and fair treatment of legal migrants.

In looking at the ASEM process as a whole, and in particular the focus and results of the Lanzarote conference, the argument here is that the problematic nature of the multinational framework discussed above – a strong built-in restrictive drive – is most likely strengthened through ASEM. ASEM in fact seems to develop into a prime example of how upward shifting blurs actor capacity, and makes it more difficult to know whose interests, which community's interests, the participants actually represent, and who they are accountable for. A shared notion of 'multinational migration control' emerges and is forged through the holding of the conference. As we look at the list above, for example, it seems that the ASEM leaders had one single motive for attending the Lanzarote conference: the strengthening of migration control. The linkage between migration and transnational crime was simply accepted as a fact. By contrast, the idea of protecting the rights of vulnerable people, migrants, asylum seekers, seems virtually invisible.[39]

More specifically, given that the ASEM process aims to act as a forum to create 'cognitive' language and 'cognitive' linkages upon which the future rules and agreements will be established,[40] it is regrettable that the Lanzarote conference was prepared and organised with minimum input from civil society groups and migrants themselves. The lack of media coverage did not help to enhance awareness of the vulnerable positions of migrants and asylum seekers in the regions, either. There is no effective debate and control over the intended outcomes of this kind of conferences. One example that springs to mind is that even though the absence of readmission programmes among the Asian members of ASEM was specifically pointed out in the beginning of the Lanzarote conference, none have been introduced yet. Inter-regionalism is fine in theory so long as what emerges is accountable to the scrutiny of people in those regions. Without popular legitimacy, inter-regionalism will simply become another means of removing ordinary people from the political decision-making process, rendering it increasingly difficult to hold any polity responsible for the infringement of people's rights.

It has been argued earlier already that 'effectiveness' – the key criteria of the subsidiarity principle – of each level in a multi-level migration control framework ought to be measured in such a way as to contribute to the core values on which the EU was founded: liberty, democracy, respect for human rights and fundamental freedoms, and the rule of law. In cases where some of them might be compromised, the EU is required to take a complementary measure to alleviate the situation. In the case of ASEM, the EU could potentially make immense contributions to the building of multinational migration control as a way of protecting human rights. Indeed, at the moment, there is no regional watchdog for human rights in Asia. In contrast, the European Court of Human Rights works as the final enforcement authority of the European Convention on Human Rights against national courts.

In this context, it is understandable that some scholars in Asia pay special attention to the deepening of EU–Asia relationship, arguing that, in addition to traditional subject areas such as trade and economic cooperation, the emphasis should now be placed on democracy and human rights.[41] In response to the recent debate on 'Asian values' which emphasises the special nature of the concept of human rights unique to Asia, politicians and academics in Europe are understandably hesitant in getting involved with human rights issues.[42] Cautious as the EU may be, however, the debate on human rights protection within an inter-regional framework at least keeps politicians in the region engaged with the issues, forces them to consider what the 'Asian values' actually are or might be. Without regional consensus in Asia over the meaning of human rights and its protection obligations, it is only the EU that can prevent its inter-regional attempt to establish mechanisms of multinational migration control from damaging human rights and provide a counter-measure to protect them if necessary. In sum, there is a lot of responsibility the EU has chosen to shoulder and not all of those duties have been satisfactorily fulfilled. More strikingly, it remains questionable whether the EU and its decision makers have actually realised the full extent of the various dimensions of responsibility the Union has taken on by engaging in the ASEM dialogue.

Conclusions

So has the EU been acting as a 'responsible' actor in the field of migration and asylum? The analyses above have revealed a rather mixed picture. Judging on the basis of recent Commission documents, the Union seems to be aware of the need to find a balance between 'internal' security through migration control and international obligations for protecting the human rights of migrants and asylum seekers. Multinational migration control frameworks in which the EU takes part show the tendency for restriction of migration and migrants rights, but then so do all the other multinational frameworks. In the case of ASEM, it has been the European members who emphasise human rights protection, although they might not push the issue in opposition to their Asian counterparts. At a time of 'global terrorism', moreover, linking trans-national crime to migration is a global phenomenon; some politicians argue that it is a natural outcome for a 'responsible' polity to try to protect its 'internal' members from 'external' threat. All in all, it is hard to see that the Union would have acted less responsibly than most other international actors.

In analysing the role of a 'responsible' polity in migration control, this chapter has suggested that – closely related to the community principle of this volume's conceptual framework – it is often necessary to make a distinction between 'internal' and 'external' responsibility; the former applies to the members of the polity and the latter to the non-members. In the increasingly globalised world, it is always controversial to define who the members are. In addition, as a polity with an in-built multi-level governance mechanism, what is seen as 'inside' and 'outside' by a member country might be different from the EU; as a result, it is often not clear-cut to conclude to whom the EU should be most responsible and why. Regardless of the criterion between the two groups, however, a 'responsible' EU needs to be aware, on the basis of its core values, of the discrepancy between 'internal' and 'external' responsibility. To fulfil this requirement, the protection of human rights could serve as a key yardstick.

Another important point made in the chapter is that the principle of subsidiarity is helpful in identifying the way responsibility is vertically distributed both within the framework of the EU and the migration control regime. What is important is that the subsidiarity question 'what is the most effective level of authority' ought to be judged, in the case of the EU, in relation to the core values on which the Union was founded, and which it has explicitly consented to promote in all its external activities. However, the present multinationalisation trend seems to be able to water down, at least to a certain extent, this principle. The Commission and leaders in member countries need to be aware that multinational migration control tends to employ more restrictive measures than national legislation. In combination with the current phenomenon of linking control of migration with that of transnational crime, measures to counter-balance excessive restriction are all the more urgent nowadays for the protection of migrants and asylum seekers.

In the case of multinational migration control within the ASEM process, the argument has been that a 'responsible' EU should be aware, not only of the impact of the current efforts of policy coordination and information exchange, but also of the future policy implications of today's dialogue. This is the final central point of this chapter: a 'responsible' EU needs to realise the huge potential it may have upon future migration control in both national and multinational settings in the Asian region. The significance of ASEM lies more in its potential to build a shared cognitive basis for solid relationship between the two regions than in the immediate results of each summit meeting. ASEM conferences on cooperation for the management of migratory flows may not immediately result in changes within the migration regime, but they eventually determine how the future form of migration control between the two regions takes shape. Without regional consensus on the protection of human rights, let alone a regional institution such as ECtHR, in Asia, the EU's responsibility on that matter is inherently significant not only for EU citizens but to people in Asia as well. With voluntarily assumed roles come real responsibilities, and setting norms within the ASEM dialogue means sharing moral responsibility for future migration policies in Asia and beyond.

Notes

1. Communication from the Commission to the Council and the European Parliament on *Integrating Migration Issues in the European Union's Relations with Third Countries*, COM(2002)703 final of 3.12.02, p. 4.
2. Green Paper on a *Community Return Policy on Illegal Residents*, COM(2002)175 final of 10.04.02, p. 5. Prior to the Treaty of Amsterdam, migration was largely dealt with inter-governmentally. The Treaty (Title IV of the Treaty and article 63 in particular) conferred competence on the European Community in the areas of migration and asylum, transferring it from the EU's third to its first pillar. Denmark, Ireland and the United Kingdom reserved the right to not to participate in this part of the Treaty (Title IV), however. See e.g. Kostakopoulou 2000 and Guild 1998.
3. See e.g. Guiraudon 1999.
4. One of the main exceptions is often the right to vote and run for national election. Permanent residents who are not citizens of member countries do not possess the entitlements of the EU citizenship such as the right of free movement within the member countries.
5. According to article 6 of the TEU, these principles are 'common to the Member States'.
6. See e.g. Soysal 1994. In looking at the rights of migrants in receiving countries (particularly in the EU), Soysal advocates the emergence of human rights regimes based on universal 'personhood', under which national governments become more accountable for protecting the rights of both migrants and citizens.
7. For detailed research on subsidiarity, see Endo 2001.
8. Ibid., 35.
9. For detailed argument of this scholarly camp, see Bigo 2001.
10. Ghosh 2000.
11. International Organisation for Migration (IOM), *Statement by the Director General to the Council*, MICEM/9/1995, 28 November 1995.
12. Commission Working Document on *the Relationship between Safeguarding Internal Security and Complying with International Protection Obligations and Instruments* COM(2001)742 final of 5.12.01.
13. Council Regulation of 11 December 2000 concerning the Establishment of 'Eurodac' for the Comparison of Fingerprints for the Effective Application of the Dublin Convention on the State Responsible for Examining Applications for Asylum Lodged in One of the European Union Member States (2000/2725/EC) of 11.12.00.
14. Cf. Communication from the Commission to the Council and the European Parliament on an *Open Method of Coordination for the Community Immigration Policy* COM(2001)387 final of 11.07.01.
15. United Nations Development Programme (UNDP), *Human Development Report 1994*, Oxford University Press, New York, p. 23.
16. Communication from the Commission to the Council and the European Parliament on the *Common Asylum Policy and the Agenda for Protection* COM(2003)152 final of 26.3.03. (Second Commission Report on the Implementation of Communication COM(2000)755 final of 22.11.00), p.3. From the member states' perspective the slow pace can be deemed as somewhat irrational: some scholars

working in the field emphasise the incentives for each country to link transnational crime to migration and to fight it through a common EU policy. They assume that there should be relatively good prospects for cooperation among member states, given that national governments tend to find it convenient to appease public anxiety in this way. See Koslowski 2001.

17. Bauman 1999, 50–53.
18. Guiraudon 2001, 32.
19. For details, see ibid., p. 34 (table 2.1).
20. Home Office, *Fairer, Faster and Firmer – A Modern Approach to Immigration and Asylum*, Cm. 4018, July 1998, ch. 4. Policy orientation remains unchanged in the latest legislation (Nationality, Immigration and Asylum Act 2002).
21. Communication from the Commission to the Council and the European Parliament on *Integrating Migration Issues in the European Union's Relations with Third Countries* COM(2002)703 final of 3.12.02., pp. 25–6.
22. Guiraudon (2001, 45–7) explains that the multinationalisation of migration control, the upward shifting, is part of what she calls venue shopping for governments to install restrictive migration measures.
23. Ibid., ch. 2.
24. For the ASEM process, this article owes a particular debt to: Gilson 2002; Preston and Julie 2001; and Yeo 2003.
25. A table of the ASEM structure is found in Yeo 2003, 29. Chapter 2 of Yeo's book also presents a chronological development of the ASEM process up to 2002.
26. European Commission, ASEM 4, *An Introduction to the Asia–Europe meeting – ASEM*, pp. 3–4, 2002.
27. Shoji 2002, 34.
28. Communication from the Commission to the Council, *Towards a New Asia Strategy* COM(1994)314 final of 13.07.94.
29. Ibid.
30. Soeya 1996, 197.
31. Yeo 2003, 18–19.
32. Ministry of Foreign Affairs of Japan, *ASEM: Asia-Europe Meeting*, April 2000, p. 1 (translation by the author).
33. For the preparation period for ASEM, see Camroux and Lechervy, 1996, 442–53.
34. ASEM2: Chairman's Statement 1998, www.asem2.fco.gov.uk.
35. Gilson 2001, chapter 6.
36. Communication from the Commission on *Europe and Asia: A Strategic Framework for Enhanced Partnership* COM(2001)469 of 4.9.01.
37. The declaration of the Lanzarote conference cited several cases of regional efforts at policy cooperation, which preceded the Conference. They are the International Symposium on Migration – ISM in Bangkok (April, 1999), the International Conference on Migration in Brussels (October 2001) and the Regional Ministerial Conference on People Smuggling, Trafficking in Persons and Related Transnational Crime in Bali (February 2002). The two UN protocols enacted in 2001 regarding trafficking are: Protocol against the Smuggling of Migrants by Land, Sea and Air, Supplementing the UN Convention against Transnational Crime and Protocol to Prevent, Suppress and Punish Trafficking in Persons, especially Women and Children, Supplementing the UN Convention against Transnational Organized Crime, res. 55/25, Annex III, 55. UN GAOR Supp. (No. 49) at 65 and 60, respectively. UN Doc. A/45/49(vol. I), 2001.
38. Details of this conference are found at http://europa.eu.int/comm/external_relations/asm/min_other_meeting/mtg.htm.

39. This invisibility is conspicuous in many other documents, too. In the 2003 communication *A New Partnership with South East Asia*, for example, the Commission mentions nothing about the protection of migrants' rights but only of controlling migratory movements and fighting the organised crime of trafficking. COM (2003)399/4.
40. Armstrong 1998, 469.
41. Tanaka 1997, 5. Professor Tanaka describes this recent type of dialogue in the EU–Asia relationship as that of the 'third generation'. According to him, the 'first generation' focused single-handedly on trade, whereas the 'second generation' included economic cooperation as well.
42. A number of works exist on 'Asian values', both in favour and against. This paper takes a similar line to those who are concerned with Western dominance over the debate on human rights, but are still critical of the way 'Asian values' is used by politicians to gain political advantages. See, for example, a compilation of articles on human rights and Asian values in *Kokusai Mondai (International Affairs)*, vol. 449, 1998.

Bibliography

Armstrong, David, 'Globalisation and the Social State', *Review of International Studies*, vol. 24, no. 4 (1998).

Bauman, Zygmunt., *In Search of Politics* (Cambridge: Polity Press, 1999).

Bigo, Didier, 'Migration and Security', in Virginie Guiraudon and Christian Joppke (eds), *Controlling New Migration World* (London: Routledge, 2001).

Camroux, David, and Christian Lechervy, 'Close Encounter of a Third Kind?; The Inaugural Asia-Europe Meeting of March 1996', *The Pacific Review*, vol. 9, no. 3 (1996), 442–53.

Endo, Ken, 'Subsidiarity & Its Enemies: To What Extent is Sovereignty Contested in the Mixed Commonwealth of Europe', *EUI Working Papers*, RSC No. 2001/24.

Ghosh, Bismal, 'New International Regime for Orderly Movements of People: What Will It Look Like?', in Bimal Ghosh (ed.), *Managing Migration: Time for a New International Regime?* (Oxford: Oxford University Press, 2000).

Gilson, Julie A., 'Europe-Asia: the Formal Politics of Mutual Definition', in Peter W. Preston and Julie Gilson (eds), *The European Union and East Asia: Inter-Regional Linkages in a Changing Global System* (Cheltenham: Edward Elgar, 2001).

Gilson, Julie, *Asia Meets Europe: Inter-Regionalism and the Asia-Europe Meeting*, (Cheltenham: Edward Elgar, 2002).

Guild, Elspeth, 'Competence, Discretion and Third Country Nationals: The European Union's Legal Struggle with Migration', *Journal of Ethnic and Migration Studies*, vol. 24, no. 4 (1998), 613–26.

Guiraudon, Virginie, 'De-nationalizing Control: Analyzing State Responses to Constraints on Migration Control', in Virginie Guiraudon and Christian Joppke (eds), *Controlling New Migration World* (London: Routledge, 1999).

Koslowski, Rey, 'Personal Security and State Sovereignty in a Uniting Europe', in Virginie Guiraudon and Christian Joppke (eds), *Controlling New Migration World* (London: Routledge, 2001).

Kostakopoulou, Dora, 'The "Protective Union": Change and Continuity in Migration Law and Policy in Post-Amsterdam', *Journal of Common Market Studies*, vol. 38, no. 3 (2000), 497–518.

Preston, Peter E., and Julie Gilson (eds), *The European Union and East Asia: Interregional Linkages in a Changing Global System* (Cheltenham: Edward Elgar, 2001).

Shoji, Katsuhiro, 'EU no tai Asia Jinken Gaiko: the First ASEM Summit (EU's Human Rights Diplomacy towards Asia: the First ASEM Summit as a Case Study)' in Ueda Takako (ed.), *21 seiki no Oshu to Asia (Europe and Asia in the Twenty-First Century)* (Tokyo: Keiso Shobo, 2002).

Soeya, Yoshihide, 'ASEAN to Sekai Chitsujyo no Yukue (ASEAN and the Future of the World Order)', *Sekai*, May 1996.

Soysal, Yasmin N., *The Limits of Citizenship: Migrants and Postnational Membership,* (Chicago: University of Chicago Press, 1994).

Tanaka, Toshiro, 'ASEM – Atarashii Taiwa no Tanjyo (ASEM – the Birth of New Dialogue)', *EU Gakkai Nenpo (Annual Review of the EU Association)*, vol. 17 (1997).

Yeo, Lay Hwee, *Asia and Europe: The Development and Different Dimensions of ASEM* (London: Routledge, 2003).

8
Coping with Historical Responsibility: Trends and Images of the EU's Development Policy

Henri Vogt[1]

Development policy, relations with the 'Third World', represents the oldest form of the international activities of the EU; it was initiated in the Treaty of Rome already. The evolution of this policy, its many twists and turns, is thus an excellent example of how the Union's global role has taken shape over the past five decades.

The following analysis of that policy is composed of two parts with rather distinct starting points, one dealing with what could be called 'real politics' and the other with 'image politics'. The first part identifies three major recent trends or changes of the EU's policy towards poorer continents. These trends cannot be attributed to the EU system only, but they also reflect post-Cold War changes of world politics more generally.

The first and most important trend is what I call *a non-reflective belief in democratic values*; it is a trend that can be found in many other, if not all, policies of the Union, but hardly anywhere in as concrete a form as in development policy. The argument is that 'liberal' values – democracy, good governance, the rule of law and human rights – now set the guidelines for EU development policies in such a self-evident manner that this may have a number of unexpected and above all negative consequences for these policies.

The second trend, called *the paradigm of dialogue*, has a long history. The ideal of dialogue based on mutual equality has been on the EU development agenda at least since the early 1970s, but it has become increasingly important over the past ten years with the evolution of the Union's common foreign and security policy. The nature of dialogue has changed simultaneously: dialogues now take place in the contexts of conditionality and globalisation, under conditions without any general principle, such as state sovereignty, that would prevent the stronger side from imposing its own ideology and norms on the weaker side. In the worst case, then, there is a risk that dialogue becomes a handy way of getting involved in the affairs of the other, a new and subtle form of imperialism.

159

The fact that *development policy is becoming*, or perhaps has already become, *a matter of power politics* is the third trend. A fairly independent area of development policy existed until the mid 1990s, but now development, economic interests and security concerns have all been included in a broad political framework; the propagators of this transformation might be willing to talk about 'a holistic understanding of development'. Whether the old aid paradigm was better or worse than the new holistic paradigm is a delicate question. In one sense the former appeared more innocent, much clearer than the latter: the rich simply helped the poor, tried to undo the injustices of the past, whereas now both the developed and the developing world sail in the same murky waters of interests, power, and winner-takes-it-all ideals.

In the second part of the chapter, the underlying idea is that it is not only the real political processes and decisions that define the agency of the EU as a development partner, but the perceptions and images that the EU has of itself, and that others have of it, are equally important. The real and the imaginary are thus mutually interdependent, albeit not in any straightforward manner: old images may continue to prevail in spite of the changes of actual policies; in the relationship between the first and third worlds this point seems particularly relevant. Moreover, even within one policy sector the central actors usually manage to create a number of competing and contradictory images, both for themselves and for others. To describe the controversial image of the European Union as a global development actor I make use of four metaphors or dramatis personae – cook, thief, bodybuilder, and mistress.[2]

The main point is, then, that *both* the recent changes of the EU's development policy and its images as a development partner constrain and determine the Union's possibilities to act in north-south politics. If the people of developing countries *believe* that the Union seeks to alleviate their problems on the basis of *their* genuine interests and not those of itself, this may significantly improve the effectiveness of the help. The EU is thus bound to take into consideration not only its actual policies, but also the images that its counterparts have of it. From the perspective of 'responsibility', the combination of the real and the imaginary may make it more difficult to know what kind of expectations others have of the EU, what the actual capacity of the Union is, and even what the nature of the human community inviting a sense of moral responsibility is (cf. the expectations, capacity, and community principles in Szigeti's chapter). Making political decisions may prove highly problematic in this kind of context. Perhaps a responsible agency would then denote nothing more than increased awareness of these contradictory trends and images and sensitivity towards the views of the other.

The EU's development policies are here understood as a fairly clearly defined phenomenon – which it is not, of course, for a number of reasons. First, as stated in the Union's new draft constitution, Article III-316-1, 'The Union's development cooperation policy and that of the Member States shall complement and reinforce each other.' Money-wise the EU is still a medium-size actor: some 80 per cent of the total aid of EU countries is chan-nelled through the member states' bilateral relationships. Often the Union has merely followed the policy guidelines designed by one or several member states – France has always had a central role in this respect – albeit mutual interaction and mainstreaming have increased in recent years.[3] Second, development policy has been a field where civil society has always had an active role, both in the preparation of national policies and on the European level; the paradigm of dialogue has further strengthened this role. In all, then, it might be sensible to speak about a European development policy *regime* rather than of EU development policy. However, to the extent it is possible, the chapter concentrates on the EU's 'own' policy as defined by the Commission and Council. Most of the empirical examples are either from the context of the EU's cooperation with the so-called African, Caribbean and Pacific states (ACP states, most of which are former European African colonies) – trad-itionally the dominant part of EU development policy – or exclusively from Africa, but it would certainly be possible to find similar examples from other cooperation contexts.[4]

Trends

Before turning to the three above-mentioned trends, the evolution of the EU's development policy is worth a brief review. In the Treaty of Rome, the then colonies of France, Belgium, the Netherlands, and Italy were simply associated with the European Community – without asking their opinion.[5] This arrangement had to be renewed quickly as most of the colonies gained their independence in the late 1950s and early 1960s. The first treaty between the former colonies (still called associate countries in a proto-neo-colonial manner) and the EC member states was signed in Yaoundé in 1963 (renewed in 1969), and since then the relationship between these two groups of countries, both now much more numerous than in 1963,[6] has been based on a detailed treaty that has gradually come to cover a vast range of different policy sectors, from agricultural to cultural cooperation, from environmen-tal issues to tourism. Between 1975 and 2000 the Convention was named after Lomé, the capital of Togo. There were four Lomé Conventions in total, the first three lasting five years and the fourth ten, with a significant mid-term revision (1995; the so-called Lomé IV bis). The present treaty, called the Cotonou Agreement, was concluded in 2000 for 20 years.[7]

Trade and *aid* have been the main elements of this cooperation framework. The first Lomé Convention (1975) was truly development-friendly in terms of its trade regulations. It guaranteed *non-reciprocal* trade preferences to the ACP countries, and thus greatly eased the access of ACP products to the EC markets.[8] These trade preferences remained the cornerstone of the Lomé framework, throughout the next quarter of a century. As for Lomé's aid pro-visions, it is worth noting that the sums delivered through the European

Development Fund increased steadily, but after the end of the Cold War in 1989, and measured in percentages, the ACP group lost its position as the single target of the EC/EU's external aid; the eastern part of the European continent now became the central concern for the Union.[9] The widely spread Western pessimism – in the African context known as afropessimism – towards third-world policies in the 1980s and 1990s certainly made this shift easier.

The first Lomé Convention was clearly informed by a structural understanding of the world, dependency theory and theories of the unequal global division of labour.[10] Responsibility was always an inherent aspect of these theories. They were based, almost in a metaphysical manner, on the historical and moral responsibility felt by the Europeans towards their former colonies. This responsibility certainly included aspects of most of the principles that may incur duties towards the other – contribution, beneficiary, community, capacity, and legitimate expectations principles but the emphasis was clearly on contribution and beneficiary principles. Interestingly, as we will see, this has clearly changed over the past 30 years: in the age of globalisation the relative importance of capacity and particularly community principles has clearly increased in the field of EU development policy.

In the Cotonou Agreement, the role of trade – but not that of aid[11] – is much less important than in Lomé, because trade regulations must now follow the rules of the WTO. The objectives may not have changed – the primary goal is still to help the ACP States 'play a full part in international trade' – but the non-reciprocal trade preferences have been buried. Therefore, to their disappointment, the ACP countries have lost their former privileged position as the Union's trading partners, and EU development policy has become more similar in different parts of the world – and thus maybe more coherent.[12] Instead of the traditional trade preferences, the trade relations between the Union and individual ACP states are now to be based on mutual, WTO-compatible trade agreements, the main aim of which is to liberalise trade between the contracting parties. The negotiations of these Economic Partnership Agreements (EPAs) should be finished by 2008.[13] In European development policy circles, there is currently a lively debate on whether the EPAs will actually promote growth and alleviate poverty in the developing countries or whether they will only serve the interests of European business and developing country elites.

This leads us to the objectives of these policies more generally. In the past the Union was often accused of not having clearly defined goals in its development policy, but in the beginning of a new century, this vagueness has clearly diminished: the main objective is now unambiguously the alleviation of poverty. This objective has also been enshrined in the Union's draft constitution, Article III-316-1 of which states that 'Union development cooperation policy shall have as its primary objective the reduction and, in the long term, the eradication of poverty.' This primary objective is usually complemented with a number of smaller objectives, such as 'support for sustainable economic and social and environmental development, promotion of the gradual integration of the developing countries into the world economy and a determination to combat inequality.[14] What is common to these objectives is that their fulfilment is essentially dependent upon a number of liberal democratic values and norms.

The non-reflective belief in values

Indeed, as all its external activities, the development policy of the European Union is now explicitly and self-evidently based on such ideals as democracy, human rights, good governance, and the rule of law. EU development documents are virtually saturated with these notions. Far too often, however, they are used in a purely rhetorical manner, without any idea of what a particular term means, without any real sensitivity to the fact that 'democracy' always includes a great number of different elements and that people interpret it in different ways. These terms have become true empty signifiers, in the sense that Ernesto Laclau has talked about them.[15] This is also why we can speak of a non-reflective belief in values; it is, in fact, this non-reflectivity that makes this trend 'new'.

The change towards the dominance of these values has been gradual, and it has reflected those changes that have been taking place in overall world politics. The first Lomé Convention (1975) consciously avoided mentioning any political values whatsoever – it appeared a purely economic agreement on the surface – as that would have violated the principle of state sovereignty, the unchallenged pillar of international affairs in those days; in cooperation with the ex-colonies that pillar was particularly important.[16] Moreover, criticism against the prevailing world economic order set the pattern of understanding the relations – the structural imbalance – between the first and third worlds at the time; the non-reciprocal trade preferences of the Convention clearly reflect this.[17]

The picture changes significantly as we come to the 1980s. Then, the World Bank and the International Monetary Fund introduced their structural adjustment policies, that is, the developing countries had to start adhering to certain macroeconomic principles in their economic policies in order to be supported by these institutions; economic conditionality entered the stage of world politics. These policies profoundly influenced the Lomé framework as well. For example, the role of financial and technical cooperation, essentially serving the goals of structural adjustment, clearly increased each time the Lomé framework was renegotiated.

The step from economic to political conditionality proved short in the 1980s; the former already showed that state sovereignty was not an inviolable principle. Moreover, capitalism and democracy were about to win, and eventually won, the Cold War. This led to two important conclusions among the Western donor community: the liberal values were apparently correct, and external pressure could indeed change the course of development in a third country. Towards the end of that decade, and especially in the 1990s, with Lomé IV, liberal political values assumed an increasingly important role in Lomé cooperation, and not adhering to them became unacceptable; political conditionality became part of the framework. In the Cotonou Agreement, then, these political principles are *the* central element of cooperation. Indeed, what was once a purely economic treaty, now primarily operates in the sphere of politics – but, *nota bene*, not necessarily of *the political*.

The role of human rights serves as a more detailed example of how the foundations of EU–ACP cooperation have changed (cf. Jurado's chapter). In the first Lomé Treaty human rights were not mentioned at all, but due to the atrocities in Uganda under Idi Amin, the EC wanted to include a human rights clause in the second Lomé Convention (1980). The ACP states strongly opposed this – successfully – the sovereignty principle proved intact. However, in the third Lomé Treaty (1985) a human rights clause was included, but only in the appendix. This time the initiative came from the ACP group that wanted to pay attention to and criticise the EC's economic relations with South Africa. The clause reads as follows; it is noteworthy how clearly the emphasis was on social and cultural rights; politics and political rights was still a very sensitive issue:

> The Contracting Parties proclaim that ACP-EEC cooperation must help eliminate the obstacles preventing individuals and peoples from actually enjoying to the full their economic social and cultural rights and that this must be achieved through the development which is essential to their dignity, their well-being and their self-fulfilment. In this respect the Contracting Parties reaffirm their obligation and their commitment under international law to fight for the elimination of all forms of discrimination based on ethnic group, origin, race, nationality, colour, sex, language, religion or any other situation. They proclaim their determination to work effectively for the eradication of apartheid, which constitutes a violation of human rights and an affront to human dignity.[18]

In the fourth Lomé Treaty, signed for ten years in 1990, human rights already played a significant role as an underlying value of the cooperation between the Community and the ACP countries – this time there were a number of references to human rights in the actual text.[19] Finally, in the Cotonou Agreement, human rights are one of the essential elements of the Treaty. It is stated, for example, that the contracting parties 'reiterate their deep attachment to human dignity and human rights, which are legitimate aspirations of individuals and peoples' (Article 9). The Agreement also remarks that human rights are, not only 'indivisible and inter-related' as was the formulation of Lomé IV, but also *universal* – whatever that may mean. What is particularly important is that if human rights are not respected, this can lead to specific consultations and eventually to sanctions:

> If the consultations do not lead to a solution acceptable to both Parties, if consultation is refused, or in cases of special urgency, appropriate measures

may be taken. [. . .] The 'appropriate measures' referred to in this Article are measures taken in accordance with international law, and proportional to the violation. In the selection of these measures, priority must be given to those which least disrupt the application of this agreement. It is understood that suspension would be a measure of last resort.[20]

We will return to the issue of sanctions in the next section. Here, instead, let us ask what this domination of liberal democratic, individualistic values and promotion by the EU actually means or can lead to. From the perspective of democratic theory, the critical point is by no means new, but one that has been well known from at least the days of Hannah Arendt: democracy requires an open sphere of the political, an idea that all principles, foundations of policies, can be discussed and argued about without any belief in the universality or eternity of them. This does not seem to be the case in European development policy at the moment: there are hardly any competing interpretations of what, say, human rights are.[21] Under these conditions, there is a risk that values become imperatives imposed from above, without any sensitivity to the practises of the other. Echoing the French philosopher Alain Badiou, the European democracy promotion may just turn into misunderstood Kantian universalism.[22]

As we read African and ACP documents on development issues, it readily becomes obvious that this risk is not at all farfetched in reality. One quickly gets the impression that liberal democracy is by no means the dominant discourse or goal in these countries, but it is still the idea of a just and equitable world, understood primarily in structural terms. Moreover, in contrast to the individualism of the European values, in many a developing country the dominant ethos of society is based on the community, on the well-being of the community, on a decent social and economic life within that community. Thus, only when 'democracy' can contribute to the creation of a structurally just world and be compatible with the community ethos may it be ok – otherwise it is basically useless, at least from the African point of view.

There is no doubt that Europeans truly believe that by exporting their 'universal' (if they are universal why do they have to be exported?) values across the globe, they can actually make the world a better place to live, create the necessary conditions for development. The underlying idea seems to be that of a global community defined in a specific way: we can all lead our lives better together if we adhere to the same basic values. We need to pose the counterfactual question, however: what would happen if there was no idea of any kind of value promotion involved in the EU's development activities? Would it be easier to simply argue that it is our *moral* responsibility, without any qualifications, to help those that we have capacity to help, members of the same humanity? There is no clear answer but the question is certainly worth asking whenever development projects are initiated.

Emphasis on dialogue

As a parallel phenomenon to the prevalence of the liberal democratic values, development policy in EU Europe is increasingly based on what could be called the paradigm of dialogue. There are a number of other notions that more or less closely belong to this paradigm; 'partnership', 'ownership', 'openness', 'accountability', 'transparency', 'effectiveness', 'consultation', are all relevant code words here. For example in the Cotonou Agreement (Article 9) 'the pivotal role of dialogue' and of 'equality of the partners and ownership of the development strategies' are listed as fundamental principles of cooperation. The point is not that these terms are newcomers on the EU or global development agenda, however. In the 1970s already, as the ACP cooperation framework was established, it was important to emphasise dialogue and partnership. But the connotation of these terms was clearly different then: they were primarily a means to emphasise that the question was of cooperation between (nominally) equal partners; dialogue was meant to create an air of equality.

The current situation is rather different, for two main reasons. First, dialogue seems to have become a value in itself. There seems to be a widespread consensus that the more dialogue there is between the cooperating societies and within them, the better results development activities may yield. In practice this has meant that the number of relevant actors has increased dramatically; it is believed that proper dialogue requires the participation of all possible actors on all levels of society, or as the term reads 'stake-holders'. This is also closely related to the shift from 'government' to 'governance' (see Raik's chapter).

In terms of democratic theory, the dialogue-as-a-value-in-itself implies that the idea of deliberative democracy has been adopted in this policy field; through deliberation between the relevant actors a meaningful compromise can be found.[23] This opens up a positive horizon: a proper political dialogue makes it possible to interpret, time and time again, the liberal political values; they may become meaningful in the sense of *the political*. In more concrete terms, this might lead to a dialogue that takes place on the political level, not only on policy and project levels as now tends to be the case.[24] It is also noteworthy that this deliberative dialogue may prove positive from the perspective of responsibility: dialogue is indeed a means to create a sense of community on which responsibilities can be based in a natural way.

Closely related to the need to include all *stakeholders* in the dialogue, there is a phenomenon that is usually called *outsourcing*; 'subcontracting' and 'the privatisation of governance' would be alternative expressions.[25] An increasing amount of official European development work – and not only on the level of implementation – is channelled through non-state actors, profit and non-profit international and national non-governmental organisations (INGOs and NGOs), and private consultancies. Often the northern actors use southern organisations and companies as subcontractors. It is, however, difficult to estimate what the actual scale of outsourcing is; it may happen on so many different levels. In the Cotonou framework, non-state actors and their activities are directly supported; some five percent of the resources allocated in total to ACP cooperation are directly given to NGOs. This outsourcing, although it primarily concerns the level of implementation, easily becomes problematic from the perspective of democracy, however: there is a risk that more outsourcing means less democratic control.

Secondly, and more critically, dialogue can also be used as a means to achieve certain political goals – and is indeed used. Let me illuminate this with an example that also continues the discussion in the previous section. In spring 2004, the small francophone republic of Togo was regarded as one of the most problematic countries in the vast African continent; the state of democracy in the country appeared to be, to say the least, questionable; consultations in the spirit of the Cotonou Agreement seemed necessary. In a draft letter to the Togolese Republic the concerns of the Union were formulated as follows:

> The European Union wishes in particular to know what steps the Togolese Republic intends to take to initiate a genuine dialogue with the various traditional opposition parties and representatives of civil society so that a true democratic process can begin with a view to full restoration and application of democracy at all political levels. The European Union also wishes to discuss the situation as regards human rights and fundamental freedoms, including freedom of the media and freedom of expression, in your country in order to ascertain what the Togolese Government has done to improve the situation and what future steps are planned.[26]

The letter well illuminates how the values of democracy are dominating the agenda, and that they actually can have a concrete meaning; in this case, opposition parties, other civic organisations and the media must be allowed to function freely. There is certainly an element of altruism: the Union truly is concerned about the fate of ordinary people in the country. However, dialogue also seems to be a means of coercive power, in two different senses at least. Firstly, the EU seeks to promote dialogue *within* the borders of Togo. Dialogue from this perspective is an imperative that others should use in the same way as Europeans and their civil societies do. Secondly, there is an inherent risk that 'dialogue' gives the EU a possibility to dictate how its weak 'partner' should organise its government and, at the end of the day, life. This is, of course, something that the once colonised countries have always vehemently opposed.

When it comes to the issue of responsibility, the implications of the paradigm of dialogue appear clear, especially if we also take into account the notion of capacity building,[27] currently one of the most widely used slogans of development jargon and closely related to 'dialogue'. Dialogue implies that responsibilities need to be shared, and to the extent it is possible, the donors, including the EU, should simply help developing countries develop such capacities that would enable them to be responsible for themselves. It is primarily the community principle that seems to inform the Union: through dialogue we come to belong to the same community but in this community everyone has certain responsibilities. And this may make it easier for the EU to evade argumentation that emphasises the Europeans' historical and moral responsibilities towards the former colonies.

From development to security

The third and final trend discussed here is logically rather different from the other two, but it is also related to some essential aspects of them. It is a fairly recent trend, one that has clearly become stronger after the catastrophe of 9/11 and the subsequent 'war on terrorism'.[28] The point is that development policy has increasingly become just one element of the EU's global political agenda, the security policy agenda in particular. Development policy has thus lost its former fairly independent position. The logic that this shift is based on is obvious: underdevelopment, poverty, and desperation tend to breed violence, in the worst case terrorism, and there can be no development without security and political stability. More importantly, it has also been realised that poverty not only contributes to local security problems; it may materialise as insecurity far away, also in Europe.

Migration issues are a good example of this new trend. They were introduced to the ACP–EU framework only in the Cotonou agreement, after difficult negations in which the ACP strongly resisted the migration clause.[29] Also, in cooperation with the Mediterranean countries migration is one of the central issues. Another example of the holistic framework is the 2004 decision to fund the so-called African Peace Facility from the Commission's development budget: funds – 250 million euros – that were originally to be used for traditional development aid or projects were now directed to peace efforts in Africa.

This does not mean, of course, that the old development aid paradigm would have disappeared from the corridors and discourses of the EU. For example within the European Commission, particularly its DG Development, one has easily come across two competing views in recent years, the defenders of this holistic paradigm and the promoters of 'traditional development work'. The latter believe that political issues, security concerns in particular, may destroy the foundations of a genuine, equality-based dialogue with the development partners needed to achieve some sort of development. In their view, if self-interest or power politics assume a central role in development work, this may obscure the goals of the actual development efforts and thus be truly harmful from the perspective of the needy. This view is, however, clearly in a minority position at the moment, to the extent that one Commission employee interviewed for this chapter even argued that 'they've killed the EU's development policy'.

I believe that there is nothing wrong, in principle, in including security and broader political concerns into the development framework; it is hard to argue that security and development would *not* be mutually connected in one way or the other. Besides, security concerns may actually make it easier to politically justify increases in the total development aid budget. The recent decisions to increase global ODA, above all the decisions made in the Monterrey Summit of spring 2002, have been heavily influenced by the new security paradigm; the pessimism that had long prevailed with regard to development work has at least momentarily given way to a belief that by giving more material resources something really can be changed. In the enlarged EU this may be particularly important: otherwise there might be a risk that all material resources will be directed to the poor new member states. It is also obvious that from the perspective of policy coherence – the lack of which is widely regarded as the biggest handicap of the Union in developing countries – this holistic framework may yield positive results.[30]

On the other hand, one can indeed argue that the EU's security and political concerns should not be determined by those worries that Europeans themselves have. The categorical moral imperative of simply helping the poor should still be the fundamental objective – which does not mean that the idea of a long-term enlightened self-interest should be completely abandoned. The notion of responsibility is relevant here again. Whereas the old development paradigm was clearly informed by a historical and moral responsibility towards the people of developing countries, now the European leaders increasingly seem to justify their actions by emphasising their responsibility towards European citizens, too. A Europe-centred community principle prevails, not the beneficiary or contribution principles.

*   *   *

To end the first part of the chapter, a few concluding words with regard to the notion of responsibility are still needed. It is striking to notice that hardly any allusion to some sort of historical, one-way responsibility can be found in newer EU development documents. The justification of development work is primarily based on the belief that through cooperation we can create a better world for all of us, to create a true global community, global humanity; all the three trends analysed above actually imply this. Another issue that one comes across in many EU development sources is the proposition that the Union has the *capacity* to act and that it should therefore act; whether some other actor would have an even better capacity is seldom pondered upon. This argument is linked to the very essence and justification of the Union, to the expectations of the Union's active role in this new global community, a role that necessarily entails power but should nevertheless be clearly different from that of traditional power-political, 'realistic' actors. In the interviews this author conducted among EU officials and activists in the spring of 2004, this kind of global role for the Union was perceived as the most important future goal for the Union. There is a risk here, however: the meaningfulness of the EU project in itself may become more important than bringing about development in the world.

Images

The trends that we have described above form only one side of the picture of the Union as a development partner. A more complete picture requires that we have some sort of understanding of the images (or identities) that the EU has of itself as a development partner and that others have or could have of it. The current fate of the US shows how crucial this is: the negative image of that country in many corners of the world surely diminishes its global power. The EU may not be that different a case; its good intentions may be in vain, if the other side does not believe that the intentions truly are good. To illustrate, in a rather untraditional and maybe controversial manner, some of the real or potential images of the Union's global development agency, I will in the following exploit the power of metaphors and introduce four satirical human figures. It is obvious that these figures, cook, thief, body-builder and mistress, cannot capture all aspects of the EU as a development actor nor define the 'true' nature of it – it would surely be possible to find other equally relevant figures – but they do reveal some essential features of their complex, history-bound agency.

The Cook

Over the years, the EU and its predecessors, along with many other actors of the materially rich world, have introduced a great number of programmes and projects – recipes – for improving the situation in the developing countries and particularly in Africa. The rhetoric of democratic values and dialogue as we have described them above are just the newest recipes, whereas capacity building, ownership, market access, to name but a few of the beautiful current development slogans, can be seen as examples of their ingredients. The Cook thus seems a highly appropriate characterisation of the EU's development policy. The EU's complex nature in general, and in development policy in particular, can also bring one's thoughts to the metaphor of a Cook – or rather Cooks: too many Cooks seldom make a tasty soup.

There is no doubt that many of these recipes have been formulated with a genuine will to fill the stomachs of the hungry. In reality, however, the meals cooked with these recipes have not always proved successful. In Africa they may even have been counter-nutritive. For example, it has often been argued that development aid and trade preferences have only helped reproduce the dependency of the poor countries on donors and that aid projects have not been able to curb the structural problems of these countries but rather helped maintain them. From this perspective, the Cook would be a metaphor for those who are profoundly pessimistic towards development cooperation, for those who cynically remark: 'All this has been done time and again in the past, but nothing changed – why would something change now? Lomé did not bring about any long-lasting development, why would Cotonou?'

Ability to defy this type of criticism has been one of the essential characteristics of the EU-development Cook, however. In other words, optimism regarding the possibilities of outsiders to bring about development has continued to have the upper hand within the EU, and it continues to draft new recipes. In this respect, the EU–Cook appears to be a fairly naïve image, but essentially benevolent.

What kind of implications does this naïve image have from the perspective of responsibility, then? Primarily positive, I believe. There is no doubt that the EU and its member states are well aware of the fact that over the decades they have often failed in their development efforts; their recipes have been false. But in spite of this, they continue their activities. Why? We have in the previous part tried to answer this with the idea of a global community, a community where the Union also has a number of interests that it seeks to defend. But that may not be a sufficiently convincing explanation; in this respect, thinking in terms of the metaphor of a naïve Cook may actually show that there has been and there still is a real altruistic element in the Union's development efforts. Contribution and beneficiary principles still play a role.

The thief

A 'thief' can personify a number of very different characters. He can be a more or less miserable creature who steals merely to survive; there is not necessarily any difference between a beggar and this sort of thief. But a thief can also be a highly skilled professional, a well-mannered, handsome and unreservedly arrogant individual, whose sense of social morals is not particularly conventional and whose charm even the chief inspector cannot resist; these gentleman thieves are familiar from dozens of films. Finally, a thief can be a hero, someone who steals from the rich and gives to the poor, a Robin Hood.

Needless to say, Europeans have been, for centuries if not millennia, the master thieves of the world. The terms vary: from the crusades to imperialism and neo-colonialism. In many materially poor parts of the world, this negative image of Europeans created by the history of European exploitation is still a popular and also politically influential factor. In the African context, above all, the negative heritage of colonialism has been and is still mentioned in many an official document, often bitterly, whereas it is virtually impossible to find an official document praising the 'civilisation' introduced by the Europeans. The following example is from the Vision of the African Union (AU) of May 2004:

> What is needed [. . .] is for the African Union Commission to show the international community that Africa is not a dying continent, but one in which the logic of marginalization practiced over centuries of forced integration (including slave trade, colonization, neo-colonization, globalization) did not succeed in eroding its rich heritage of knowledge and expertise, both theoretical and practical. [. . .] That this material civilization

has survived despite attempts at cultural cannibalism and ethnic genocide should compel us to revisit the phenomenon of under-development and to resituate it in a wider historical perspective, thereby making it an episode limited in time and which can be overcome. Emphasis should be placed on History, History approached not as refuge but as a recourse, bearing in mind, in the words of Césaire, that the short cut to the future is through deeper knowledge of the past.[31]

Two points are particularly interesting in this extract. First, globalisation is listed as a new form of colonialism. This may be interpreted as a warning: if Europeans believe that they are building a new global community as we have tried to describe it earlier, it is precisely this global community that may be despised in the African continent. Indeed, there is a strong sense in many parts of the world that globalisation happens because the rich world wants it. Second, although the idea is clearly to resist the influences of the outside world and instead seek inspiration from the continent's own cultural heritage, it is the 'international community' that seems to be the primary target of argumentation.

This indicates that the Thiefness of Europe needs some elucidation. What is particularly interesting is the ambivalence with which Europeans have always been regarded by those who were once colonised by them. Europeans have been accused of the current misery, but European culture has been simultaneously admired and imitated; Europe is where the elites have been studying; and the new AU institutions have been designed after the EU's model. Especially in older African documents dealing with the continent's development problems, the basic message was 'stay out of my business, but come here and help me'.[32] From the donors' perspective, this contradiction has been, of course, *the* essential problem of all development work – a problem that the paradigms of values and dialogues can cleverly circumvent. In all, the most appropriate characterisation of Europe in the minds of many Africans is possibly that of a gentleman thief, this charming paradoxical image.

But to what extent has the European Union inherited (and will inherit) the image of a Thief from its member states, from the former colonisers? Two points are worth mentioning. First, it is obvious that people's views in developing countries vary a great deal. Some see the whole rich world, including all its major organisations, as part of the problem. For example, in most interviews that this author has made with African officials recently, the attitude was that 'we don't make any distinctions between the EU, France or the US . . . just give us access to your markets, and get rid of the dumping of agricultural products.' Many African civil society actors also seem to share this view. The lack of policy coherence thus seems to reproduce the negative historical image of Europe, now attached to the European Union. But there are also people who make clear distinctions between different global actors. One European Commission official interviewed in the spring of 2004 emphasised that in many African countries it is much easier to get access to state executives as an EU bureaucrat than as a representative of the US or some member state.

Secondly, at least in the past, the distinction between the EC/EU and its member states has also made cooperation more possible. Especially during the days of the Cold War, the EC was regarded as a fairly neutral actor not burdened by the past; its activities were not interpreted as a challenge to the newly won independence. For example, as Dieter Frisch mentions, in Ethiopia in the 1980s development cooperation took place primarily within the framework of the EC, while cooperation with France or Britain would not otherwise have been possible.[33] Even today, at least in Africa, the Union is widely understood as an international organisation rather than a state-like creature.

This leads to an important conclusion: being 'only' an international organisation may be a value in itself. If the EU assumes new state-like features, it may lose the specific space of manoeuvre that it has traditionally had.

The bodybuilder

For the 'bodybuilder', the size of his muscles is important in itself; he is not particularly concerned with what the muscles can be used for. The bodybuilder thus lives in the world of images; his self-respect correlates with the circumference of his biceps, for he believes that the shape of his body guarantees him a certain aura of respect in the eyes of the others. Yet the bodybuilder is never really happy with his musculature; the percentage of fat could always be lower, his buttocks firmer. And at the end of the day, the bodybuilder no longer knows why he actually is a bodybuilder.

Development policy has always been an important exercise for the bodybuilder–EU. It has guaranteed the Union a certain amount of goodwill, say, in global decision-making. In fact, given its long-standing special relationship with the ACP countries, the often used metaphor of an 'economic giant and political dwarf' – that is, the argument that the Union cannot use its power at the international stage to the extent its economic resources would make it possible[34] – has always been more than questionable. Particularly for France, the EU's development sector has been important. It has even been argued that the French have simply used EU development policy, its relative neutrality, as a means to retain their influence in the world. A telling anecdote is that until 1985 all development commissioners were French.

In the EU's current development rhetoric it is very easy indeed to find examples of how development policy still follows the logic of bodybuilding. One random example: the former President of the Commission Romano Prodi and the Commissioner for Development Cooperation Poul Nielson stated, after the Union had promised to raise the level of its ODA in conjunction with the 2002 Monterrey Summit 'Financing for Development', as follows: 'This achievement, which builds on the conclusions of the Gothenburg and Laeken European Councils, shows that Europe is not complacent about being the world's number one aid donor.'[35] The statement indicates that the image created through development activities is in fact more important than the actual fact, the increase of development funding. It is simply important to be a big actor, to have large biceps, even though this does not necessarily serve any clearly defined purpose. Moreover, one can also wonder whether the idea is to build up the internal legitimacy of the Union: being big as a development actor is thought to contribute to the emergence of a common European identity.

This brings us to the overall goals of the EU again. At the moment, if one talks to people working in the EU bodies, they will soon tell that one of the problems is that the Union no longer has a great, overarching goal. After the milestones of Maastricht, the introduction of the Monetary Union, and the big-bang enlargement of 2004, no goal of this magnitude seems visible – maybe not even possible (the Constitution is apparently not big enough). As we mentioned earlier, building a new kind of global role for the Union may be the only real goal that is perceived as significant enough. The preceding analysis suggests this goal should be accompanied by an important qualification: global role-seeking should not follow a self-expansive bodybuilder logic. That would not serve the ideal of a responsible international actor; a responsible actor knows why she does what she does – the bodybuilder does not know.

Finally, an extensive use of conditionality and even dialogue in the sense we have described it above can be seen from the perspective of the Bodybuilder metaphor. Conditionality is always a form of control, and although it is meant to serve the interests of the partner, this ability to control simultaneously increases the muscles of the actor. This is obviously the case with dialogue as well, at least when dialogue is the first step of conditionality.

The mistress

Whilst the three images described above are essentially images that others may have of the EU as a development partner, the image of a 'mistress' primarily reflects the EU's own understanding of itself. The word mistress has two distinct meanings. According to the new Oxford Dictionary of English, a mistress is 'a women in a position of authority and control' and 'a woman (other than a wife) having a sexual relationship with a married man'. Both these meanings are relevant here.

With regard to the latter meaning, the metaphor here refers to a purely *pragmatic* relationship between two persons or agencies. Apart from the satisfaction of bodily needs, there are very few mutual expectations in this relationship. The 'mistress' does not really expect anything from the Lover, no security, no economic benefits. There are no such deep emotions as in marriage, and no signs of any kind of humiliation. Instead, the relationship is based on mutual trust, on mutually accepted values and rules – or that is what the partners at least hope for.

Belief in this kind pragmatism appears to be widely spread in the Union's development circles. The argument goes as follows: 'Yes, we are well aware that our values may be foreign to our development partners and conditionality may in some cases be problematic, but let us look at the results, let us be pragmatic. We do bring development to many parts of the world; positive conditionality is indeed a useful means to make others change their undemocratic policies.' Moreover, this pragmatic Union is believed to be a very different actor than for example the US, the policies of which are essentially based on a certain ideology.

Pragmatism may certainly be positive in terms of responsibility: the EU has decided to act in the developing world, and act with a long time-span, because it simply realises that in the long run it is a very good investment; the question is simply of pragmatic, enlightened self-interest. Yet we can pose, once again, a critical question: because of this pragmatism, is there any room for development idealism in the sense it prevailed in the 1970s? Should not development work be based on idealism as well? Besides, pragmatism can easily turn into an ideology; anything can be said to be pragmatic, and therefore right and true. This is how pragmatism – *qua* effectiveness or accountability – is often used in the current neo-liberal paradigm.

The current EU development discourses also bring to mind the other definition of 'mistress'. They often convey a very strong awareness of the authority the Union has in many corners of the world, of the fact that it is indeed a success story in many respects. The sense of this authority, based on the Union's exemplary nature, can be read in many EU documents. The following two examples illuminate this well. In a speech in the African Union Summit in Maputo in July 2003, Romano Prodi remarked, among other things, that 'authority comes from deeds. It is not the result of declarations. This is our experience in the European Union. We offer it for your consideration.' In a speech on EU-Latin America relations, the External Affairs Commissioner of Prodi's Commission, Chris Patten made a similar point and tied it to the Union's overall democracy promotion and regionalisation paradigm:

> Regional integration is [. . .] important for stability and conflict prevention. Closer cooperation can be a catalyst for democracy and improved human rights. Regional integration provides opportunities for countries to become more active and influential partners in, rather than dependant spectators of, global, political, economic and social developments. And it allows countries to work more effectively together to combat global challenges such as narco-trafficking and drugs production.
> *Naturally I speak from the experience of the peace, stability and prosperity that Europe enjoys. This is to a large extent the result of our commitment to the goals of European integration.*[36]

It is not difficult to find a historical parallel for this pattern of argumentation. Needless to say, it does not differ logically from the originally French idea of *mission civilisatrice* or 'leading by example'. In this respect, the pragmatism of the 'mistress' easily includes an element of arrogance which may encounter opposition in the counterpart, at least in the long run.

Concluding remarks

We have above followed two rather different lines of argumentation. These have had, however, a number of common reference points. First of all, the different trends and images that we identified have sought to show how complex a phenomenon EU development policy is. The point has been that however much the EU promotes its fundamental values or seeks to apply a holistic framework on development, the way others understand these politics and policies is dependent on a number of potential interpretative frameworks. For example, the historical Thiefness of Europe, and the fact that the others are well aware that the Union also seeks to build its own body through its development activities, necessarily determine and often constrain the way in which the Union's values can make an influence in the outside world. In fact, it is hard to think about any other policy sector where the role of historically evolved images would be as significant as in development policy, in relations between the rich and the poor.

Another theme that we have repeatedly touched on is the thin line between altruism and self-interest. If we think about our four images, the 'cook' is clearly an altruistic figure, perhaps the 'mistress' as well, whereas the 'thief' and the 'bodybuilder' act only in the name of their own selfish interests. Values and dialogue are certainly meant to serve altruistic purposes, but there is always a risk that they in reality lead to the creation of a global community where the rich define the correct modes of life. What is obvious, however, is that in the world of politics, in the world of realism, altruism and self-interest must be combined in a fruitful manner, if we want to achieve development. It is not realistic to assume that aid flows to Africa would increase rapidly, if no element of (enlightened) self-interest were involved. If it makes tough political decisions possible, even the bodybuilder image may be useful.

We have also made a few other points that deserve to be repeated here. First, the image of the Union as an organisation rather than a state is something that the Union should not simply give away; in many instances an organisation may have more capacity to act than a state. Second, the prevailing pragmatism and, closely related to it, a holistic understanding of development, should not substitute idealism, idealism that is primarily connected with traditional development work. The idea of a pure moral responsibility is always relevant, for that is what we, the western world, should sense in relation to the poor of the humankind. Third, we have noted how crucial policy coherence is; it is of primary importance for creating trust between the Union and its development partners. From this perspective, it is hardly positive that it proved so easy to draft contradictory images of the EU as a development actor.

What does all this indicate in terms of the EU's possibilities to be and become a responsible global actor? The point must simply be repeated: the EU needs to understand and bear in mind the contradictory aspects of some of its activities and some of the principles it follows in its development policies, and that its image in the world may vary a great deal despite its own positive self-understanding. Awareness of these contradictions possibly creates a Union that can enter into dialogue with its partners in a modest, humble manner – humbleness is the starting point of responsibility, of finding out what the expectations of the partner actually are, be they legitimate or not. And true political dialogue as a means in itself should be further cultivated as one of the fundamental values of the Union for only it can make the liberal democratic values somehow meaningful.

Finally, we have noted that capacity and (global, West-dominated) community principles instead of beneficiary and contribution principles now seem to determine EU development policies. It must be emphasised, however, that the idea of a global community may actually be harmful from the perspective of development: it may lead to the evasion of responsibility. The question of who is, at the end of the day, guilty of underdevelopment may no longer be posed.

Notes

1. The author wishes to thank Elena Jurado, Matti Hautsalo, and Suvi Virkkunen for their excellent comments on earlier versions of this chapter.
2. These images have got their inspiration from Peter Greenaway's film, *The Cook, the Thief, His Wife and Her Lover*. The film was released in 1989, and was then interpreted as a powerful satire against the Thatcherite rule in Britain. The Cook was seen to embody the obedient civil servants of Thatcher's government; the Thief personified Thatcher's policies that humiliated the needy and promoted the greedy; the Wife was the suffering Britain; and the Lover the far too weak leftist and intellectual opposition.
3. See e.g. Roberts 2002.
4. As for empirical sources, the chapter is based on a wide range of EU documents related to the Union's development policy, on interviews with people working with development issues both within the EU and European NGOs, as well as documents produced in Africa, particularly under the auspices of the African Union and the New Partnership for Africa's Development (NEPAD).
5. The treaty also initiated the first European Development Fund (EDF), established in 1959. Most of the EC/EU development aid has been channelled through the EDF ever since. The EDF has not been part of the Community budget but has been managed directly by the Council of Ministers. Bringing the Fund into the Community budget – the so-called budgetisation – is currently a heatedly debated issue among those concerned with EU development policies.
6. The group of ACP countries was formally founded with the treaty of Georgetown, the capital of Guyana, on June 6, 1975. Before that the group of former colonies was called Associated African and Malagasy States (AAMS). See the list of ACP countries in Chapter 9, by O'Shaugnessy, note 6.

7. See e.g. Brown 2002; Kauranen & Vogt 2003.
8. Article 2 of Lomé I states: 'Products originating in the ACP States shall be imported into the Community free of customs duties and charges having equivalent effect, but the treatment applied to these products may not be more favourable than that applied by the Member States among themselves.'
9. The Lomé IV 2nd financial protocol (1995) was close to 13 billion ecus (euros), whereas the aid channelled to Eastern Europe and former Soviet Central Asia through *TACIS* and *PHARE* programmes amounted to some 9.5 billion ecus in 1995–1999 (www.eu.int). Mentally the latter form of aid seemed more important, however.
10. Cf. e.g. Hewitt and Whitemann 2004, 141.
11. The first EDF under Cotonou Convention for the period 2000–2005 amounts to 13.5 billion euros, i.e. a little more than that of the Lomé IV bis.
12. Hewitt and Whitemann (2004, 146). In addition to ACP cooperation, the Union cooperates with developing countries through a number of other cooperation agreements. In Asia, the aid programme is called ALA; in the Mediterranean region MEDA; and in CIS countries TACIS. There is reason to believe that the importance of these regional forms of cooperation will increase. In Africa, the establishment of the African Union (AU, 2002) and the New Partnership for Africa's Development (NEPAD; 2001) have created new forums for cooperation.
13. In addition to WTO compatibility, these agreements are based on three main principles: partnership, regional integration, and development. Article 36 of the Cotonou Agreement states: 'The Parties agree to conclude new World Trade Organisation (WTO) compatible trading arrangements, removing progressively barriers to trade between them and enhancing cooperation in all areas relevant to trade.' Indeed, the fact that EU development policies increasingly need to follow rules that have been set elsewhere – particularly within the UN system and the WTO (e.g. Millennium Development Goals; Doha) could have been listed as the fourth major recent trend, but because this is by no means solely a matter of the Union's own policies, this has not been done.
14. The European Community's Development Policy. 'Statement by the Council and the Commission', 10 November 2000, Article 7. Poverty eradication is also the main gain goal of the UN's Millennium Development Goals, which serve as the overall guideline for EU's policies. A new Commission proposal was introduced in the summer of 2005, after the bulk of this chapter had been finished (there was no need to revise the interpretations presented in the chapter). In that proposal, poverty reduction is clearly the most important objective: 'Halving poverty in the world between now and 2015 is the major challenge of the years to come.' 'Proposal for a Joint Declaration by the Council, the European Parliament and the Commission on the European Union Development Policy, "The European Consensus"', COM2005 311final.
15. Laclau 1996.
16. The Treaty was signed 'on the basis of complete equality between partners, close and continuing cooperation, in a spirit of international solidarity'.
17. The preamble of the Treaty notes, among other things, that the signatories are 'Resolved to establish a new model for relations between developed and developing States, compatible with the aspirations of the international community towards a more just and balanced economic order.' This is a direct reference to the Programme of Action on the Establishment of New International Economic Order (NIEO), approved by the United Nations in May 1974.

18. Appendix of the Lomé III Treaty, article 1.
19. The Treaty was amended in 1995, and Article 5 of this renewed version stated: 'Respect for human rights, democratic principles and the rule of law, which underpins relations between the ACP States and the Community and all provisions of the Convention, and governs the domestic and international policies of the Contracting Parties, shall constitute an essential element of this Convention.'
20. Cotonou Agreement, from Article 96.
21. In the field of international law, we could talk about a deformalisation process.
22. Badiou 1998. Social scientists and international lawyers have naturally given a great deal of attention to this problem of simple universalism and sought ways out from it. For example Klaus Günther (1999, 124) argues that 'A European approach to human rights has to make an argument out of the European history of human rights. What matters is not the foundation of the claim to universalism in moral principles and discourses but the insufficient sensitivity to negative experiences of human beings under the regime of well established and sufficiently justified human rights. Complex universalism of human rights has to be sensitive to the voices of those human beings who suffer from pain and humiliation, who live with fear, and who reject it as injustice.'
23. It is noteworthy that dialogue is originally a very republican idea; there must be a polis where a dialogue between equals is pursued. This interpretation of dialogue seems, however, less relevant in the context of EU development policies.
24. Cf. e.g. Olsson and Wohlgemuth 2003.
25. Ojanen 2004; Cutler 2001.
26. Annex to the Council of the European Union document 7286/04.
27. Capacity building is in fact a problematic notion, for it can easily be interpreted in 'imperialistic' terms: it implies that the other does not possess a capacity to act, she is immature, a child.
28. The trend has not emerged overnight, however. Already in the preamble of the renegotiated Lomé IV (Lomé IV bis) the following addition was made: 'Wishing to strengthen further their links through greater political dialogue and its extension to issues and problems of foreign policy and security and those of general interest and/or of common interest to a group of countries.'
29. Kauranen and Vogt 2003.
30. In recent years the Union has paid increasing attention to this problem, although the consistency principle was already introduced in the Treaty of Maastricht (Arts 2004, 105). There is now, for example, a special coherence unit within the DG Development. The draft constitution also explicitly talks about policy coherence. 'The Union shall ensure consistency between the different areas of its external action and these and its other policies. The Council and the Commission, assisted by the Union Minister for Foreign Affairs, shall ensure that consistency and shall cooperate to that effect.' Article III-292-3.
31. Vision of the African Union and Missions of the African Union Commission, March 2004, p. 31; printed from www.africa-union.org on 30 May 2004. The Organisation of African Unity, OAU, transformed into the AU in July 2002.
32. See e.g. the Lagos Plan of Action from 1980.
33. Frisch 1997.
34. E.g. Ginsberg 1999.
35. www.eu.int; visited on 26 April 2002.
36. Canning House Lecture 'EU–Latin America Relations' by Chris Patten, External Relations Commissioner, London, 4 February 2004; emphasis added.

Bibliography

Arts, Karin, 'The ACP in the European Union's network of regional relationships: still unique or just one in the crowd?', in Karin Arts and Anna K. Dickson (eds), *EU development cooperation. From model to symbol* (Manchester and New York: Manchester University Press, 2004).

Badiou, Alain, *L'éthique: Essai sur la conscience du mal* (Paris: Editions Hatier, 1998).

Brown, William, *The European Union and Africa: The Restructuring of North–South Relations* (London & New York: I.B.Tauris Publishers, 2002).

Cutler, Claire, 'Critical reflections on the Westphalian assumptions of international law and organization: a crisis of legitimacy', *Review of International Studies*, vol. 27 (2001), 133–50.

Frisch, Dieter, 'The political dimension of Lomé', *The Courier ACP–EU*. November–December 1997, 78–82.

Ginsberg, Roy, *The European Union in International Politics. Baptism by Fire* (Lanham *et al.*: Rowman & Littlefield Publishers, 2001).

Günther, Klaus, 'The Legacies of Injustice and Fear', in Philip Alston (ed.), *The EU and Human Rights* (Oxford: Oxford University Press, 1999).

Hewitt, Adrian and Kaye Whiteman, 'The Commission and development policy: bureaucratic politics in EU aid – from the Lomé leap forward to the difficulties of adapting to the twenty-first century', in Karin Arts and Anna K. Dickson (eds), *EU development cooperation. From model to symbol* (Manchester and New York: Manchester University Press, 2004).

Kauranen, Soile & Henri Vogt, *Piilopolitiikasta politiikkaan. Afrikan, Karibian ja Tyynenmeren valtioiden ja Euroopan unionin yhteistyön kehitys*. UPI Report 3/2003. The Finnish Institute of International Affairs.

Laclau, Ernesto, *Emancipation(s)* (London: Verso, 1996).

Ojanen, Julia, 'Selling Development? EC Development Policy as a field of private governance'. Paper presented at the SGIR Conference, The Hague 9–11 September 2004.

Olsson, Jan & Lennart Wohlgemuth (eds), *Dialogue in Pursuit of Development* (EGDI/ Almqvist & Wiksell International, 2003).

Roberts, Hugh, 'Dancing in the Dark: The European Union and the Algerian Drama', in Richard Gillespie and Richard Youngs (eds), *The European Union and Democracy Promotion. The Case of North Africa* (London & Portland Or: Frank Cass, 2002).

9
The European Union – A Responsible Trading Partner?

Terry O'Shaughnessy

Is the EU a responsible member of the world trading system? To answer, we need to address a second question: to whom should the EU be responsible when it weighs and adopts policies which have impacts on trading relations with other countries? This chapter sets out to answer these two questions by examining some (not all) areas of trade policy where the EU has found itself in conflict with its trading partners.

The answers to these two questions are interesting in their own right, but they may also help to illuminate more general features of the EU's role as a global actor. Using trade policy as a case study to do this has two advantages. The first derives from the fact that a common commercial policy is an exclusive Community competence rather than a national or a shared competence. This principle was established in the Treaty of Rome, so we have over forty years of evidence of EEC/EC/EU trade policy-making and implementation on which to draw.[1]

The second advantage of using external trade policy to evaluate whether the EU acts responsibly is that there is, arguably, more consensus about the effects of different trade policies on the interests of both EU citizens' welfare and the welfare of non-citizens than is the case in other spheres in which the EU is a global actor. To the extent that there is such a consensus about trade policy, it derives from relatively well-established principles about the relationship between trade liberalisation and economic welfare and from the fact that trading relations between the EU and other countries take place within a rule-based system under the auspices of the WTO. These principles and rules can be used to evaluate particular actions and policies of the EU and of other international actors in a way which is much more difficult in other policy areas.[2]

To whom, then, should the EU be responsible when it makes and implements its trade policies? There appear to be five possible answers, answers that will essentially guide the analyses of this chapter:

1. Those EU residents who would be adversely affected by moves towards freer trade and lower subsidies for the industries and enterprises in which

they work and lower prices for the factors of production which they own. Responsibilities to these EU residents will be labelled 'R1' in what follows.

2. EU residents generally. ('R2' responsibilities.)
3. Residents of former European colonies, particularly those which are classified as Developing Countries or Least Developed Countries ('R3').
4. The international trading system ('R4').
5. Residents of the world at large ('R5').

There is a clear connection between this question and these answers and the principles which are set out in Chapter 1 by Andras Szigeti and which provide a theoretical framework for this volume. Thus what we are describing here as the EU's 'R1 responsibilities' derive from the 'contribution principle', that is, those who cause a situation to arise have a duty to mitigate its harmful consequences. Or, to take another example, the EU's 'R3 responsibilities' could be seen as deriving from the 'beneficiary principle', if it is accepted that European countries have in the past benefited from colonial arrangements that have involved a loss or harm to these countries. (R3 responsibilities have also arisen as a result of the 'legitimate expectations' and 'consent' principles.) A third case might be the way in which the EU's 'R4 responsibilities' (to the international trading system) derive from the 'community principle', in that the EU is a major exporter and importer and a key World Trade Organisation member and, as such, has a responsibility to other WTO members and to the multilateral trading system as a whole. (R4 responsibilities also derive from the 'beneficiary principle' to the extent that the EU benefits from a rule-based trading system with a well-established mechanism for settling disputes.)

The list of these different responsibilities clearly raises some questions, too. Why, for example, distinguish between R1 and R2? There is clear evidence that EU policy-makers have often given more weight to losses or potential losses on the part of some residents than they have given to gains or potential gains on the part of others. An example of this is the McSharry reforms to the Common Agricultural Policy (CAP) in 1992. These reforms substituted direct payments to European farmers for the previous system of price support for farm products. Direct payments were made on the basis of historic yields and production entitlements, so their distribution was heavily skewed in favour of large arable producers in northern member states.[3] Entitlement was thus based on farmers' expectations of future income and not on the fact that the losers in this case constituted a particularly disadvantaged group. The same principle appears to be operating in the current WTO agriculture negotiations. In these negotiations the EU has adopted a position which is defensive of European farmers' interests even though a more liberal position could secure large benefits for European consumers (as well as for producers in exporting countries, including low-income exporters).[4]

When it comes to the matter of responsibilities to those who live outside the EU, there is evidence that the EU, member states and EU residents support giving assistance to poorer countries. This can take the form of official aid,[5] financial and in-kind aid provided by non-governmental organisations and private individuals, and by extending preferential treatment to such countries in trade matters. Examination of the countries benefiting from aid flows and from preferential trading arrangements suggest that particular responsibility is felt for the former European colonies which are members of the ACP (African, Caribbean and Pacific) group of countries, some (but not all) of which are classified as 'least developed countries'.[6]

A final distinction that the list above raises is between responsibilities to the international trading system and responsibilities to residents of the world at large. The distinction is important because it is by no means obvious that the international trading system as presently constituted – or even some ideal version of the system, following thoroughgoing trade liberalisation and institutional reform of the WTO – reflects the interests of residents of the world at large; if it did, the EU could meet its R5 responsibilities simply by meeting its R4 ones. To the extent that the international trading system falls short of providing the benefits which an ideal system could provide, there will be additional scope for conflict between R4 and R5 responsibilities.

As far as R4 responsibilities are concerned, these have always been expressed in forceful terms in EU documents. Moreover, the EU is, in a real sense, the creature of the international trading system, in that it was set up under the auspices of Article XXIV of the General Agreement on Tariffs and Trade (GATT). This article allowed for the formation of customs unions and free trade areas, even though these arrangements violated the key GATT principle of non-discrimination in trade matters. Since the histories of the EEC/EC/EU and of the GATT/WTO have long been bound together, it is perhaps unsurprising that the EU tends to act in ways which it believes will strengthen and legitimise the rule-based trading system centred on the WTO. Moreover, the EU, like the WTO, was created out of a series of torturously-arrived-at international agreements and, like the WTO, has developed an extensive jurisprudence. These institutional and cultural commonalities clearly play a role in explaining the EU's commitment to the WTO, to the rule-based trading system it oversees. The contrast to the policies of the United States is significant: the US tends to play a less active role in promoting the GATT/WTO institutions.[7]

Taking a global view: the EU's responsibilities to the world at large

Where does this leave R5 responsibilities? In other words, how should we think about claims on the EU by residents of the world at large? This is a large question, aspects of which other contributors to this volume have addressed; for our purposes here it is useful to confine attention to dimensions of people's welfare which may be influenced by trade policy. This comes down, in the end, to incomes, employment and consumption possibilities. If EU trade policy restrains incomes, restricts consumption possibilities and discourages employment in other countries, then residents of these countries arguably have a claim against the EU. Moreover, if they are poorer than EU residents, their claim, presumably, is stronger. The fact that the EU provides economic aid to and supports preferential trade access for poor non-EU countries shows that the existence of these responsibilities is accepted. But this leaves important measurement questions unanswered. In particular, what precisely should the EU care about when it decides about matters which will impact the economic welfare of non-EU residents? Also, to what extent is it legitimate to discriminate between different people living in different countries when making these decisions?

One way to approach this systematically is to posit a social welfare function for the EU defined over the utilities of all the world's residents:

$$W(u_{11}, u_{12}, \ldots, u_{1k}, \ldots; u_{21}, u_{22}, \ldots u_{2l}, \ldots; \ldots u_{im} \ldots)$$

where u_{im} is the utility of person m in country i. Now suppose that it is predicted that a trade liberalisation measure will increase the income of someone in country i (say, person k) while reducing the income of person l in country j. Suppose also that the fall in y_{jl} (the income of person l in country j) is less than the increase in y_{ik}, so that

$$\Delta y_{ik} = -\varphi \Delta y_{jl} \qquad \varphi < 1$$

(This will usually be the case for such a measure such as trade liberalisation, since the income gains to winners will be greater than the losses to losers.) To see whether the welfare gain is positive, a policy-maker would need judge whether:

$$\Delta W = \frac{\partial W}{\partial u_{ik}} \frac{\partial u_{ik}}{\partial y_{ik}} \Delta y_{ik} - \frac{\partial W}{\partial u_{jl}} \frac{\partial u_{jl}}{\partial y_{jl}} \Delta y_{jl} > 0$$

or whether

$$\frac{\partial W}{\partial u_{ik}} \frac{\partial u_{ik}}{\partial y_{ik}} > \frac{\partial W}{\partial u_{jl}} \frac{\partial u_{jl}}{\partial y_{jl}} \varphi$$

This is more likely to be satisfied if

(I)   the gainer's initial income is low, since her marginal utility of income is likely to be high;
(II) the gainer's initial level of utility is low, since the policy-maker is likely to give more weight to improving the utility of those with low initial utility; and
(III) φ is low.

But there is a troubling question raised by (II). To what extent will the weight the policy-maker places on person k in country i – that is $\partial W/\partial u_{ik}$ – depend only on this person's initial utility, rather than also on k, the country they reside in? If this weight is simply a (negative) function of u_{ik} irrespective of k, the policy-maker is treating all the world's residents alike. On the other hand, more weight could be given to residents of particular countries, so that

$$\frac{\partial W}{\partial u_{ik}} = \beta_k f(u_{ik})$$

with $\partial f(u_{ik})/\partial u_{ik}$ [<0] being the same across countries but with the 'country weights' (the β_k) differing between countries.

A policy-maker committed to non-discrimination between countries would be permitted to take into account incomes in different countries and the extent to which income changes can raise individuals' utilities. She would also be permitted to take into account the distribution of utilities across countries and, if she chose, give more weight to those whose utility is low. However, she would not be permitted to apply different 'weights' to those whose utilities were the same but who happen to reside in different countries.[8] This provides a criterion for judging whether a policy of apparently discriminating in favour of particular individuals or groups of individuals or countries should be seen as a way of meeting the EU's R5 responsibilities to residents of the world at large or as evidence of failure to meet these responsibilities by favouring special interests.

Case studies

In order to see how the EU meets its responsibilities in trade matters, it will be useful to examine briefly three areas of trade policy within which the EU has been active: disputes settlement, agricultural trade reform and trading relations with developing countries.

Disputes settlement

A major innovation that came with the replacement of the GATT by the WTO in 1994 was the creation of an effective disputes settlement procedure. Under the GATT, disputes could not be dealt with effectively, since it was possible for any contracting party to the GATT to block the establishment of a disputes panel or (if a panel was established but its report was unfavourable) to block the adoption of a panel report. In the WTO such vetos are not available to member countries since panel reports can only be blocked if all members of the Dispute Settlement Body (effectively the whole WTO membership) agree to do so.[9] As a consequence, a number of WTO members have become very active in using the disputes procedure. In particular, the

Table 9.1   WTO disputes brought by the US and EU, January 1995–October 2005

	1995	1996	1997	1998	1999	2000	2001	2002	2003	2004	2005 (to Oct)
Total	25	39	50	41	30	34	23	37	26	19	9
Brought by US	7 [3]	16 [3]	19 [8]	11 [8]	11 [4]	8 [1]	1 [1]	3 [1]	3 [1]	4 [2]	0 [0]
Brought by EU	2 [0]	6 [3]	14 [3]	16 [5]	6 [4]	6 [5]	3 [2]	3 [2]	4 [1]	5 [3]	2 [0]

Source: WTO website, accessed 1 November 2005.

Table 9.2   WTO disputes, January 1995–October 2005. Number of disputes launched by and launched against countries most heavily involved in the disputes settlement system

Complainant	Respondent										
	US	EC	Jap.	Bra.	Kor.	Mex.	Arg.	Aust.	India.	Can.	Other
US		32	6	5	6	6	4	4	4	4	12
EC	28		6	3	4	2	6	2	7	4	5
Japan	8		1							1	2
Brazil	7	7			1	2				3	2
Korea	7	3	1								1
Mexico	6	3									6
Argentina	2	2									3
India	6	5	1				1				3
Australia	2	2		1					1		1
Canada	12	7	1	1	1			1	1		1
Other	16	14		2	1	4	2	3	4	1	36

Source: WTO website, accessed 1 November 2005.

US and the EU have initiated a large number of disputes, as well as finding themselves to be respondents to a similarly large number of disputes. Between January 1995 and the end October 2005, a total of 333 disputes have been initiated, of which 83 were brought by the US and 67 by the EU. Table 9.1 shows the total number brought in each year, together with the numbers brought by the US and by the EU. (The number of disputes brought by the US and the EU *against each other* are shown in brackets in the appropriate rows of the table.)

In Table 9.2, which focuses on the most active users of the disputes settlement system, complainants are listed vertically in the first column and respondents are shown in successive columns across the table. From this table it is clear that both the EU and the US have each been involved in a number of disputes with most of the countries listed as both complainants and respondents, but

Table 9.3 WTO disputes, January 1995–October 2005. Number of disputes and share of world trade

	Total disputes as complainant	% of total disputes	Total disputes as respondent	% of total disputes	% share of world trade (2002)
US	83	23.8	94	26.9	18.6
EU	67	19.2	75	21.5	18.5
Japan	12	3.4	14	4.0	7.5
Brazil	22	6.3	13	3.7	1.1
Korea	12	3.4	13	3.7	3.1
Mexico	15	4.3	13	3.7	3.3
Argentina	7	2.0	15	4.3	0.4
India	16	4.6	17	4.9	1.0
Australia	7	2.0	10	2.9	1.4
Canada	25	7.2	13	3.7	4.8
Other	83	23.8	72	20.6	40.3

that these other pairs of countries have not, on the whole, been involved in mutual disputes (the exception is Brazil-Canada). What is also clear from Table 9.2 is that Japan has been involved in relatively few disputes, given its role in world trade.

To explore this issue further, Table 9.3 compares numbers of disputes with countries' share of world trade. Here Argentina, Australia, Brazil and India stand out as heavy users of the system while, as suggested, Japan is exceptional in the other direction. But what is also striking is that the US and the EU play a more prominent role in WTO disputes than their trade shares would lead us to expect. Even more striking are the data on bilateral disputes: EU/US bilateral trade is approximately 3.4 per cent of world trade, while EU/US disputes make up 16.8 per cent of all disputes.

In Table 9.4 the focus is on the EU as complainant and as respondent. Countries classified under 'Other' in Tables 9.2 and 9.3 are listed individually. What is striking here is the large number of cases in which countries appear in both columns.[10]

From these data it is clear that the EU is playing a very active – even a disproportionately active – role in the WTO's disputes settlement mechanism. Is this evidence of responsible behaviour, in that the EU is helping to establish the legitimacy of a rule-based international trading system? Or is this evidence of the fact that the EU is thought by its trading partners to be behaving irresponsibly by breaking too many trade rules (hence its role as a respondent) while using the mechanism to bully these same partners (though its role as a complainant)?

As far as the question of building the legitimacy of a rule-based trading system is concerned, the case can be made that using the system is better than not using it. This is especially so if the alternative to using the system is a

Table 9.4   WTO disputes, January 1995–October 2005. The EU as complainant and respondent

EU as complainant	EU as respondent	
US (28)	US (28 + 4 joint)	Guatemala (3 joint)
India (7)	Canada (7)	Honduras (3 joint)
Japan (6)	Brazil (7)	Peru (2)
Argentina (6)	India (5)	Chile (2)
Korea (4)	Thailand (4)	New Zealand (1)
Canada (4)	Korea (3)	Norway (1)
Chile (3)	Mexico (3 joint)	Panama (1 + 1 joint)
Brazil (3)	Argentina (2)	Uruguay (1)
Australia (2)	Australia (2)	Ecuador (1 joint)
Mexico (2)		
Indonesia (1)		
Pakistan (1)		

reversion to an older form of trade diplomacy which rested more directly on countries' economic and political power. Someone who accepted this case would take a favourable view of the EU's active role in the disputes settlement mechanism. However, this case rests on a characterisation of GATT/WTO evolution which has been disputed by some recent analyses. Thus Dunne questions, in a 2002 article, whether the GATT/WTO process involves a transition from 'power orientation' to 'rule orientation', a view he locates in the influential work of John Jackson from 1978. While Jackson's view is superficially plausible – in that influential parties such as the US and EU have lost GATT/WTO cases and have appeared to comply with adverse judgements – a careful examination of the historical record throws up a more complex picture. Dunne uses the *EU–Bananas* dispute[11] to make the case for a 'contextual' analysis (in contrast to Jackson's 'realist' view). According to Dunne, power orientation and rule orientation are 'symbiotic rather than mutually exclusive'.[12] Rules cannot constrain power or make asymmetries of power irrelevant. In his view, the international system is an environment in which 'power-orientated negotiations serve as the primary means of dispute settlement, rule-orientated regimes provide the yardsticks by which behaviour is measured, and the international community acts as the arbiter and enforcer of common norms.'[13]

Busch and Reinhardt also raise serious questions about the development of the GATT/WTO disputes settlement mechanism. Their focus is on one of the supposed benefits of a move to a more rule-based system: better access for developing countries. They point out that many observers felt that developing countries had been ill-served by GATT's diplomacy; these observers hoped and expected that matters would be better for developing countries under the WTO, precisely because of the latter's greater 'legalism'.[14] But historical experience has shown otherwise. Busch and Reinhart demonstrate this by examining 380 GATT/WTO disputes filed between 1 January 1980 and 31 December 2000. Of these, 154 occurred under WTO rules. The outcome of each dispute is classified in terms of (i) which party succeeded in having its interests served by the outcome of the dispute and (ii) when in the dispute settlement process this outcome emerged – they distinguish between disputes which were settled by consultation, those which were settled during panel deliberations in advance of a ruling, and those on which a panel ruled.[15] Using an ordered probit analysis, they show that disputes settlement under the WTO is more effective for developed countries but no better[16] for developing ones. Using the examples of India and Australia, two countries with similar GDPs in 2000 ($US460 billion in 1995 dollars) but very different GDP/capita figures ($459 and $23,837, respectively), Busch and Reinhardt estimate that India would have a 41 per cent chance of getting the average defendant to concede, while Australia's probability of success in identical circumstances is estimated to be 73 per cent.

Busch and Reinhardt provide an interesting explanation for their results. They believe that access to legal resources is a crucial advantage, but this advantage is greatest early in the disputes process when opponents are most likely to settle. Hence, they argue, providing legal resources to poorer countries during the later stage of a dispute (once a panel has been established) will not correct the imbalance between rich and poor countries. One suggestion they offer is to provide more assistance to poorer WTO members during the initial stages of a dispute, even though the overall impact of such assistance may not be very great. They conclude that 'the rule of law does not of itself guarantee efficient outcomes. For that, one also needs an adequate level of legal capacity and expertise to realise the full promise of such a system'.[17]

An implication of these more sceptical views about the benefits of a rule-based disputes mechanism following the establishment of the WTO in 1995 is that we should interpret the activities of large, rich players like the EU in a more power orientated way, even if this is not the way in which EU policy-makers would like to describe their actions. Of course, it is possible that analysts could reach different conclusions if they focused on different disputes; for example, it may be that *EU–Bananas* provides evidence which is unfavourable to the view that the EU acts responsibly within the WTO, but that this case is extreme and not typical. On the other hand, the fact that so few middle- and low-income WTO members have succeeded in holding the EU to account through the disputes settlement mechanism, while the EU has made such active use of this same mechanism to pursue its interests, suggest that a more sceptical view of the EU's role in the WTO is appropriate. Moreover, the EU's increased economic weight in the world trading system following the 2004 enlargement will increase the temptation to exploit the enhanced probability of winning disputes, especially against smaller and poorer opponents.

Agricultural trade reform

The aspects of its trade policy for which the EU is most often criticised are its approach to agricultural protection and its resistance to the liberalisation of world trade in agricultural products. Its stance on these issues was a major factor in preventing the Uruguay Round from securing substantial progress on agriculture. Since then, the WTO has been attempting to find a way to create a new basis for reform in this area, in the context of Article 13 of the Agreement on Agriculture adopted at the end of the Uruguay Round (the 'peace clause'). The peace clause exempted a range of government subsidies for agricultural goods from challenge under the disputes settlement mechanism. Initially to be in effect for six years, the peace clause was extended to nine years as part of the final Uruguay Round settlement.[18] This period expired on 31 December 2003 without the peace clause being renewed. This puts pressure on negotiators, especially those from WTO members whose subsidy regimes would be vulnerable to challenge (such as the EU's CAP), but so far to little effect.[19] Additional pressure is coming from developing countries, many of which see agricultural trade reform as an essential aspect of the Doha Development Round.[20] They are joined, on this issue, by a number of developed and middle-income agricultural producers in the Cairns group.[21] A number of these countries have liberalised their own agricultural sectors and believe that they would benefit from a more liberal international trading regime in agricultural products.[22]

The EU's reluctance to agree to a reduction in agricultural subsidies and an increase in market access for agricultural goods is usually explained in terms of the political influence of farming interests, especially those in temperate Europe, where the largest subsidies apply.[23] However, new factors are increasingly playing a role in agricultural policy, including food safety issues and environmental concerns.[24] These issues mean that a wider constituency than that made up of producer interests is becoming involved in this area of policy, but it is not clear whether this will reduce the effectiveness of producer lobbies. On the contrary, it is very possible that policy entrepreneurs will attempt to create coalitions involving producers, consumer interests and environmental activists around policies which will extend protection to agriculture, albeit with different justifications and through different mechanisms.[25]

In order to examine the issue of to whom EU policy is responsible, it is useful to compare two proposals for reform. The first comes from the OECD, and the second from two academic critics of the CAP, Carsten Daugbjerg and Alan Swinbank.[26] The OECD analysis is striking in its theoretical austerity. It relies entirely on traditional welfare economic justifications for intervention in markets: that is, the existence of externalities,[27] public goods or distributional concerns. In each case it argues that support for the agricultural sector as a whole or for particular products is likely to be a third-best policy. Even if the importance of positive externalities from rural activities can be established, a preferable policy would be to subsidise the activity directly.[28]

Similarly, if redistribution of income is desired, this will be best achieved by income transfers through the usual tax-benefit system,[29] rather than via subsidies to or protection of particular activities, such as farming. While the OECD analysis does not explicitly employ the 'mathematical' framework developed above, it would be consistent with such an approach to evaluating the welfare benefits of redistribution.[30]

Daugbjerg and Swinbank take a different approach. They favour the wholesale transformation of existing CAP subsidies into tradable bonds. These bonds would be given to existing agricultural producers in exchange for them foregoing subsidies, tariff support and other forms of protection. The bonds would pay an annual amount which reflects the value of the current level of agricultural protection received by each producer. Producers would then be free to produce agricultural output and trade this output within the EU or on the world market, with transactions on both markets being at similar prices.[31] Producers would also be free to sell any land they owned, though the prices they would receive for land would be well below current prices of agricultural land. The reason for this is that current land prices are inflated by the capitalised value of expected future subsidies. When the subsidies are permanently removed, land prices will fall to reflect this.

The advantage of the Daugbjerg-Swinbank plan is that it makes farmers no worse off while improving the welfare of consumers. The disadvantage is that the coupon payments on the bonds given to farmers would have to be raised by (distortionary) taxation. Daugbjerg and Swinbank envisage these payments continuing for ten or twenty years, possibly at a reducing rate.[32] Nevertheless, during this period, there will be a significant burden on taxpayers, though it will be no greater than the current burden of tax-financed subsidies. Taxpayers, of course, in their role as consumers, will benefit from being able to buy agricultural goods at world prices.

Despite the logic of their proposals, Daugbjerg and Swinbank are aware that they currently lack widespread political support, though they are optimistic about being able to build support in the future. Previous versions of their proposals were strongly opposed by agricultural producers. Given the fact that, under the plan, producers' incomes and wealth would be protected, this may be difficult to account for, though producers may have feared that making financial transfers to them in this transparent way would leave them vulnerable to a future decision to renege on coupon payments.[33] Daugbjerg and Swinbank believe that the current version of their plan may prove more attractive. One reason they put forward is that the CAP is no longer the only policy which holds the EU together. Another is that the 2004 EU expansion will increase the fiscal burden of the current CAP regime. Of course, this latter point raises the issue of whether farmers in the accession countries should be eligible for the bond scheme. This, in turn, is linked to the concept of producers' legitimate, historically evolved expectations which is key to the plan.

The difference between the OECD and Daugbjerg-Swinbank proposals is that the latter respects (and in fact guarantees to fulfil) the income expectations of current producers. A global (or EU-wide) welfare analysis would not do this. After all, the income expectations of other groups of producers, such as workers in declining manufacturing industries, are not guaranteed in this way (though individuals are protected from negative income shocks through the tax-benefit system). The only possible reasons for treating rural producers differently are (i) because they are particularly vulnerable to income shocks, or (ii) because the rest of society has a special responsibility to protect them from income shocks, or (iii) they are favourably placed to deploy political and ideological resources (their own and those of their allies) to protect their incomes. If careful analysis suggests that (i) and (ii) do not provide good explanations, we end up at (iii). In this case the conclusion surely is that a better policy would be to take a more global approach (or one based on an EU-wide welfare analysis) to income support, while addressing directly the political and ideological factors which have distorted policy outcomes in this area in the past.

Trading relations with developing countries

As noted above, the EU's trading relationships with developing countries have been greatly influenced by historical factors and especially by the history of European colonialism (see also Vogt's chapter). The ACP group of countries, most of which are former European colonies, were given special status under the Yaoundé (1963, 1969) and Lomé (1975, 1980, 1985, 1990) Conventions. In 2000 Lomé expired and was replaced by the Cotonou Agreement. The history of Yaoundé/Lomé/Cotonou provides useful insights into the way in which the EU has viewed its responsibilities to residents of countries (some of) its member states formerly colonised and which are today some of the poorest countries in the world.[34]

Both Lomé and Cotonou are products of their times. Lomé I was negotiated at a time when developing countries were seeking to promote what was described as a New International Economic Order. The ACP countries expressed their interests in a more self-confident way than they had previously and were, to some extent, treated as equals rather than as supplicants.[35] The EU felt itself able to offer non-reciprocated trade concessions and supported arrangements to stabilise some ACP countries' export earnings (the Stabex scheme). In doing so, the EU seemed to acknowledge a special responsibility to these countries and to accept that non-market mechanisms may sometimes produce welfare-enhancing outcomes.

By 2000 the political and ideological climate had changed dramatically. It was widely accepted that most development initiatives (including those associated with the Lomé process) had failed to improve the plight of the poorest in the ACP countries. The collapse of communism and the shift of both centre-right and centre-left political parties in Europe (and elsewhere) towards a more market-oriented stance (reflecting similar shifts in the research community and in international organisations), had a major impact on development thinking. At the same time, the EU's development focus was shifting to Eastern Europe, as were flows of aid. New concerns – particularly about migration into Europe – began to influence the EU's attitudes to events and policies in poor countries. Finally, the issue of Lomé's incompatibility with GATT/WTO rules had taken on new salience, given the EU's commitment to a rule-based international order.[36]

The EU's stance during the Cotonou negotiations reflected these changes but it also exposed serious differences between interest groups within Europe which were sometimes expressed by different member states. For example, Forward distinguishes four key players, Germany, France, 'the Nordics' (this group includes the Netherlands) and the UK, and various possible outcomes.[37] These ranged from extending the ACP countries' privileges to all developing countries (advocated by Germany and the Nordics) to merely enhancing existing Lomé provisions (the French position). Forward's players also differed over the weight they gave to WTO compatibility and over how important it was to reach an agreement on the EU's negotiating mandate.

The outcome was a new framework within which relationships between the EU and the developing world have still to be worked out, but within which certain patterns are already clear. The most significant break with the past is that Cotonou introduces what Arts describes as 'drastic differentiation' among the various ACP states.[38] Whereas Lomé's benefits were, in principle, available to all ACP countries, under Cotonou differentiation is a key feature. In particular, maximum benefit will only be available to the 40 least developed countries listed above in footnote 5. The other ACP countries will be strongly encouraged to negotiate new agreements known as Economic Partnership Agreements (EPAs) with the EU. The EU's intention is that the non-LDC ACP countries should form regional groups and these groups should enter into an EPA with the EU. Crucially, EPAs will be free trade agreements based on reciprocal trade concessions. In this, they differ from the Lomé arrangements they replace, since under Lomé the concessions granted to ACP countries did not require reciprocal rights of access for EU exports to these countries. As free trade agreements they are designed to be GATT/WTO compatible under Article XXIV of GATT 1994 and the Uruguay Round Understanding of that Article.

Many ACP countries doubt the benefits of taking the EPA route, and they are probably right to be sceptical. Analysis of the likely impact of an EPA involving Kenya, Tanzania and Uganda (the East African Cooperation countries) carried out by Milner, Morrissey and McKay suggests that the welfare effects (excluding the impact of lost tariff revenue) are likely to be negative for Tanzania and Kenya and only slightly positive for Uganda. The negative impact on Tanzania arises because the country shifts its demand for imports away from more efficient producers in the rest of the world and towards less efficient EU producers. Even though Tanzanian consumers benefit from the fact that they no longer have to pay tariffs on these imports, trade diversion towards the EU is welfare reducing. (The effect in Uganda differs due to a different pattern of trade in the pre-EPA situation.) Kenya suffers because its exports to Tanzania and Uganda fall as a result of more intense competition from EU exports to these countries. If we add in the effect of lost tariff revenue, the assessment is even bleaker.[39]

The EU's proposals for regional EPAs also presents the less developed ACP countries with a dilemma. Several potential EPAs contain both LDCs and non-LDCs. For example, in the East African case examined by Milner, Morrissey and McKay, Uganda and Tanzania are classified as LDCs but Kenya is not.[40] Should LDCs join more developed ACP countries in regional EPAs or should they hang on to their privileged non-reciprocal access to the EU market and forego the benefits (assuming they are potential Ugandas rather than Tanzanias) of belonging to an EPA? It is hard to see how less developed members of the ACP group could make informed decisions about this, given that calculating the benefits and costs joining an EPA is a difficult, data-intensive task which inevitably rests on many assumptions about future domestic and international developments about which even well-informed observers are uncertain.[41]

Compounding these uncertainties are those arising from the fact that it is very difficult to predict the outcome of the Doha Round of multilateral trade negotiations. ACP countries have not played a prominent role so far in these negotiations though Tanzania and Zimbabwe both joined the G20, led by Brazil, South Africa, India and China.[42] The G20 emerged as a major player in Cancún meeting in September 2003 and its key members are likely to play a pivotal role in the WTO negotiations during the later stages of the Doha Round, and beyond. However it is unclear how successful they will be in maintaining the coherence of the G20 and in attracting new members. Some ACP countries may find the stance adopted by Brazil, South Africa, India and China attractive and may come to see a possibly reconstituted G20 as a useful counterbalance to the EU. The EU, on the other hand, would certainly see this development as threatening. It may calculate that on some WTO issues the ACP countries (or at least those that retain non-reciprocal trading privileges with the EU) are its natural allies. As such these countries may offer the EU some support in a series of difficult negotiations where the EU's inflexible negotiating mandate means that opponents are growing in number and becoming more impatient and potential friends are few. In the light of these considerations, ACP defections to a reconstituted G20 would be very unwelcome.[43] In fact, the EU may well find itself making concessions to some ACP countries in order to reduce the probability of its own isolation in current and future multilateral negotiations. However, these concessions would not, of themselves, provide evidence that the EU was putting particular weight on its responsibilities to these ACP countries – what we have defined above as its 'R3' responsibilities. Recent developments in trade policy towards developing countries suggest that the EU has placed less weight on these responsibilities than it has on achieving WTO-compliance in its trading relations with these countries and on seeking an outcome in wider WTO negotiations which gives most weight to its own agricultural interests. The Union's policy has thus been effectively driven by a combination of R1 and R4 responsibilities.

Conclusion

In this chapter we have examined to what extent the EU has behaved responsibly when it has made and implemented its trade policies. In order to do so we first asked: *to whom* should the EU be responsible in these matters (especially given its capacity within and commitment to the international trading system and the expectations it has more or less consciously sought to raise in the outside world)? We identified five possible answers to this question by distinguishing the EU's responsibilities to (i) EU residents who are likely to lose from changes in trade policy ('R1 responsibilities'); (ii) EU residents generally ('R2'); (iii) residents of former colonies, especially those classified as least developed countries ('R3'); (iv) the international trading system ('R4') and (v) residents of the world at large ('R5'). With respect to this last set of responsibilities, we have shown that some apparent discrimination towards particular individuals or groups may be justified and that the degree of discrimination will depend on the policy instrument being employed. We illustrated this by comparing the impact of trade reforms with the impact of tax-financed aid and argued that the EU should be more willing to take an R5 view when it is contemplating trade reform than when it is considering an increase in its aid budget.

The case studies we have examined show that the EU rarely acts in the way such a disinterested 'R5' stance requires. Instead, at different times the EU appears to take one of its R1-R4 responsibilities most seriously, at the expense of its other responsibilities. For example, in its current stance on agricultural trade reform in the Doha Round the EU is giving more weight to its R1 responsibilities (in this case, to farming interests) than to its responsibilities to EU consumers (R2), to the ACP countries (R3) or to the integrity of the WTO system itself (R4). The EU's position is also at odds with the welfarist stance adopted by, for example, the OECD which sees itself able (at least on this issue) to adopt an 'R5' stance. On other issues other responsibilities are given salience. For reasons that we can well understand, the EU does act as if it has a particular responsibility to a rule-based international trading system ('R4'). It promotes and uses the WTO mechanisms in trade disputes and places significant weight on acting in a WTO-compatible way, even when this involves disappointing the expectations and acting against the interests of, for example, citizens of the ACP countries.

What we have not done is provide an ordering of these responsibilities in either a positive or a normative sense. In other words we have not claimed that R1 responsibilities *will* always trump, say, R2 responsibilities (though they often have). Nor are we claiming that, say, R3 or R5 responsibilities *should* always trump, say, R4 responsibilities (though perhaps they should have in the Cotonou case). What we have provided is a framework for understanding the various responsibilities the EU acknowledges in the arena of trade policy. The fact that the EU has accepted that it has responsibilities along all these dimensions means that arguments about acting responsibly in trade matters sometimes have force and practical effect; this is the positive dimension of the analysis we have provided. But the fact that the EU has acknowledged that it has these responsibilities also means that other actors, whether individuals, groups or states, can hold the EU to account for its actions in this arena. This introduces an irreducibly normative dimension into the analysis of trade policy.

Notes

1. As Eeckhout (2004, 347) puts it: 'The common commercial policy is clearly the EU's most developed external policy.'
2. The contrast drawn in this paragraph between trade policy and other policy areas should not be overstated. For a start, there are some critics of trade liberalisation and of the WTO who would reject the consensus view I am appealing to here. On the other side, there are principles and international rules pertaining to these other policy areas which may be deployed in a successful normative analysis – in fact, several of my fellow contributors to this volume are doing just that. Nevertheless, it remains true that it is easier to appeal to agreed principles and rules when it comes to trade policy than it is in these other areas.
3. Daugbjerg and Swinbank 2004, 101.
4. WTO, 2004 provides a summary of the negotiations, as of 20 April 2004. According to one study of the effects of agricultural trade liberalisation, a 50% cut in agricultural support across the world would lead to over half the total benefit ($28.3 bn a year out of a total of $53.2 bn) accruing to the EU. See Freeman *et al*. 2000, 2.
5. In 2003 EU member countries' net official development assistance totalled $36.8 bn, or 0.35% of GNI. In addition, a further $8.1 bn was provided by the EC, which brought the ODA/GNI ratio to 0.43%. This compares with 0.14% for the US, 0.20% for Japan, 0.23% for New Zealand, 0.25% for Australia and 0.92% for Norway. Source: http://www.oecd.org/dataoecd/57/30/35320618.pdf, accessed 1 November 2005.
6. The least-developed ACP States are Angola, Benin, Burkina Faso, Burundi, Republic of Cape Verde, Central African Republic, Chad, the Comoros, Democratic Republic of the Congo, Djibouti, Ethiopia, Eritrea, the Gambia, Guinea, Guinea-Bissau, Equatorial Guinea, Haiti, Kiribati, Lesotho, Liberia, Malawi, Mali, Mauritania, Madagascar, Mozambique, Niger, Rwanda, Samoa, São Tome and Principe, Sierra Leone, the Solomon Islands, Somalia, Sudan, Tanzania, Timor Leste, Tuvalu, Togo, Uganda, Vanuatu, Zambia. ACP States which are not classified as 'least developed' are Antigua and Barbuda, the Bahamas, Barbados, Belize, Botswana, Cameroon, Congo (Brazzaville), the Cook Islands, the Ivory Coast, Dominica, the Dominican Republic,

Fiji, Gabon, Ghana, Grenada, Guyana, Jamaica, Kenya, the Marshall Islands, Mauritius, Micronesia (Federated States of), Namibia, Nauru, Nigeria, Niue, Palau, Papua New Guinea, St Kitts and Nevis, St Lucia, St Vincent and the Grenadines, Senegal, the Seychelles, South Africa, Surinam, Swaziland, Tonga, Trinidad and Tobago, Zimbabwe.

7. See e.g. Woolcock 2000, 374.
8. This analysis of non-discrimination in trade policy reform can be adapted to the analysis of official aid. Aid is funded by taxation in donor countries and such taxation (in common with taxation for all other purposes) will be, to some extent, distortionary. This means that the income loss to the taxpayer in the donor country will be greater than the income gain to recipients. (This is in addition to administration costs in both countries and other inefficiencies associated with the distribution of aid.). If the distortionary effect of taxation in the donor country is captured by using a value of φ which is *greater than one* by the appropriate amount, an analysis similar to that in the text provides a characterisation of optimal non-discriminatory aid. It is clear that an income gain to a poor country which results from trade liberalisation ($\varphi < 1$) is much more likely to pass the policy-maker's test for a welfare improvement than would a policy based on aid ($\varphi > 1$).
9. Woolcock 2000, 387.
10. Nine countries appear in both columns out of a total of twelve in column one. Eighteen countries are listed in column two but if we exclude those which have not brought individual disputes but were involved only in the joint *EU–Bananas* disputes (DS16, DS27 and DS158), the number of countries in column two falls to fifteen.
11. On *EU–Bananas,* see Ierley 2002 and Badinger *et al.* 2002.
12. Dunne 2002, 331.
13. Ibid., 342.
14. Busch and Reinhardt 2003, 719.
15. In their sample, a large proportion (58%) of WTO era disputes were resolved or dropped before a panel decision was obtained.
16. Or at least not *significantly* better, in the sense that, for a developing country, there is substantial overlap in the 90 per cent confidence intervals for the estimated probabilities of 'winning' in the GATT and WTO eras. For developed countries, the probability of winning did rise significantly, from 40% to 70%, with no overlap of the 90 per cent confidence intervals.
17. Ibid., 734.
18. Morgan and Goh 2003, 977.
19. WTO 2004. See also Landau 2001 and O'Connor 2003.
20. The collapse of the Cancún Conference in September 2003 was, in large part, the consequence of the failure to meet developing countries' demands for progress on agricultural subsidies and market access for their agricultural products.
21. Argentina, Australia, Bolivia, Brazil, Canada, Chile, Colombia, Costa Rica, Guatemala, Indonesia, Malaysia, New Zealand, Paraguay, the Philippines, South Africa, Thailand and Uruguay.
22. For an Australian analysis of the benefits of agricultural trade liberalisation, see Freeman *et al.* 2000.
23. Ackrill 2000; Gaisford and Kerr 2001.
24. Skogstad 2001; Roederer-Rynning 2003.
25. For a sceptical view of the benefits of providing environmental public goods through agricultural subsidies, see OECD 2002.

26. OECD 2002; Daugbjerg and Swinbank 2004.
27. 'Externalities' are benefits or costs which are by-products of the production or consumption decisions, but for which there is no separate market. For example, a pleasant countryside may be a by-product of some farming activities; this would be a positive externality. (Negative externalities, such as pollution, may also be generated in agriculture.) Externalities lead to the mis-allocation of resources. The best way to deal with externalities would be for beneficiaries to pay for the benefits they receive (in the case of positive externalities) and for those harmed to be compensated (in the case of negative externalities). Usually this is not possible, in which a case a 'second best' outcome would be to subsidise production of the benefit. Less efficient still (hence 'third best') would be to subsidise the product of which the externality is a by-product.
28. This is a second-best policy because the subsidies will have to be raised by distortionary taxation on incomes or expenditure in the rest of the economy. It is only when policy-makers have a non-distortionary (lump-sum) tax available that the first-best solution (of paying an optimal subsidy for the activity) can be implemented. Given policy-makers' incomplete information about residents' characteristics (such as their endowments of skill and of other resources, and their preferences) non-distortionary taxation is never available in practice, so the second-best outcome is the best we can hope for.
29. Again, this will be a second-best outcome, due to the distortionary effect of the taxation required to provide income transfers and the disincentive effects of the resulting benefit payments.
30. Note that the account of redistribution provided in the first section of this chapter is couched in terms of global welfare concerns, whereas the context of the OECD's discussion is a national level analysis.
31. Prices will not be identical because of transport costs, possible price premia on freshness and possible consumer preferences for locally-produced goods. Naturally, many agricultural products currently subsidised under the CAP would not be produced at world prices, so the scale and composition of farming activity would change dramatically, though this should not be of concern to policy-makers.
32. Daugbjerg and Swinbank 2004, 110.
33. The bonds created for this scheme would trade on the same markets as other government liabilities, so it is not clear why the fear of default on the part of government would be any greater for these bonds than it is for other government bonds.
34. See Lister 1997, 1998.
35. Clapham 1996, 99; Hurt 2003, 162.
36. GATT allowed for preferential trade regimes with developing countries where all developing countries are treated alike. Lomé discriminated between ACP countries and others and required a waiver from the GATT/WTO.
37. Forward 2001.
38. Arts 2003, 99.
39. Milner *et al.* 2005. Low income countries typically raise over a quarter of total tax revenue from taxes on international trade. Tariff revenue as a share of GDP has tended to fall over the past quarter century as some trade liberalisation measures have taken effect, but other revenue sources have not expanded sufficiently to compensate. See Baunsgaard and Keen 2004.
40. Burundi and Rwanda (both LDCs) have attended meetings of the East African Cooperation group and could ultimately join.
41. A number of multilateral organisations, NGOs and research institutes provide technical assistance to ACP countries involved in EPA negotiations. See, for example,

the UN Economic Commission for Africa (www.uneca.org), the International Centre for Trade and Sustainable Development (www.ictsd.org) and Stevens and Kennan 2005. Nevertheless, the uncertainties referred to in the text remain.

42. Cuba is a member of G20 and in December 2000 was admitted to the ACP Group. However, Cuba is not a signatory of the Cotonou Agreement, which is why it is not listed in footnote 5 above.

43. There may be an analogous tension in the relationships between the United States and those Latin American countries that supported the G20 position in Cancun. Oxfam (2003) claims that a number of these countries soon afterwards came under 'unprecedented pressure' to withdraw from the G20 and to support instead the US's initiative for a Free Trade Area of the Americas (FTAA).

Bibliography

Ackrill, Robert, 'CAP Reform 1999: A Crisis in the Making?', *Journal of Common Market Studies*, vol. 38, no. 2 (2000).

Arts, Karen, 'ACP–EU Relations in a New Era: The Cotonou Agreement', *Common Market Law Review*, vol. 40, no. 2 (2003).

Badinger, Harald, Fritz Breuss and Bernhard Mahlberg, 'Welfare Effects of the EU's Common Organization of the Market in Bananas for EU Member States', *Journal of Common Market Studies*, vol. 40, no. 3 (2002).

Baunsgaard, Thomas and Michael Keen, *Tax Revenue And (Or?) Trade Liberalization* (Washington: Fiscal Affairs Department, International Monetary Fund, 2004).

Busch, Marc and Eric Reinhardt, 'Developing Countries and the General Agreement on Tariffs and Trade/World Trade Organization Dispute Settlement', *Journal of World Trade*, vol. 37, no. 4 (2003).

Clapham, Christopher, *Africa and the International System: The Politics of State Survival* (Cambridge: Cambridge University Press, 1996).

Daugbjerg, Carsten and Alan Swinbank, 'The CAP and Eu Enlargement: Prospects for an Alternative Strategy to Avoid the Lock-in of CAP Support,' *Journal of Common Market Studies*, vol. 42, no. 1 (2004).

Dunne III, Matthew, 'Redefining power orientation: A reassessment of Jackson's paradigm in light of asymmetries of power, negotiation, and compliance in the GATT/WTO disputes settlement system', *Law and Policy in International Business*, vol. 34, no. 1 (2002).

Eeckhout, Piet, *External Relations of the European Union – Legal and Constitutional Foundations* (Oxford: Oxford University Press, 2004).

Forward, Genevra, 'The Road to Cotonou: Negotiating a Successor to Lomé', *Journal of Common Market Studies*, vol. 39, no. 3 (2001).

Freeman, Fran, Jane Mélanie, Ivan Roberts, David Vanzetti, Apelu Tielu and Benjamin Beutre, *The Impact of Agricultural Trade Liberalisation on Developing Countries*, ABARE Research Report 2000.06 (Canberra: Australian Bureau of Agricultural and Resource Economics, 2000).

Gaisford, James and William Kerr, *Deadlock in Geneva: The Battle over Export Subsidies in Agriculture*, Department of Economics Discussion Paper Series no. 2001-07 (Calgary: University of Calgary, 2001).

Hurt, Stephen, 'Cooperation and coercion? The Cotonou Agreement between the European Union and ACP States and the end of the Lomé Convention', *Third World Quarterly*, vol. 24, no. 1 (2003).

Ierley, Douglas, 'Defining the factors that influence developing countries compliance with and participation in the WTO dispute settlement system: another look at the dispute over bananas', *Law and Policy in International Business*, vol. 33, no. 4 (2002).

Jackson, John, 'The Crumbling Institutions of the Liberal Trade System', *Journal of World Trade*, vol. 12, no. 2 (1978).

Landau, Alice, 'The Agricultural Negotiations in the WTO: The Same Old Story?', *Journal of Common Market Studies*, vol. 39, no. 5 (2001).

Lister, Marjorie, *The European Union and the South: Relations with Developing Countries* (London and New York: Routledge, 1997).

Lister, Marjorie (ed.), *European Union Development Policy* (London and New York: Macmillan, 1998).

Milner, Chris, Oliver Morrissey and Andrew McKay, 'Some Simple Analytics of the Trade and Welfare Effects of Economic Partnership Agreements', *Journal of African Economies*, vol. 14, no. 3 (2005).

Morgan, David and Gavin Goh, 'Peace in Our Time? An Analysis of Article 13 of the Agreement on Agriculture', *Journal of World Trade*, vol. 37, no. 5 (2003).

O'Connor, Bernard, 'A Note on the Need for More Clarity in the World Trade Organization Agreement on Agriculture', *Journal of World Trade*, vol. 37, no. 5 (2003).

OECD, *Agricultural Policies in OECD Countries: A Positive Reform Agenda* (Paris: OECD, 2002).

Oxfam, *From Cancun to Miami: The FTAA Threat to Development in the Hemisphere* (Oxford: Oxfam, 2003).

Roederer-Rynning, Christilla, 'From "Talking Shop" to "Working Parliament?" The European Parliament and Agricultural Change', *Journal of Common Market Studies*, vol. 41, no. 1 (2003).

Skogstad, Grace, 'The WTO and Food Safety Regulatory Policy Innovation in the European Union', *Journal of Common Market Studies*, vol. 39, no. 3 (2001).

Stevens, Christopher and Jane Kennan, *Preparing for Economic Partnership Agreements: Trade Analysis Handbook* (Brighton: University of Sussex Institute of Development Studies, 2005).

Woolcock, Stephen, 'European Trade Policy', in Helen Wallace and William Wallace, *Policy-Making in the European Union*, 4th edn (Oxford: Oxford University Press, 2000).

WTO, *WTO Agriculture Negotiations: The issues, and Where We Are Now* (Updated 1 December, 2004) at www.wto.org/english/tradtop_e/agric_e/agnegs_bkgrnd_e.pdf

10
Citizens' Perceptions of the EU as a Global Actor

Joakim Ekman[1]

Public opinion generally defines the acceptable boundaries of politics, and stakes out the space within which political elites can resolve controversies.[2] In the context of this chapter, the crucial issue is in what ways public opinion constrains or shapes the possibilities to develop the global agency of the EU. The questions posed are thus: What are people's general attitudes towards the EU as a global political actor? Do they believe that it is the responsibility of the EU to get involved in world affairs? And if they do, of what kind should this involvement be? Ultimately, do today's Europeans somehow envisage a normatively conscious – and therefore responsible – global agency for the Union?

It is worth noting that people's views have been to a large extent neglected in the literature on the external affairs of the EU, although the theme has generated a great deal of scholarly interest in recent years.[3] One can even wonder whether this neglect has indirectly helped reproduce the democratic deficit of the Union – external affairs have remained a particularly elite-driven sector of Union policies. The point this chapter wants to make, then, is that whatever the future form of the Union, it should not be constructed without a proper anchorage to the views of 'ordinary' citizens; only this can guarantee the legitimacy of the entire integration project in the long run.

The following analyses are based on the major European cross-national public opinion surveys, the *Eurobarometers* and the *Candidate Countries Eurobarometers* in particular. In such a short text as the present one, it is of course impossible to exploit the total empirical wealth of these materials, but it has not been the idea either: the aim has simply been to provide an overview of public attitudes to the emerging global role of the European Union and to do this in the context of the themes that have been raised in the preceding chapters. The findings of the chapter are thus somewhat sketchy or snapshot-like – also because surveys are always contingent upon the historical situation in which they are conducted. What is particularly important with these survey materials is that they make cross-country comparisons possible. As will be seen, it is by no means self-evident that people across the European continent hold similar attitudes to the EU's global agency.

Pointing out some of these differences is one of the sub-aims of the ensuing investigation.

The chapter breaks down into four sections, each of which focuses on a different external policy field of the EU. The first and most extensive section deals with the notion of a Common Foreign and Security Policy. The second section reviews EU citizens attitudes to the US and transatlantic relations, while enlargement and the borders of the EU is the topic of the third section. The fourth section deals with globalisation and development aid. In the conclusion, the main argument – the fact that there indeed is a great deal of public support for an internationally active European Union – is put into the perspective of the normative framework of this book.

*   *   *

Before we turn to the analysis of people's attitudes towards the EU's role in international politics, we need to take a quick view of what they think about the process of European integration in general. Needless to say, these general views are in one way or the other related to the public support for EU external affairs, although – and this is what we are interested in – not necessarily in any straightforward manner.

In Figure 10.1, we have summarised generalised public opposition to EU membership in the old member states between 1991 and 2004, drawing on the pooled data of standard *Eurobarometer* surveys, and in the new member states and the candidate countries between 2001 and 2004, based on the *Candidate Countries Eurobarometer*. All these surveys have had approximately one thousand respondents per year in each country under scrutiny, so that we speak of very respectable 'N's indeed. Here the specific question posed to the respondents reads: 'Generally speaking, do you think that our country's membership of the EC/EU is [or will be] a good thing, a bad thing, or neither good nor bad?' In Figure 10.1, only the percentages for 'a bad thing' are shown.

The figure shows unambiguously that *overall*, the European integration has been accepted by a clear majority of people in most European countries. The geographical pattern that emerges is quite distinct, however, and there also seems to be, albeit to a lesser extent, a visible cultural, that is, Protestant-Catholic, dimension. Among the 15 old member states, the Eurofriendly group include the Benelux countries and Southern Europe (Italy, Spain, Portugal, and Greece) alongside with Ireland and the six counties of Ulster (Northern Ireland). Germany and France could perhaps be included in the pro-EU camp as well. The sceptical camp comprises non-continental Europe: Great Britain and the Nordic countries (Denmark, Sweden, Norway, and Finland), alongside with Austria.

The historical experiences of integration also seem to matter. Austria, Sweden and Finland became members only in 1995. Denmark and the UK have admittedly been members for a longer period of time, since 1973, but these two countries have always figured as outspoken EU sceptics; after 1995

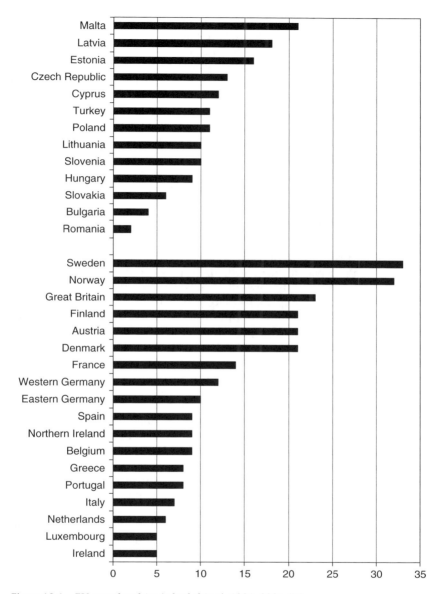

Figure 10.1 EU membership: 'a bad thing', 1991–2004 (%)
Sources: *Candidate Countries Eurobarometer* 2001; 2002; 2003.2; 2003.4; 2004.1; *Eurobarometer* 36 (1991) to 62 (2004).

they have been joined by Sweden. None of these three countries are members of the euro zone, for example. Norway, finally, is not even a EU member, but has been included here as a point of reference. The country fits neatly into the sceptical, non-continental camp; the Norwegian voters have twice advised against membership (in 1972 and 1994). Generally speaking, Euroscepticism thus seems to be – at least partly – related to lack of long-term experience with European integration. It is certainly not a coincidence that the pro-EU camp includes the six founding members of the European Communities.

It is more difficult to find distinct patterns among the new member states. The *Candidate Countries Eurobarometer* surveys conducted in recent years show that, as a rule, the citizens of these countries tend to be rather supportive towards the EU. The most Eurosceptical voices are found in Malta, Latvia and Estonia – the two latter with close historical ties to the Protestant Nordic countries with high levels of Euroscepticism – and to a lesser extent, in the Czech Republic. In the remaining countries, articulate opposition is not particularly widespread, and in the candidate countries Romania and Bulgaria, only two to four per cent on average find the prospect of a future EU membership a bad idea. Indeed, these two countries have repeatedly shown the most EU-friendly views of all, possibly because their expectations *vis-à-vis* Union membership are so high; people believe that they have a lot to win. All in all, Euroscepticism/optimism is clearly a multi-dimensional phenomenon, dependent on a great number of factors.[4] The Union's external relations are, of course, one of them.

Public support for a common foreign policy

From the start, the European integration process has primarily been geared to create economic wealth and stability, and it is therefore likely that it is the economic aspects – or at least internal policies – that are most clearly evaluated in the survey items such as the one discussed above. However, and as this book also shows, the foreign political dimension of the EU has become more and more important ever since the CFSP was officially introduced in the Treaty of the European Union in 1992.[5] Indeed, in recent efforts to redesign the Union and its institutions, foreign and security policies have played a central role. The EU's determination to shoulder a larger share of responsibility for global security has become increasingly evident. The draft Constitution also clearly reflects these ambitions, by making two particularly significant amendments to the provisions of earlier treaties: the creation of a new institution, a Minister of Foreign Affairs, and the creation of a European External Action Service.

Two problems have been particularly conspicuous in the development of the EU's foreign policy, however.[6] First, due to the complicated, multidimensional nature of the Union, it has remained unclear what 'European foreign policy' actually stands for. It seems to encompass almost all of what the EU *and* its member states do or do not in world politics; 'the EU has not been able to speak with one voice' is the best known simplification of this problem. The profound disagreement between the member states over the war on Iraq (2002–2003) is undoubtedly the most significant example of this. Tony Blair and José Maria Aznar broke ranks with Gerhard Schröder and Jacques Chirac, and supported President Bush's plans to invade Iraq.[7] Second, even in those cases in which the Union has basically been able to formulate a common view, it can be argued that at least until recently the EU did not have any (power-political) means to fulfil its objectives. The crisis in Kosovo in 1998–99 saw NATO and UN action, while the EU appeared weak, far from the image envisaged in the Maastricht Treaty.[8] As Hanna Ojanen explains in detail in her chapter, the Union is currently taking significant steps towards the creation of military capabilities of its own. Whether this is positive or negative from the perspective of the EU's international standing and global order remains to be seen.

Foreign and security policies have traditionally belonged to the core functions of the state, and it is therefore indicative for the entire integration process as to how people generally regard the efforts to move decision-making and even military power in these fields from the national to the European level – whether they actually wish that the Union speaks with one voice. It would also be interesting to know to what extent they express unanimous views about the above-mentioned problems.

The *Eurobarometer* surveys provide us with some useful empirical insights in this respect. Table 10.1 lists the 15 old EU member states, the 10 new member states, and the remaining candidate countries – Turkey, Bulgaria, and Romania – in terms of their public support for and opposition to a common European foreign policy. Sweden stands out as the most sceptical country in the sample, with 44 per cent explicitly against the notion of a common foreign policy for the EU members. The UK, Denmark, and Finland score high on the sceptical dimension as well. In contrast, the respondents of the original six member states – France, Germany, Italy and the Benelux countries – overwhelmingly support the idea of a common foreign policy; the percentages in favour range between 66 and 77 per cent. Among the new member states and candidate countries, we find significant cross-national variation as well: in the Czech Republic, Estonia, and Malta, almost one-fourth of the respondents are explicitly *against* a common foreign policy. In the two post-communist countries left outside the 2004 expansion wave – Bulgaria and Romania – as many as 74 per cent of the respondents are in favour. In all, thus, a clear majority of the respondents in *both* the old *and* the new EU member states are in favour of a common EU foreign policy (65 per cent and 68 per cent, respectively).

What is important, however, is the clear similarity between Table 10.1 and Figure 10.1 above. This seems to suggest that we could use a rather simple point of departure in this chapter: support for the EU's role in world affairs seems to correlate positively with generalised support for the EU as such, and the correlation is fairly high. Indeed, hesitation regarding a common European foreign policy is most common in countries that are generally Eurosceptical – Finland,

Table 10.1   Opinions on a common foreign policy (%)

15 Old EU member states	2004 EU member states	Remaining EU candidates	Against	In favour
Sweden			44	49
UK			39	39
Denmark			39	50
Finland			36	55
	Malta		24	50
	Czech Republic		23	57
	Estonia		23	62
France			22	66
Austria			21	62
Netherlands			21	69
Portugal			18	62
		Turkey	17	47
	Latvia		17	67
Spain			17	69
Belgium			17	71
Ireland			16	66
	Poland		16	70
Germany			16	74
	Hungary		14	70
	Slovakia		14	74
	Slovenia		14	76
Greece			14	78
Luxembourg			13	77
Italy			12	77
	Lithuania		10	61
	Cyprus		9	81
		Bulgaria	6	74
		Romania	6	74

Sources: *Eurobarometer* 61 (2004) and *Candidate Countries Eurobarometer* 2004.1.

Denmark, Sweden and the UK among EU15, and Malta, Latvia, Estonia and the Czech Republic among the new EU members. Conversely, 'pro-common-foreign-policy' attitudes seem to be combined with a general pro-EU stance.[9]

Intuitively, we could expect the ESDP, introduced in 1999 (see Ojanen's chapter), to be the most sensitive part of the CFSP for EU citizens; security and defence has traditionally been *the* core function of the nation-state. From this perspective, it is not surprising that the ESDP is a latecomer on the Union agenda, and that NATO still is, and has been ever since it was founded in 1949, the primary mechanism of military cooperation in Europe. After the end of communism, it was equally, if not more, important for the countries of Eastern Europe to join the transatlantic framework as it was to join the EU.

In spite of this newness – or because of it – the public opinion surveys reveal a rather unambiguous picture: public opposition to a European defence policy is *not* widespread within the Union today. Some 72 per cent of citizens in the old member states and 79 per cent of citizens in the new member states support the notion of a common European defence and security policy.[10] The same pattern that we encountered before is manifest here as well. The Eurosceptical countries are, as expected, also the most ESDP-critical countries: Austria, Sweden, Finland, Denmark, and the UK. In these countries, between 28 and 38 per cent of respondents are against a common defence policy. In pro-EU countries, we find very few critical voices, in most cases under 15 per cent of the respondents. Interestingly, Eurosceptical Estonia and Latvia have rather few opponents to a common defence policy. The explanation for this is certainly the delicate geo-political and historical position of these two countries. Estonians and Latvians may feel ambivalent towards Brussels – some of them even see it as a replacement of the Soviet Union – but nevertheless appreciate the EU as a provider of security.

Support for 'one voice' in world politics

The empirical investigations above have demonstrated that a majority of EU citizens seem to accept the notion of a common European foreign policy and a common defence and security policy. We have also noted that the differences between public attitudes in the old and new member states are generally relatively small. Table 10.2 seems to confirm these observations. In it, we

Table 10.2 Support for various elements of a common European foreign policy (%)

Elements	15 old EU member states	10 new EU member states
When an international crisis occurs, EU member states should agree a common position	81	83
The EU should guarantee human rights in each member state, even if this is contrary to the wishes of some member states	79	80
EU foreign policy should be independent of United States foreign policy	77	75
The EU should work to guarantee human rights around the world, even if this is contrary to the wishes of some other countries	76	67
The EU should have a rapid military reaction force that can be sent quickly to trouble spots when an international crisis occurs	70	72
The EU should have its own seat in the United Nations Security Council	65	62
The EU should have its own Foreign Minister, who can be the spokesperson for a common EU position	64	61

Sources: *Eurobarometer* 61 (2004) and *Candidate Countries Eurobarometer* 2004.1. The percentages indicate the share of affirmative respondents.

compare these groups of countries by using a battery of questions that tap public support for various elements of a common European foreign policy, including defence and security issues.

Eight out of ten EU citizens agree that an international crisis justifies a common EU position. When it comes to the specific implementation of such a common position, the citizens are somewhat more hesitant. Still, a respectable 63 per cent agree that the EU should have its own Foreign Minister, and approximately 64 per cent that the EU should have its own seat in the United Nations Security Council. As many as 71 per cent of the respondents support the creation of a European military reaction force.

Some 80 per cent of the respondents feel that the EU has a responsibility to guarantee human rights within the Union, even if this should be contrary to the wishes of a member state. Opinions are more divided when it comes to the EU's global responsibility to promote human rights. 76 per cent of citizens in the old member states and 67 per cent in the new member states agree that the EU has such a duty. Finally, about three-quarters of the EU citizens think that EU foreign policy should be independent of US foreign policy. These are very interesting results indeed: they clearly support the idea of an internationally active EU, a Union that acts independently and is also willing to sacrifice the principle of state sovereignty for the sake of suffering individuals anywhere in the world.

Before we move on, we need to return to the point we made in the beginning of this section, to the relative importance of a common foreign and security policy in the minds of European citizens. In the standard *Eurobarometer* surveys, respondents are regularly asked about the most important issues facing their own country at the moment. When polled in the autumn of 2004, unemployment (46 per cent), the economic situation (27 per cent) and crime (24 per cent) were the most common answers. No more than 2 per cent identified defence/foreign policy as a timely issue.[11] It would seem that foreign policy remains a rather abstract or remote policy field. A significant part of the public support for the CFSP and the ESDP can thus be labelled as *uninformed support*. Citizens lend support for these particular policy fields without knowing or caring too much about them.[12] We therefore also need to treat the figures of the above analysis with caution.

Attitudes to the United States

Following the Second World War, the United States helped re-build Western Europe, and a transatlantic community was established. The threat of communism justified a continued American presence on the continent. This presence was repeatedly contested over the years, however. In the late 1960s, anti-American sentiments spread throughout Western Europe along with the ideas of the New Left, the criticism of capitalism and liberal democracy in general and the Vietnam War in particular. The peace and environmental movements of the 1970s and 1980s in many respects inherited this anti-American platform, although, as it became more and more apparent that the US was to win the Cold War, these sentiments gradually waned. The collapse of the communist regimes in 1989–91 profoundly changed the security constellation in Europe, and made many ask whether the US presence was still justified. In the spring of 1999, the NATO bombings of the former Yugoslavia again fuelled anti-American sentiments in Europe, although most European governments actually backed the NATO action. The Iraq war in 2003, finally, brought the transatlantic relations into a deep crisis. Today (summer 2005), anti-American feelings still appear strong in Europe, although the most difficult phase is probably over. It remains to be seen whether the post-war transatlantic friendship is slowly coming to its end.[13]

In the context of this book, the crucial point is that European public attitudes to the US can be seen as an indicator of what kind an international actor the EU should become. The argument is simply that the more negative the European attitudes to the US are, the more different from this country should the EU be, or develop into, as it pursues its foreign policy around the globe. In other words, opposition to the US and its unilateralism can be interpreted as support for a multilateral system and for EU agency within that system.

How widespread, then, have anti-American sentiments been among European publics in the aftermath of 9/11 and during and after the Iraq war? It may be needless to say, but the war itself was disapproved by a clear majority of EU citizens. For example, in the *Flash Eurobarometer* 151, conducted in the autumn of 2003 in the old EU member states, respondents were explicitly asked about the righteousness of the war, and two thirds, 68 per cent, of them were of the opinion that the military intervention was not justified. The same survey also included a question tapping respondents' perceptions of threats to world peace. The question read: 'For each of the following countries, tell me if in your opinion, it presents or not a threat to peace in the world?' In Table 10.3, we have listed the affirmative percentages for each country.

Israel scores highest in Table 10.3, with 59 per cent, which reflects, no doubt, the negative image given by the Western media of the Israeli–Palestinian conflict. The US too scores high, with more than half of the respondents seeing the country as a threat to the world. The world's only superpower is on par with Iran and North Korea (53 per cent, respectively) and, ironically, scores higher than both Iraq (52 per cent) and Afghanistan (50 per cent). Pakistan comes close, with an affirmative rate of 48 per cent, whereas the traditional Cold War enemies and nuclear weapon states – Russia, China, and India – stand out as rather moderate threats. Greece, Spain, Finland and Sweden are the most US-sceptical countries in EU15, but even in allied countries in the Iraq war, a majority of citizens share the opinion that the US poses a threat to peace in the world: in Spain 61 per cent, and in the UK 55 per cent.

Figure 10.2, based on *Eurobarometer* 59.1 from spring 2003, gives us a somewhat more detailed and complex picture of how Europeans perceived

Table 10.3 Countries perceived as a threat to peace in the world (%)

	SP	SWE	GR	F	I	A	FIN	B	DK	G	P	UK	IRL	L	NL	EU15
Israel	56	52	61	55	48	69	60	63	64	65	55	60	62	66	74	59
Iran	41	44	26	55	58	49	48	54	55	57	56	54	54	62	64	53
North Korea	37	49	30	49	42	69	57	49	63	65	59	59	66	65	70	53
United States	**61**	**54**	**88**	**52**	**43**	**63**	**63**	**59**	**52**	**45**	**53**	**55**	**60**	**55**	**64**	**53**
Iraq	42	41	27	50	55	45	53	54	50	57	59	54	54	56	61	52
Afghanistan	36	36	23	50	58	40	44	48	47	54	54	49	55	54	61	50
Pakistan	38	41	23	53	49	53	39	46	46	52	48	44	50	57	58	48
Syria	25	29	17	44	41	36	25	37	35	35	40	41	37	44	51	37
Libya	24	29	13	42	27	33	34	37	33	39	42	43	40	42	52	36
Saudi Arabia	32	23	25	44	37	33	29	40	38	31	45	34	38	41	43	36
China	27	27	28	24	27	32	31	29	36	26	39	40	37	36	43	30
India	13	22	14	20	18	26	23	23	24	22	26	28	27	28	34	22
Russia	19	19	23	20	16	24	29	21	23	19	30	27	31	27	25	21
Somalia	6	11	7	15	19	15	10	11	13	17	24	20	17	20	20	16
EU	9	11	14	6	5	3	6	8	9	4	13	18	12	6	7	8

Source: Flash Eurobarometer 151 (2003a). N = ca. 500 in each country. Acronyms: Spain (SP), Sweden (SWE), Greece (GR), France (F), Italy (I), Austria (A), Finland (FIN), Belgium (B), Denmark (DK), Germany (G), Portugal (P), United Kingdom (UK), Ireland (IRL), Luxembourg (L), Netherlands (NL), and the average for EU 15.

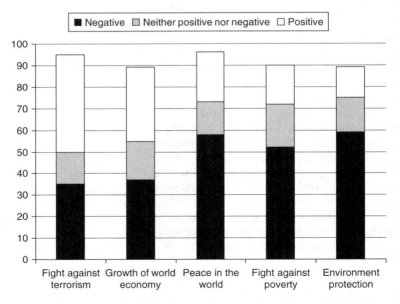

Figure 10.2 The image of the US in the world among the citizens of EU15 (%)
Source: Eurobarometer 59.1 (2003).

the United States in the early 2000s. The respondents were asked to assess the role of the US in the world with respect to five different themes: the fight against terrorism, growth of the world economy, world peace, the fight against poverty, and the protection of the environment. Perhaps the most interesting observation is that 45 per cent of EU15 citizens think that the US plays a positive role in the global fight against terrorism – somewhat more than the number of those who view this role in negative terms. This may imply that a significant part of Europeans actually think that the war on terror is in itself justified, but the invasion of Iraq was not the right means to wage that war. The Bush administration's war on terrorism is condoned in particular by citizens in the UK (68 per cent), Denmark (64 per cent), Sweden and the Netherlands (56 per cent, respectively). In Greece, by contrast, 80 per cent disagree with Washington's post-9/11 crusade.

As for the four other items in Figure 10.2, the respondents prove more critical than supportive towards the US. The peacekeeping role of the US is perceived as negative by 58 per cent of all respondents. Again, the Greece citizens stand out as particularly critical, with 91 per cent opting for the 'negative' alternative, followed by the Eastern part of Germany (78 per cent) and France (73 per cent). At the less anti-American end of the spectrum, we find Denmark (35 per cent negative) and the UK (32 per cent negative). Furthermore, it is fair to say that most EU citizens remain unimpressed with US efforts to fight poverty or protect the environment. As regards the promotion of economic growth in the world, the picture is more balanced; 37 per cent of the respondents are negative and 34 per cent positive.

It has been argued that the inclusion of the former communist states into the EU might make the Union friendlier towards the US. Many post-communist citizens share the view that they owe their freedom to the US, the victor in the ideological battle of the Cold War. It is in any case true that the 2004 enlargement brought a number of new NATO members, and thus perhaps deeper feelings of pro-Americanism, into the Union. It is also likely that the US enjoys credibility as a safeguard against Russian imperialist aspirations, especially in the Baltic States.[14]

Unfortunately, all the questions in Figure 10.2 were not asked in the *Candidate Countries Barometers*. However, in the *Eurobarometer* 62 (autumn 2004), respondents throughout EU25 were asked to evaluate the role of the US with respect to the country's ability to guarantee peace in the world and fight against terrorism. As for the role of the US as a promoter of peace, a majority of all respondents in EU25 were more critical (58 per cent) than supportive (22 per cent). Only three countries had a predominantly positive perception of the US in this respect – none of these belong to the old member states: Romania (53 per cent), the Czech Republic (47 per cent), and Lithuania (43 per cent).

The east–west divide was more evident with regard to the US's fight against terrorism. A relative majority (46 per cent) of citizens in EU15 believed that the

US plays a predominantly *negative* role in the world in this respect. Among the new member states, it was rather the other way around: 53 per cent of the respondents thought *positively* of the US as an enemy of terrorism. Again, pro-American sentiments were especially manifest in the Czech Republic (67 per cent), Romania (66 per cent), and Lithuania (61 per cent). In light of these figures, the division between the new and old Europe has not been entirely unfounded.

To sum up, it seems that the US has a rather tarnished public image in Europe, and there is no doubt that the country's foreign policies in the new millennium – Afghanistan, Iraq, Kyoto, Guantánamo – have significantly contributed to the construction of this image. It is hard to tell whether such profound anti-American sentiments are temporary, however, and how much long-term impact the Iraq war and its aftermath actually will have on public opinion in Europe. For the time being, Europeans, especially in EU15, are hesitant to regard the US an ally.

The EU and the borders of Europe

We will now turn to an analysis of public opinion and the borders of the EU, of who are regarded as 'insiders' and who as 'outsiders'. According to the official homepage of the EU (www.europa.eu.int), the May 2004 enlargement entailed 'a historical opportunity to unite Europe peacefully after generations of division and conflict'. The expansion would supposedly 'extend the EU's stability and prosperity to a wider group of countries, consolidating the political and economic transition that has taken place in Central and Eastern Europe since 1989'. Among the political elites, there were surprisingly few influential critics of this historical enlargement, but as will be seen, the views of ordinary citizens have been less harmonious.

In Table 10.4, we have summarised attitudes towards enlargement in the old EU member states. Two different survey items are used: in the first column, respondents have been asked specifically about the May 2004 enlargement; the second column is based on the respondents' attitudes towards future enlargements in general. In the table, only the percentages of negative or disapproving respondents are shown.

Support for the 2004 enlargement was far from overwhelming: 39 per cent were explicitly against it, and only 42 per cent were in favour. Again, cross-national differences can largely be explained with reference to the general pro/contra EU dimension. One may at least assume that many Eurosceptics in the Nordic countries reckon that the enlargement of the Union will work as an obstacle to intensified and deepened integration, and they are thus in favour of enlargement. By the same logic, the rather large share of negative respondents in Luxembourg, Belgium, France and the Netherlands could be interpreted as a wish to deepen integration within a more narrowly defined European Union.

Table 10.4   Against the enlargement of the EU (%)

	Against the enlargement of the EU in 2004	Against further enlargements of the EU
Germany	56	60
Austria	52	59
Luxembourg	51	53
Belgium	49	49
France	47	52
Netherlands	45	43
Finland	44	55
UK	40	40
Sweden	37	48
Denmark	31	43
Portugal	27	28
Italy	25	28
Ireland	22	30
Greece	19	23
Spain	18	17

Source: *Eurobarometer* 61 (2004).

There are also other explanations for the cross-national differences. When polled in the spring of 2004, 72 per cent of the respondents in EU15 feared that the enlarged Union would entail 'the transfer of jobs to other member countries which have lower production costs', and 53 per cent deemed that it would lead to the loss of their social benefits. Some extremist politicians have naturally tried to capitalise on such fears – Jörg Haider in Austria is possibly the most evident example – but even 'mainstream' leaders have not been able to steer clear from the populist road entirely. For example, former German Chancellor Gerhard Schröder has branded suggestions by German industrial leaders to move facilities eastwards as 'unpatriotic'. Not surprisingly, the least enthusiastic respondents in Table 10.4 are found in Germany and Austria, that is, the countries with borders to the old 'Eastern Europe'. Here, enlargement has clearly been perceived as a potential threat.

The second column in Table 10.4 displays the share of respondents who are against any further enlargements of the Union. A majority of EU15 citizens oppose the idea: 43 per cent are against it, 37 per cent are in favour, and 20 per cent express no opinion at all. Again, Germans and Austrians are the most disapproving (around 60 per cent). Though not explicitly stated, this means that the citizens of Western Europe do not regard Turkey, the Balkan countries and Orthodox Eastern Europe as self-evident members of the European family.[15] In the terminology of this volume, they have a limited sense of a large European community – the community principle does not necessarily apply.

Table 10.5   Support for a larger and more powerful Union (%)

	More members – more security	More members – more influence in the world
Cyprus	84	85
Bulgaria	76	79
Romania	74	72
Slovakia	72	75
Malta	71	81
Hungary	70	72
Poland	69	69
Czech Republic	67	69
Slovenia	67	73
Estonia	64	72
Latvia	61	71
Lithuania	59	62
Turkey	53	56
2004 members	68	66

Source: *Candidate Countries Eurobarometer* 2004.1.

Support for enlargement has been clearly more pronounced in the new member states, however. When polled in early 2004, as many as 71 per cent of the respondents supported the 2004 enlargement in general. Approximately 60 per cent were in favour of further enlargements of the EU.[16] Furthermore, just before 1 May 2004, respondents in the candidate countries were asked to evaluate the consequences of EU enlargement. In Table 10.5, we have high-lighted the outcome for two statements, one about regional security ('The more countries there will be in the EU, the more peace and security will be guaranteed in Europe') and one about the EU's global role ('The more member countries within the union, the more important it will be in the world'). Judging on the basis of these two items, citizens in the new member states are generally in favour of including new members into the EU: 68 per cent agree that more members equals more security in Europe, and 66 per cent feel that more members will make the EU a more influential actor in the world.

Immigrants and asylum seekers

Another way of analysing the sense of community among the EU citizens is to take a look at their views on immigrants and asylum seekers. Here, we will look at public attitudes towards 'outsiders' on a fairly general level: do EU citizens support the notion of a common European immigration policy and a common asylum policy?

Table 10.6 shows that approximately 70 per cent of all respondents – in the old as well as in the new member states – support a common immigration and asylum policy. This does not necessarily entail a more *generous* policy,

Table 10.6   Support for a common European immigration and asylum policy (%)

	15 old EU member states	10 new EU member states
The EU should have a common immigration policy towards people from outside the EU	71	68
The EU should have a common asylum policy towards asylum seekers	70	68

Sources: *Eurobarometer* 61 (2004) and *Candidate Countries Eurobarometer* 2004.1. The percentages indicate the share of affirmative respondents.

however. It may merely tell that fighting against illegal immigration and human trafficking and guaranteeing fair and equal treatment of legal migrants in the Union are perceived as highly important issues on today's European political agenda.

Analyses conducted for the Vienna-based EU agency *European Monitoring Centre on Racism and Xenophobia* (EUMC) may shed further light on this issue. In March 2005, the EUMC published a summary report on *Majority Attitudes towards Migrants and Minorities*.[17] This comprehensive report, based on recent European cross-national surveys, indicates that a clear majority of European citizens – maybe three out of four – claim that they do not have problems living in a multicultural society. However, when asked more specific questions about minority groups and multicultural societies, more critical opinions seem to emerge. For example, in the *Eurobarometers* conducted between 1997 and 2003 in the old member states as many as 60 per cent felt that multiculturalism had already reached its limits. The corresponding figure among the candidate countries in 2003 was 42 per cent. The surveys thus seem to confirm the widely held perception that people of other races, religions or cultures are far from wholeheartedly accepted in contemporary Europe.

*   *   *

To conclude this section, it has become obvious that it may not be all that easy to find supporters of a Union that coincides with the geographical boundaries of Europe, from the Atlantic to the Urals, in the current EU member states. The eastward enlargement in 2004 was only half-heartedly accepted by citizens in EU15, and opposition to further enlargements is widespread. In Central and Eastern Europe, we find stronger support for a larger Union, but it is not self-evident that public support for a 'united Europe' will survive there either in the years to come, if the material sacrifices for further enlargement are expected to be too significant. The European community obviously has its outer borders. A nagging suspicion is, indeed, that the high levels of support for a common European immigration policy and a common asylum policy documented in Table 10.6 are in fact motivated by a desire to keep outsiders out.

The EU and globalisation

The final empirical section of this chapter deals with issues that are somehow related to the processes of 'globalisation', including the promotion of democracy and human rights around the world. The *Eurobarometer* surveys contain a few items that may be employed to assess public attitudes towards globalisation. One recently used is a question about which actors are believed to be able to regulate globalisation. The options given to the respondents included, for example, political parties; the EU; trade unions; consumer rights associations; multinational companies; the WTO; the UN; the World Bank and the IMF; or the US government.[18]

Interestingly, the EU comes out as the *most* trusted actor; 27 per cent of all respondents in EU25 give their vote to it. By contrast, the WTO is regarded capable of taming the negative aspects of globalisation by 17 per cent in the old and by 15 per cent in the new EU countries; trust in the UN is on approximately the same relatively low level. National governments are trusted even less throughout the Union: only 13 per cent of citizens in the new member states and 19 per cent in the old ones believe their own government to be able to harness globalisation. The World Bank and IMF are mentioned by 10 per cent of the respondents, and the US government is trusted by a meagre 4 per cent.

What about the perceived advantages and disadvantages of globalisation? It seems that people generally have mixed feelings about the phenomenon; they see both threats and opportunities in it. For example, in *Eurobarometer* 61 (spring 2004), conducted in EU15, approximately the same number of respondents, 39 per cent, agreed and disagreed with the statement 'overall, globalisation is a good thing for our country'; the views were somewhat more pessimistic when the enquiry concerned the respondent him- or herself and not his/her country (29 versus 45 per cent). A 2003 *Flash Eurobarometer* provides us with another example. In it, as many as 80 per cent of the respondents thought that globalisation facilitates cultural exchanges; 64 per cent felt that globalisation entails solidarity between countries. Yet, only 41 per cent believed that globalisation improves the unequal situation between the North and the South, and only 54 per cent that developing countries benefit from globalisation.[19]

What is particularly important in the context of this volume, however, is that those who support the EU are clearly the most optimistic group in terms of attitudes towards globalisation.[20] Conversely, it does not seem implausible that for many of these people, the EU's perceived ability to regulate or resist globalisation is one of the most important reasons to support the Union. This in turn indicates that to the extent the Union can take an active role in the international efforts to control and regulate globalisation, this will actually give a dose of legitimacy for the Union. It would be a prime example of responsible global agency from the perspective of EU citizens themselves.

The perceptions of the EU's relationship to globalisation vary significantly across the European continent. For the Nordic countries and the UK in particular – generally globalisation beneficiaries – the EU's role should be that of a regulator of the most negative effects of globalisation; the Union should see to it that globalisation proceeds smoothly. By contrast, in Southern Europe, people are much more wary about globalisation and want the EU to help slow it down. Given these differing views, the way the EU posits itself in relation to globalisation is bound to be one of the most important political questions within the Union in the near future.[21]

The EU and the Middle East

The final item that we want to take a look at here – the EU's contacts with the Mediterranean countries – is logically somewhat different than the previous ones, but it also tells a great deal about the role people are willing to give for the European Union. In addition to assessing the EU as a promoter of peace and stability and economic growth, it may also reveal something about the willingness of Europeans to get involved in political affairs far away from the European peninsula, and thus even about the legitimacy of its development and human rights policies.

In Figure 10.3, the citizens in the old EU member states have been asked about the EU's involvement in the Middle East, more specifically in the Israeli–Arab conflict.[22] The overall impression is clear: citizens throughout EU15 are indeed ready to endorse the EU as an influential actor in this respect. On average, 36 per cent 'totally agree' and another 45 per cent 'rather agree' that the EU ought to actively help resolving the Middle East conflict. The usual pattern can be found in terms of the cross-national variation. In Eurosceptical Finland, the UK, Austria and Sweden, citizens are not entirely convinced of the need for the EU to get involved in the Middle East. At the other end of the spectrum, we find pro-EU countries like Greece, Italy, Ireland, Luxembourg and Portugal. Germany is a deviant case: citizens in both Eastern and Western Germany could be classified as rather Eurofriendly, but just above one-fifth of the German respondents 'totally agree' that the EU should get involved in Middle East politics. This is in all likelihood a reflection of Germany's post-war self-consciousness and the consequent cautiousness of its foreign policy.[23]

To sum up, the above somewhat randomly chosen survey items are hardly sufficient for mapping out public attitudes to such a complicated phenomenon as globalisation, not to speak about the EU's efforts to promote democracy and respect for human rights in the world. What we can say, however, is that given the Europeans' awareness of the need to solve the problems of globalisation – for example, how to cope with the fact that globalisation has often worsened the prospects for economic growth in the developing countries – a globally ever more active EU seems to be a course of development which they widely endorse. Moreover, it appears safe to argue that in their view, this development should be based on some sort of normative premises and objectives.

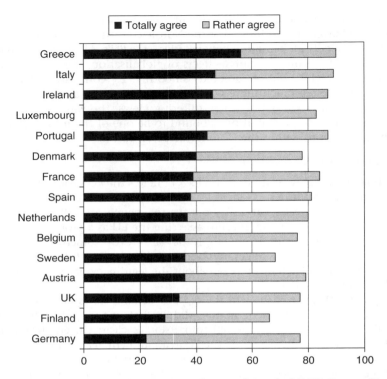

Figure 10.3   The EU should play an active role in resolving the Middle East conflict (%)
Source: *Flash Eurobarometer* 151 (2003a).

Concluding remarks

The most important findings of this chapter are roughly summarised in Table 10.7. The empirical analysis of the first section indicated that European publics are willing to accept a Common Foreign and Security Policy for the EU (Table 10.1), including a common defence policy. A majority of EU citizens also supports the idea of a single voice in world politics. Eight out of ten agree, for example, that an international crisis justifies a common EU position (Table 10.2). As for EU–US relations, the survey data analysed here do not indicate that Europeans in general support the notion of a transatlantic community. The US's military might is widely seen as a possible threat (Table 10.3). Likewise, EU citizens remain unimpressed with the US in terms of its civilian power (Figure 10.2).

EU enlargements also seem unpopular at the moment. The May 2004 enlargement was only half-heartedly accepted, and a clear majority of EU15 citizens oppose the idea of future enlargements (Table 10.4). There is, in other

Table 10.7 Citizens' perceptions of the EU as a global actor: a summary

Public opinion characterised by:	A common foreign and security policy			Transatlantic relations		Enlargement and borders of the EU			EU and the world	
	CFSP	ESDP	Single voice	US: military power	US: civilian power	Enlargement	Community	Immigrants	Regulate globalisation	Middle East
Support	X	X	X			(X)		(X)	X	X
Ambivalence						X	X	X		
Rejection				X	X	X				

words, no overwhelming public support for a wider European community encompassing the whole continent (cf. Aalto's chapter). Not surprisingly, citizens in the new member states are clearly more positive about further enlargements (Table 10.5). It remains to be seen whether the former outsiders will become more narrow-minded, once inside the Union themselves. We have also seen that the majority of EU citizens support common European immigration policy and a common asylum policy (Table 10.6). This could be interpreted as a common wish to guarantee immigrants fair treatment, but it could also mean support for a more restricted immigration policy – and a limited sense of a global community.

The final empirical section dealt with Europeans' attitudes towards various aspects of globalisation. The overall impression was that EU citizens regard globalisation with a certain degree of ambivalence; they see both threats and opportunities. Importantly, they tend to trust the EU as a potential regulator of the negative aspects of globalisation. In the same section, by using the EU's involvement in the Middle East as an example (Figure 10.3), we noted that Europeans do acknowledge the EU's efforts to promote economic growth and democratic development throughout the world. Moreover, more than two thirds of them believe that the EU should work to guarantee human rights around the world (Table 10.2).

It is obvious that these survey indicators may be regarded as too vague for drawing any far-reaching conclusions about citizens' perceptions of the EU's developing global agency. But in spite of the limitations of our – or indeed any – survey-based analysis, at least one general conclusion appears unproblematic: EU citizens are ready to accept an increasingly important role for the European Union in global political arenas. Throughout the member states, citizens support a Union speaking and acting as one, a Union that opposes US unilateralism and favours multilateralism, a Union that seeks to diminish the negative effects of globalisation, and a Union that promotes democratic values and human rights throughout the world. This could be a Union with a joint military task force, a military dimension, but – in contrast to the US – this should only complement the Union's essentially civilian nature. We have also seen that these attitudes are closely linked to people's general support to the EU. Even though national interests persist, and people in different countries have somewhat different attitudes to the process of integration, to the extent they support the EU – and most of them do, in fact – they also support its global agency.

This does not mean, however, that we could matter-of-factly contend that the citizens of Europe would explicitly demand a globally responsible EU, whatever that may mean. Surveys seem to say fairly little about the hoped-for *nature* of the EU's global role. Yet, and this is the important point, assuming that a globally more responsible EU agency in many senses requires a more active and stronger agency, too, public opinion will hardly become an obstacle, if the European political elites are willing to take action towards that end. This sort of agency would, in other words, be within the acceptable boundaries of EU politics, as defined by EU citizens themselves. Moreover, given the high level of support to the overall integration process, and therefore to its basic values, it appears reasonable to argue that in average Europeans' view, this active global role should include a responsible – rather than irresponsible – dimension; Europeans hardly want to see the Europe of the past even in the field of external relations.

The current European attitudes to the US no doubt also support the latter argument. As we have shown, the acceptance of the EU as a global actor tends to go hand in hand with a rejection of the US's role in the world. This does not indicate, however, that in order to satisfy its citizens, the EU (as an institution) has a 'responsibility' to turn its back to the US. Rather, the general idea among European citizens seems to be that the EU should be something *different* from the US, and because of this need to be different it should shoulder a larger share of responsibility for what is happening in the world. This is also significant when we think about the implications of 'responsibility' to the relationship between the general public and political elites. Responsible (EU) agency is not and should not be primarily a matter of inner accountability (within the Union): public opinion can only set the outer limits of political decision making; political leaders need to have a considerable space of manoeuvre. Simultaneously, however, these political leaders should not let themselves believe that they could educate the wider public to any considerable degree in today's world.

Finally, it is obvious that the above analyses are closely related to this volume's conceptual framework of the sources of responsibility, two of these sources in particular. First of all, the expectations principle appears highly relevant. The EU has sought to brand itself in terms of democracy and respect for human rights; the EU citizens have indeed a legitimate reason to expect that it follows these principles around the world in a coherent and consistent manner, and that it does this primarily with civilian, or civilised, means. Expectations regarding Europe's international role have risen not only among the political elites but also among ordinary Europeans. Secondly, we may view the current European public attitudes in terms of the capacity principle. Europe's citizens may reason, as they try to advance the idea of dissimilarity *vis-à-vis* the US, that as an economic superpower, the EU indeed has the capacity to make a difference in many external policy fields worldwide. Therefore, even though the EU may often be a less appropriate actor than some other international organisations, say, NATO or the UN, it could all the same be held responsible for *not* acting to help those in need of help, to avert a genocide or to prevent war. The EU citizens have a right to expect the EU to promote democratic and economic development in, for example, Eastern Europe, the Balkans and Minor Asia, simply because it *can* do so.

Notes

1. Some of the formulations, tables, and figures presented in this chapter are also used in *The Making of the European Union: Foundations, Institutions and Future Trends*, co-authored by Sten Berglund, Joakim Ekman, Henri Vogt and Frank H. Aarebrot (Edward Elgar, 2006).
2. Dalton 2002; Sinnott 1995.
3. Christiansen and Tonra 2004; Holland 2004; Smith 1999; Smith 2004; Soetendorp 1999.
4. See Theiler 2004.
5. The failure to stop the atrocities in the former Yugoslavia is possibly the most significant reason for the recent development of EU external affairs. Only a few months after the outbreak of the Bosnian war, in the Treaty of the European Union (1992), a Common Foreign and Security Policy was initiated (section 5, article 11, paragraph 1 and 2): 'The Union shall establish and conduct a common foreign and security policy that comprise of all areas within foreign and security policy. [. . .] The member states shall in an active and unconditional manner support the Union's foreign and security policy in a spirit of loyalty and mutual solidarity'. The CFSP has subsequently been reinforced through the introduction of more coherent instruments and more efficient decision-making, in the Amsterdam Treaty and the Nice Treaty. In 1999, the EU assumed a more explicitly military dimension into its sphere of activities, by initiating the European Security and Defence Policy (ESDP).
6. Bomberg and Stubb 2003, 195–213; Holland 2002; 2004; Christiansen and Tonra 2004.
7. Bale 2005, 259–62; Bretherton and Vogler 1999; Hill 1996; 1998; Peterson and Smith 2003, 196–8; Smith 2003.
8. Bale 2005, 259–62.
9. It is worth noting that men are generally clearly more positive towards the EU than women. For example in *Eurobarometer* 61 (2004), 53 per cent of men and 47 per cent of women thought that their country's EU membership was a good thing. It is thus not surprising that men also support the creation of a common foreign policy, and trust in the EU's capacity to control globalisation, more often than women. Of the other socio-democraphic background factors, high level of education also

seems to increase people's sympathy towards the EU, whereas the urban–rural dimension and age have reasonably little explanatory value.
10. *Eurobarometer* 61; *Candidate Countries Eurobarometer* 2004.1.
11. *Eurobarometer* 62.
12. See Manigart 2001. The level of knowledge is undoubtedly getting better. When asked about what the EU means to the respondents personally, the item 'a stronger say in the world' was picked by a respectable 26 per cent of citizens in the new member states, and by 28 per cent of citizens in EU15 (*Eurobarometer* 61; *Candidate Countries Eurobarometer* 2004.1). For almost twice as many, however, the Union primarily denoted 'freedom to travel, study and work anywhere in the EU'.
13. Bale 2005, 251; Habermas 2004; Markovits 2005; Peterson and Pollack 2003.
14. Berglund *et al.* 2004; Fawn 2003; Stent and Shevtsova 2002; Wiatr 2004.
15. Cf. Hansen 2000; Kohli 2000.
16. *Candidate Countries Eurobarometer* 2004.1.
17. *Majority Attitudes Towards Migrants and Minorities: Key findings from the Eurobarometer and the European Social Survey* (data from 1997–2003). European Monitoring Centre on Racism and Xenophobia, 2005.
18. *Eurobarometer* 61; *Candidate Countries Eurobarometer* 2004.1.
19. *Flash Eurobarometer* 151 (2003b).
20. *Eurobarometer* 61; Berglund *et al.* 2006, 177.
21. Berglund *et al.* 2006, ch. 7.
22. A number of efforts are currently being made at the EU level to promote cultural and political exchanges between European and Arabic countries, most notably within the framework of the Barcelona Process, launched in 1995 as a cooperation project between the EU and the Mediterranean countries. The key objective of the programme is to turn the Euro–Mediterranean region into a stable and peaceful area, by developing a free-trade area between the EU and the Mediterranean partners and by promoting understanding between cultures in the region. The partners have agreed to develop the rule of law and democracy in their respective political systems, and the year 2010 has been set as the target date for the establishment of a free trade area.
23. See, for example, Ekman 2001.

Bibliography

Bale, Tim, *European Politics: A Comparative Introduction* (Basingstoke: Palgrave, 2005).
Berglund, Sten, Joakim Ekman and Frank H. Aarebrot (eds), *The Handbook of Political Change in Eastern Europe*, 2nd edn (Cheltenham and Northampton: Edward Elgar, 2004).
Berglund, Sten, Joakim Ekman, Henri Vogt and Frank H. Aarebrot, *The Making of the European Union: Foundations, Institutions and Future Trends* (Cheltenham: Edward Elgar, 2006).
Bomberg, Elizabeth and Alexander Stubb (eds), *The European Union: How Does it Work?*, (Oxford: Oxford University Press, 2003).
Bretherton, Charlotte and John Vogler, *The European Union as a Global Actor* (London and New York: Routledge, 1999).
Candidate Countries Eurobarometer 2001; 2002; 2003.2; 2003.4; 2004.1, Machine-readable data files and publications, Brussels, European Commission.
Christiansen, Thomas and Ben Tonra (eds), *Rethinking EU Foreign Policy: Beyond the Common Foreign and Security Policy* (Manchester: Manchester University Press, 2004).

Dalton, Russel J., *Citizen Politics: Public Opinion and Political Parties in Advanced Industrial Democracies* (New York and London: Chatham House Publishers, 2002).

Ekman, Joakim, *National Identity in Divided and Unified Germany: Continuity and Change* (Örebro: Örebro Studies in Political Science, 2001).

Erskine, Toni, (ed.), *Can Institutions Have Responsibilities?: Collective Moral Agency and International Relations* (Basingstoke and New York: Palgrave, 2003).

Eurobarometer 36 (autumn 1991) to 62 (autumn 2004), Machine-readable data files and publications, Brussels, European Commission.

Fawn, Rick (ed.), 'Ideology and National Identity in Post-communist Foreign Policies', Special issue of the *Journal of Communist Studies and Transition Politics*, vol. 19, no. 3 (2003).

Flash Eurobarometer 151 (2003a) 'Iraq and Peace in the World', Brussels, European Commission, Directorate-General 'Press and Communication'.

Flash Eurobarometer 151 (2003b) 'Globalisation', Brussels, European Commission, Directorate-General 'Press and Communication'.

Habermas, Jürgen, *Der gespaltene Westen* (Cologne: Edition Suhrkamp, 2004).

Hansen, Peo, *Europeans Only?: Essays on Identity Politics and the European Union* (Department of Political Science, Umeå University, 1996).

Hill, Christopher (ed.), *The Actors in Europe's Foreign Policy* (London: Routledge, 1996).

Hill, Christopher, 'Convergence, Divergence and Dialectics: National Foreign Policies and the CFSP', in Jan Zielonka (ed.), *Paradoxes of European Foreign Policy* (London, Kluwer, 1998).

Holland, Martin, *The European Union and the Third World* (Houndmills and New York: Palgrave, 2002).

Holland, Martin, 'When is Foreign Policy not Foreign Policy? Cotonou, CFSP and External Relations with the Developing World', in Martin Holland (ed.), *Common Foreign and Security Policy: The First Ten Years* (London: Continuum, 2004).

Howorth, Joylan and John T.S. Keeler (eds), *Defending Europe, NATO and the Quest for European Autonomy* (Basingstoke: Palgrave Macmillan, 2003).

Kohli, Martin, 'The Battlegrounds of European Identity', *European Societies*, vol. 2, no. 2 (2000), 113–37.

Lundestad, Geir, *No End to Alliance: The United States and Western Europe: Past, Present and Future* (Basingstoke: Palgrave Macmillan, 1998).

Manigart, Philippe, *Public Opinion and European Defence* (Royal Military Academy, Belgium, 2001).

Markovits, Andrei, *European Anti-Americanism and Anti-Semitism in a Changing Transatlantic Relationship* (Princeton: Princeton University Press, 2005).

Peterson, John and Michael E. Smith, 'The EU as Global Actor', in Elizabeth Bomberg and Alexander Stubb (eds), *The European Union: How Does it Work?* (Oxford: Oxford University Press, 2003).

Peterson, John and Mark Pollack, *Europe, America, Bush* (London: Routledge, 2003).

Sinnott, Richard, 'Bringing Public Opinion Back In', in Oskar Niedermayer and Richard Sinnott (eds), *Public Opinion and Internationalised Governance* (Oxford and New York: Oxford University Press, 1995).

Smith, Karen E., *The Making of EU Foreign Policy: The Case of Eastern Europe* (Basingstoke and New York: Palgrave, 1999).

Smith, Karen E., *European Union Foreign Policy in a Changing World* (Cambridge: Polity Press, 2003).

Smith, Michael E., 'CFSP and ESDP: From Idea to Institution to Policy', in Martin Holland (ed.), *Common Foreign and Security Policy: The First Ten Years* (London: Continuum, 2004).

Soetendorp, Ben, *Foreign Policy in the European Union: History, Theory and Practice* (London: Longman, 1999).

Stent, Angela and Lilia Shevtsova, 'America, Russia and Europe: A Realignment?, *Survival*, vol. 44, no. 4 (2002), 121–34.

Theiler, Tobias, 'The Origins of Euroscepticism in German-speaking Switzerland', *European Journal of Political Research*, vol. 43, no. 4 (2004).

Wiatr, Jerzy J., 'Central Europe and NATO after the Iraqi Crisis', in Algimantas Jankauskas *et al.* (eds), *Central Europe beyond Double Enlargement* (Institute of International Relations and Political Science, Vilnius University and Konrad Adenauer Foundation, 2004).

Conclusion: The Global Responsibility of the European Union: From Principles to Policy

Hartmut Mayer and Henri Vogt

At a time when the EU seems to be less and less confident internally and more and more ambitions in global affairs, when it admits to be uncertain about its economic fate under globalisation, but at the same time claims to be a 'successful example of "globalisation" on a regional scale',[1] there is a serious need for reflection over the Union's global role and direction. This book has intended to respond to the challenge by not offering another volume on what the EU does, but what it ought to do. The aims of the book have been at least threefold:

First, and primarily, we have sought to go beyond the simple assumptions that tend to shape the foreign policies of the European Union. We have wanted to question the often unsubstantiated wishes to make the Union an ever more important global actor and the more or less hollow rhetoric generally accompanying these wishes. We have *not* argued, however, that the EU should try to minimise its international role, but instead emphasised that whatever that role will be, it should be a result of conscious, careful political assessments – assessments that should, ideally, involve an ethical component. We have sought to find out, why, why on earth, the EU should take certain action and refrain from others in today's world.

Second, in order to allow us to make such critical judgements and normative claims – which the EU so often makes without foundation and precision – we have applied what we believe is an innovative framework for defining institutional responsibility in international affairs. We have tried to understand whether, or in what ways and to what extent, the EU is or could be *responsible* for developments in its neighbouring countries, in other continents, or in the global regimes in which it already plays a significant part. More specifically, we have asked: if we can reasonably suspect that the Union bears a responsibility towards someone or within some policy sector, what could the sources of this responsibility be? The six sources of responsibility that we have utilised – the contribution, community, beneficiary, capacity, legitimate expectations and consent principles – provide, if nothing else, a mental map for asking a number of relevant questions related to ethical institutional agency. The map thus not only applies to the EU, but to all international organisations. Hence, while the book focuses on the EU, it also makes a significant contribution to the growing literature on institutional responsibility in global politics in general.

Third, each of our contributions looked at a specific policy area and assessed the EU's record in this field. Often, as we have seen, it is possible to identify many different sources of responsibility. Usually (but not always) these sources reinforce each other, although their consequences may differ significantly: sometimes it seems that the Union should become a more active and influential actor in a specific policy sector, more capable of speaking with one voice, sometimes that it should rather limit its own scope of action and seek cooperation with other actors. What is particularly important, however, is that while each chapter made a number of interesting discoveries and identified responsible as well as irresponsible behaviour, they all helped to shape our understanding of the EU's international agency as a whole. Indeed, through our openly normative perspective we have told a great deal about the development of EU external affairs in general and even about the nature of the current world order. This conclusion therefore not only draws together the individual findings of the chapters, but also ventures to offer more general conclusions about the EU and its global responsibility.

Principles and arguments

Of the six principles incurring responsibilities, the *community principle* – or rather the 'community problem' it brings forth – has proved the most significant from the perspective of this book. The essential question of several chapters is clearly a derivative of the community principle: it may be legitimate, or at least understandable, to give special attention and care to those who belong to our own community – it is after all human to defend one's own family – but how do we demarcate this community in grand political terms? Where is Europe, who is Europe, where does it end and what is it for? Is EU–Europe alone the appropriate community which incurs certain duties or do we need a larger sense of home, possibly a wider European order, the West, Eurasia or, ultimately, the global community? And if the potential responsibilities towards these different communities conflict, and they inevitably do, does closer to 'home' also mean closer to 'morality'?

Pami Aalto's and Kristi Raik's chapters explicitly deal with the borders of 'Europe'. Aalto argues that Russia ought to be regarded as a member of a wider European community. Given the mutual interests between Russia and the EU, above all the fact that they are economically highly interdependent, this would not only be culturally and historically justified but also pragmatic. A sense of community would make these two actors mutually responsible for developments in the realm of the other actor and thus facilitate their cooperation. From the EU's point of view, it would be much easier to plan common policies, to negotiate with Russia, and even be critical of that country's decision-making apparatus. However, one might wonder whether such a sense of community could offer the Union a comfortable excuse for inaction, if democratic values in Russia would deteriorate permanently. The EU, so we would claim, has to strike a fine balance between embracing and 'harnessing' Russia, once it takes its own values seriously.

Kristi Raik's review of the EU's new neighbourhood policy closely resembles Aalto's call for a larger sense of community. Since the Union's policies and general appeal clearly have an impact on the development of its new neighbours – through what Raik calls 'extended governance' – irrespective of whether full membership is on offer or not, this creates specific responsibilities to the Union; extended governance relocates the borders of the European community somewhere beyond the EU. Because most of the neighbouring countries have introduced basically similar changes of policy, it is hardly justifiable that, for example, the financial resources allocated to the new neighbourhood policy are modest in comparison with what is given to countries with official candidate status. Despite this weakness and the possibly irresponsible two-class system, one must, however, praise the EU for its activities in this area. One could hardly imagine an institution better placed for providing regional stability and security in the wider European community.

The potential discrepancy between the global and European communities has also repeatedly come forth, most explicitly in Terry O'Shaugnessy's and Henri Vogt's chapters. Vogt argues that the EU now increasingly understands its development policy in terms of a global community. This is primarily positive, but there is always the risk that the rich and powerful single-handedly decide what the nature, norms, and aims of this community are. 'Pure', altruistic development goals can therefore easily be undermined by other objectives, especially those related to Western security concerns. Moreover, there are historical limitations to this sense of community: 'Europe' with its colonial heritage still generates negative reactions in the developing countries, which may damage the very principles and aims of EU development policy.

Choosing and defining the appropriate community and disentangling the overlaps between different responsibilities towards members of distinct communities are at the heart of O'Shaugnessy's chapter. While analysing the world trading system, he thinks in terms of 'nested' communities, from the level of those EU residents directly influenced by EU trade policies to the residents of the world at large. His conclusion is that there is indeed often a conflict of interests between these different communities. The only 'solution' is, then, that the Union should become more and more aware of these different levels with possibly contradictory interests, and consciously try to formulate policies that would satisfy people on all the levels to the extent it is possible.

In Hartmut Mayer's chapter on transatlantic relations, the potential distinction between transatlantic/western and global communities is also strongly present. Rejecting a crystal-clear juxtaposition between European and American values, he argues in favour of a united West; the interests of the world would best be served if the EU and the US cooperated constructively in the future. However, for the sake of a functioning global community, the EU should seek to balance the US power in case Washington's behaviour endangers stability and order in the world. Thereby, Mayer actually invokes a primary notion of a global community towards which the European Union – and the US as well – should be responsible. Joakim Ekman's chapter is closely related to this, as it concludes that the EU citizens are indeed willing to see the EU assuming a central role on the international political scene, although, at least for the time being, this role ought to be significantly different from that of the United States.

One crucial point related to the community principle still deserves to be mentioned: the importance of dialogue. Several contributors would like to see a stronger element of dialogue in EU external affairs. Ideally, dialogue can create a real community, a community based on equality, to the extent it is possible in the world of highly differing capacities. The notion of dialogue implies that the EU's external affairs may not only be based on pre-fixed ideas, on absolute-truth-like common values, but also on pure political pragmatism. As already indicated with regard to Russia, the extent to which this pragmatism is allowed to undermine such values as democracy and the rule of law is one of the central political questions that the Union has to cope with in its daily policies.

The *capacity principle* has also proved highly useful for conceptualising some aspects of EU external affairs. Elena Jurado's and Rieko Karatani's chapters may seem to contradict each other in this respect. Jurado advocates a sensible division of labour between the EU and human rights organisations, the UN and the Council of Europe in particular. The Union does not have to try to develop into a full-fledged human rights actor, but it should leave the stage open for organisations that are better equipped for doing the tasks in question – and this would in fact prevent the Union from compromising its values, from sooner or later making itself guilty for double standards. On a more general normative note to be discussed in detail shortly, the EU should have a much clearer and systematic approach to inter-institutional burden sharing with other well-equipped agencies.

Karatani, in turn, as she analyses the global migration regime in the context of the Asia-Europe-Meeting, believes that the EU should forcefully use its capacity to promote human rights in the sense suggested by its founding treaties. At the moment migration control is drifting away, both downwards and upwards, from the Union and its member states, and this seems to lead to ever more restrictive migration policies at the expense of human rights. There is, however, not necessarily any disagreement with Jurado's view here: Karatani's argument is simply that whatever the EU does, it needs to be aware of its *already existing* capacity and thus responsibility to advance the cause of human rights. This does not indicate that the Union should assume an ever stronger and larger capacity in this field. The chapter also raises the more general problem of the 'model EU' approach to global governance. A responsible EU must be fully aware of the sometimes unwanted consequences of inter-regional cooperation and dialogue. Restricting migrants' rights ought not to be the result even if other benefits of inter-regionalism appear to be of overriding importance.

In Hanna Ojanen's chapter the question of capacity is also crucial. As the EU seeks to develop military capabilities of its own, it needs to be aware of the responsibilities that these capabilities undoubtedly carry with them. Her analysis of the current state of affairs is fairly optimistic: because the Union seems to be assuming a specific view of security – its security outlook is based on norms, conflict prevention, and the aim of well-functioning states – there are good chances that the Union's activity in this field can actually lead to improved security globally; capacity and norms are thus intertwined. The idea of burden-sharing, particularly relations with NATO and the UN, is also relevant here. Again, the notion of a global security community with different institutional roles and contributions towards stability and conflict-prevention ought to be the ultimate reference point.

These kinds of normative prescriptions lead us to two of our other principles, namely the *legitimate expectations* and *consent principles*. As we have repeatedly seen in the preceding chapters, the latter principle materialises through the values that the Union has promised to respect and promote in its activities. Such promises and consent have been written into its founding treaties in particular but also into countless other policy documents. The former principle, in turn, relates to the expectations that the Union has raised, more or less consciously, both within its own polity and outside it. They are enhanced by the advocacy of these very same values, by a rhetorical emphasis on its own uniqueness as a political actor, and by the formulation of grandiose future goals. Identity politics often seems to determine these expectations: they must be elevated in order to create a common European identity that would legitimise the whole European project in the long run.

These two principles potentially lead to a number of difficulties in the EU context: expectations may turn out to be unjustified and the common values may remain only a dead letter in practice. The raising of expectations in particular involves a severe potential risk. The gap between expectations and capacities may eventually become so wide that this can invalidate the whole European project; the legitimacy of the Union should ultimately not be based on ever increasing expectations. A more concrete example of these general problems is well formulated in Raik's chapter. The question is: if the Union closed its gate to the neighbouring countries despite their fulfilment of all the specific membership criteria, what would this mean for the credibility of the Union? It is notable how easily the other sources of responsibility could be used to 'solve' this problem – for good or bad, depending on one's perspective. The EU could simply state that it does not have the capacity to take these countries onboard, or say that these countries do not belong to the same community. This is a good example of how the different principles may lead to contradictory conclusions.

The *beneficiary* and *contribution principles* have played a somewhat more limited role in most empirical chapters of this book. However, in the fields of development and trade policies, that is, in fields where structural explanations of the world bear some validity, these principles are highly relevant. It is fully legitimate to argue, in the age of globalisation perhaps more than ever before, that the EU contributes to the creation of a world where the rich and the poor, the North and the South, have completely different conditions of life, and that it also benefits from this profoundly unequal state of affairs. From an ethical perspective, therefore, the EU has a duty to try to alleviate the suffering of the poor of the world. Also in the case of neighbourhood and Russia policies the question can be formulated in terms of the beneficiary and contribution principles: if the EU somehow contributes to developments in these regions, and perhaps benefits from their resources, this easily brings duties upon it.

*   *   *

All in all, the six principles of responsibility that have guided the studies of this volume can indeed generate a great number of questions, considerations, and problems concerning the global role of the European Union. We acknowledge that these principles do not help us to overcome all the inherent contradictions of EU external affairs and cannot free policy makers from political choice and judgement, but they certainly help them – and us – to ask appropriate questions and formulate policies in a much more coherent and ethical way.

As an attempt to illustrate the manifoldness and multidimensionality of the questions related to the EU's ethical international agency, Table C.1 combines the book's main policy areas with its conceptual framework of the sources of responsibility. We have in other words cross-tabulated, with the help of a number of questions, the six principles incurring responsibilities and the policy fields or areas that the empirical chapters have investigated. Some of the questions are directly derived from the preceding chapters, some are not. Because the implications of contribution and beneficiary as well as expectations and consent principles are often so close to each other, we have reserved just one column for each of these two pairs. What is important is that, although the number of questions in the table may seem impressive, the questions represent just one possibility within each combination of a principle and policy area, a possibility which may not even be the most important one. The table is thus meant to display only a minor part of the complexity of the EU's external dimension, and by no means simplify it. It is a model for phrasing relevant questions rather than a claim for exclusivity or an attempt to provide answers.

The table generates at least two general conclusions, conclusions that we have alluded to throughout the book. Firstly, there is no doubt that an actor of the EU's calibre carries a great number of responsibilities in the world. The problem is, however, that it is hardly possible to judge with certainty whether there are, in some specific contexts, other actors with even greater responsibilities. In the real world, it is often highly difficult to know who the primary actor should be. Fortunately, one often does not need a clear allocation of institutional responsibilities as long as one is aware that the EU, among others,

Table C.1 Examples of questions generated in various policy fields by the six principles incurring responsibilities

	Community	Capacity	Beneficiary/contribution	Expectations/consent
Security and defence policy	For whose security is the EU responsible for, European or global?	To what extent is it sensible to create own military capabilities?	Provided that Europe has contributed to conflicts, should it not try to solve them by military means?	Is it sensible to raise the expectations of others? Is there a gap between consent and capacity?
Trans-atlantic relations	To what extent do Europe and the US belong to the same value community?	Does the EU have the capacity to balance US power? And what does 'power' mean?	Should the US' historical contribution to the peace of Europe still be emphasised?	Do others have legitimate reasons to expect that the EU behaves differently from the US?
Neighbourhood policy	Where are the borders of Europe?	The EU changes the policies of its neighbours – what duties does this create?	The 'West' helped to divide the continent, and that division may still not be undone?	Has the EU really made them believe in, or even promised, full membership?
Relations with Russia	Why would Russia be part of the same community?	To what extent has the EU capacity to contribute to developments in Russia?	Because the EU benefits from Russian resources, should it not try to help?	Does the EU avoid problematic human rights and democracy issues in Russia?
Human rights agency	Should not human rights issues be discussed in forums in which the whole global community can participate?	What would be a responsible division of labour between the EU and other organisations?	Does Europe somehow contribute to human rights abuses, directly or e.g. through the WTO?	Is the protection of human rights not a treaty-based obligation for the EU?
Migration policy	How does migration change the borders of community?	Does the vertical migration regime not blur capacity, and evade democratic control?	Do the EU's policies somehow contribute to the worsening of migrants' rights?	Is the protection of migrants' rights not a treaty-based obligation for the EU?
Development policy	Should the EU focus on neighbours rather than far-away countries?	Wealth brings along obligations but to what extent?	Does Europe still benefit from poverty, poverty that it itself helped to create?	Do not the poor have a legitimate right to expect Europe to help?
Trade policy	Should the EU think in terms of the global community or try to improve the lot of EU citizens?	Does Europe not have capacity to pursue 'alternative' trade policies?	Does Europe still benefit from global poverty, poverty that it itself helped to create?	Which are more important: common values or economic interests?

has to contribute in one form or the other. That leads us to the second main point: as a first condition of responsible agency, the Union should be much better aware of the multidimensionality and complexity of the ethical foundations of its external affairs than it is at the moment; the promotion of 'common' values around the globe is only a minor (and sometimes problematic) part of them. Indeed, including a conscious ethical dimension in EU policies makes the formulation of these policies even more complicated than is perhaps generally realised. But that does not mean that we should not try to do this. We must, in fact.

A list of priorities for the EU as a responsible global actor

The above explorations and the table as well as the findings of the individual chapters, reveal precious little about what the most important global duties of the European Union are, or how it should use its resources in the most responsible way, or what it should do in practice to meet the moral requirements potentially linked to its external roles. To take at least a preliminary step towards answering these questions, we, the editors of this volume, would like to formulate in the following a list of the most important policy priorities and political measures with the help of which the EU can develop its external dimension in the future. This short list of priorities and measures is, of course, only one possibility, and some of our contributors may in fact disagree with it. We are also well aware of the fact that presenting this kind of a list may in one way or the other violate the principles of responsibility that we have discussed above, although we have tried to hold them as very serious guidelines. Concrete political priorities cannot be based solely on moral principles, but they necessarily involve more traditional foreign policy considerations as well, such as different forms of power and demands of geography. Ideally, the EU should, of course, deal successfully with all the issues mentioned in the list, but in reality it may have to follow a certain order of preference.

Let us first present the list and then explain in detail how we came to this order by applying the principles of the sources of responsibility:

1. Internal Institutional Consolidation
2. Transatlantic Relations
3. Russia
4. New Neighbourhood Policy
----
5. Inter-Institutional Burden Sharing, that is, cooperation with the UN, NATO, WTO, OSCE and Council of Europe
----
6. Middle East
7. Africa
8. Larger Sustainable Development Agenda
9. Larger and Independent Asia Strategy.

The first point of the list is *internal institutional consolidation,* both in general terms in the aftermath of the referendum crisis of 2005 and specifically in the field of foreign policy. This is of primary importance for the entire development of the EU: without internal consolidation, it is hard to envisage a Union having the capacity to act in a responsible manner externally. Internal institutional consolidation also leads to a better definition of the Union's identity, Europe's identity, and therefore makes the application of the community principle more meaningful. It is equally important from the point of view of the consent and legitimate expectations principles: without it, there is a risk that the promises and pledges the Union habitually makes remain unfounded.

We do not simply mean that the EU should learn to speak with one voice (which is certainly often, but not always, useful) and that it should invest much more time and resources on its external dimension. What is more important is that it must be better aware of what its role, power and capacity are in the world and, above all, what they should be. The makers of Union policies should think ever more seriously about what they see as the Union's ultimate position in the world of the new millennium, about Europe's preferred relationship with the rest of the world. In this respect, there is a clear linkage between internal consolidation and the emerging global order.

Two notes of caution need to be made, however. Firstly, internal consolidation should not lead to some sort of political pre-determinism. The EU must remain an open-ended polity that time and again makes a new decision of what it should do and why. The general logic guiding Union policies should not read: 'Because we have assumed this specific role in the world, this is the only political option that we have.' Closely related to this, internal consolidation should not mean that *democracy* within the Union is in any way undermined. The views of ordinary people must be listened to, understood and ultimately respected. Only this way the idea of an open-ended polity can become a reality.

The three next points of our list, transatlantic relations, Russia and neighbourhood policy, represent what could be called *external consolidation.* Together with the first point, we regard these as the EU's core responsibilities, because the Union with its notions of community and its actual capacities is better equipped than any other international organisation with regard to these tasks. In addition, the fact that the EU has in countless declarations and policy programmes committed itself to playing a leading role in these areas, brings the consent, expectations and even contribution principles into the equation. It is of paramount importance that the EU uses the global community, the global economic and security order, as its primary point of reference as it seeks to fulfil these core duties. 'A wider Europe' or 'the West' are far too often seen as synonyms for 'the World', which makes it potentially very easy to think solely in terms of Europe's own interests, in spite of more global intentions.

The first priority within 'external consolidation' is the transatlantic linkage. The way Europeans cooperate with the US is and will be crucial for the development of the world order. The EU should (continue to) forcefully advocate its soft-power approach in the contexts where the US is also active, but this should be done in a way that is not conducive to mutual antagonism between the two actors. The second and third priorities, Russia and the new neighbourhood policy, are obviously very closely related. With Russia, a lively dialogue is in itself a crucial goal. With regard to its new neighbours, the EU must make it clear where the limits of its enlargement are, that is, who can possibly dream of full membership and who cannot. And if full membership is not an option, what can come instead must be outlined as clearly as possible.

Recognising the limits of the EU's capacity and the extent to which the concept of community can be stretched, the fifth point of our list suggests a debate on inter-institutional cooperation. While we have seen that there are currently efforts to initiate this kind of cooperation, several of our chapters have shown that much still needs to be done in this respect. Although the Union can perceive itself as an advocate of multilateralism, it shows a large extent of rivalry and self-interested power politics in its relations with other, often more appropriate and competent actors in selected policy areas. For example environmental, migration and human rights issues are clearly sectors where cooperation must be consciously sought with these other actors. In development policy, particularly in Africa, Europe needs to cooperate with a great number of actors, and also support the activities of its member states – sometimes they are better positioned to make an impact than the Union itself. Specifically in Africa, cooperation with the newly established African Union is of primary importance. Indeed, the EU does not have to try to do everything, to become a universal political project.

A clearer sense of burden-sharing would also enable the EU to better address some other global concerns, that is, points 6 through 9 in our list. Some readers might be surprised to see areas such as the Middle East and sustainable development so low in the list. Let us stress, however, that this by no means reflects a lower importance of these issues in world affairs; it simply reflects the somewhat lesser extent to which the EU on its own can make a significant and responsible contribution in these fields – although by virtue of its treaty-based consent, its capacity and its present involvement, it is widely and legitimately expected to make some sort of contribution. In fact it is argued that some of these concerns can only be sensibly addressed in conjunction with other institutions and are therefore somewhat subsumed in point 5 of the list. The expectations in some of these regions of the EU's ability to play an independent role are indeed relatively low, even though policy-makers in Brussels might believe otherwise. For example, the recognisable presence of the EU, as distinct from the role and the legacies of some of its member states, is indisputably limited in many, if not most, parts of Africa. In the example of the crisis in the Middle East, the efforts of the EU should not be disregarded – they should in fact be praised and encouraged – while at the same time recognising that any EU involvement must be seen as a concerted effort with at least the US and the UN.

To conclude, we are inclined to see the EU's global responsibility as consisting of four core responsibilities, primarily based on community and capacity principles, surrounded by a second layer of responsibilities which can only be dealt with through a clear sense and strategy of inter-institutional cooperation. A more general conceptual point is that if individual international organisations do indeed have responsibilities, so have collectives and networks of relevant international institutions. The research agenda on institutional responsibility on international relations should be broadened in this respect.

A responsible Europe?

It is obvious that this book is only the first effort to think about EU external affairs in normative terms and that we have not been able cover all relevant policy sectors and geographical areas; for example environmental policies and relations with Latin America have not figured on these pages at all. Further research has to be done, new conceptual frameworks developed and, above all, more thinking exercised in order to strengthen the ethical dimension of EU external affairs. Many a reader may of course contend that it is far too idealistic to believe that this strengthening would really take place in the foreseeable future. But then we can simply reply that the entire process of European integration has been based on a great degree of idealism.

True to our idealistic frame of mind, let us finish with what has possibly been the most crucial normative point of this book, and formulate it in semi-mathematical way: Studies of the EU's global role have traditionally started off by analysing the nature of the EU's agency – 'x' – and logically concluded that because of this nature the Union should act in the world in a certain way, $f(x)$. We have sought to argue instead that the EU's global role and its development should be based on a meticulous analysis of the world and of the (normative) principles needed to make it better – the result of this analysis is y; the future nature of the Union should then be a function of these principles, $f(y)$.

Indeed, it is the global community that should be the primary reference point for the European Union in its international activities. This global perspective might not only guarantee that the Union is and will be *a* responsible actor in the world. Given the general nature of today's international politics, we are bound to ask whether we could even use the definite article, envision the EU as *the* responsible power in and for the future.

Note

1. Commission of the European Communities, *European Values in the Globalised World. Communication from the Commission to the European Parliament,* Brussels, 20 October 2005.

Index